FLORIDA

100 BEST PLACES TO VISIT

BUCKET LIST

Thank you for buying my book!
I hope you like it.

Your feedback is important to me, and I would greatly appreciate it if you could take a moment to share your thoughts by leaving an online review.

Your review will not only help me improve as an author but also assist other potential readers in making informed decisions.

Once again, thank you for your support and for considering leaving a review.

Warm regards,
Max

ABOUT FLORIDA

Florida is a state located in the southeastern region of the United States. It is bordered to the west by the Gulf of Mexico, to the northwest by Alabama, to the north by Georgia, to the east by the Bahamas and the Atlantic Ocean, and to the south by the Straits of Florida and Cuba. It is the only state that shares its borders with both the Gulf of Mexico and the Atlantic Ocean. With a population exceeding 21 million, it ranks as the third-most populous state in the nation and is the eighth most densely populated as of 2020. Covering an area of 65,758 square miles (170,310 km2), it ranks 22nd in size among the 50 states. The largest metropolitan area in the state is the Miami metropolitan area, which includes the cities of Miami, Fort Lauderdale, and West Palm Beach, with a population of 6.138 million. Jacksonville is the most populous city in the state, with a population of 949,611. Other major population centers in Florida include Tampa Bay, Orlando, Cape Coral, and the state capital, Tallahassee.

Various Native American groups have inhabited Florida for at least 14,000 years. In 1513, Spanish explorer Juan Ponce de León became the first known European to make landfall in the region, naming it "La Florida" for its lush greenery and the Easter season (Pascua Florida in Spanish). Florida subsequently became the first area in the continental United States to be permanently settled by Europeans, with the establishment of the Spanish colony of St. Augustine in 1565, making it the oldest continuously inhabited city. Florida was the subject of repeated disputes between Spain and Great Britain before being ceded to the United States in 1819. It was admitted as the 27th state on March 3, 1845. Florida played a significant role in the Seminole Wars (1816–1858), which were the longest and most extensive of the Indian Wars in U.S. history. The state seceded from the Union on January 10, 1861, becoming one of the original seven Confederate States, and it was readmitted to the Union after the Civil War on June 25, 1868.

Since the mid-20th century, Florida has witnessed rapid demographic and economic growth. Its economy, with a gross state product (GSP) of $1.4 trillion, is the fourth-largest of any U.S. state and ranks 16th globally. Major sectors of the state's economy include tourism, hospitality, agriculture, real estate, and transportation. Florida is renowned worldwide for its beach resorts, amusement parks, warm and sunny climate, and nautical recreation. Attractions such as Walt Disney World, the Kennedy Space

Center, and Miami Beach draw tens of millions of visitors each year. Florida is a popular destination for retirees, seasonal vacationers, and domestic and international migrants, hosting nine out of the ten fastest-growing communities in the U.S. Its close proximity to the ocean has profoundly influenced its culture, identity, and daily life. The state's colonial history and successive waves of migration have left a mark with African, European, Indigenous, Latino, and Asian influences. Florida has been a source of inspiration for some of the most prominent American writers, including Ernest Hemingway, Marjorie Kinnan Rawlings, and Tennessee Williams, and continues to attract celebrities and athletes, particularly in golf, tennis, auto racing, and water sports. Florida has been a closely watched state in American presidential elections, notably in 2000, 2016, and 2020.

About two-thirds of Florida is situated on a peninsula between the Gulf of Mexico and the Atlantic Ocean. It boasts the longest coastline of any contiguous U.S. state, spanning approximately 1,350 miles (2,170 km), not including numerous barrier islands. Florida has 4,510 islands that are at least ten acres (4.0 hectares) in area, the second-highest number after Alaska. Much of Florida is at or near sea level and is characterized by sedimentary soil. Florida is the flattest state in the country, with the lowest natural high point of any U.S. state, measuring just 345 feet (105 meters).

Florida's climate varies from subtropical in the north to tropical in the south. It is the only state besides Hawaii to have a tropical climate. Florida is also the only continental state to have both a tropical climate in the southern part of the state and a coral reef. The state boasts unique ecosystems, including Everglades National Park, which is the largest tropical wilderness in the U.S. and one of the largest in the Americas. Unique wildlife in Florida includes the American alligator, American crocodile, American flamingo, Roseate spoonbill, Florida panther, bottlenose dolphin, and manatee. The Florida Reef is the only living coral barrier reef in the continental United States and is the third-largest coral barrier reef system globally, after the Great Barrier Reef and the Belize Barrier Reef.

A significant portion of Florida is located on a narrow piece of land between the Gulf of Mexico, the Atlantic Ocean, and the Straits of Florida. Florida spans two different time zones and stretches towards the northwest, forming a panhandle that extends along the northern Gulf of Mexico. It shares its northern borders with Georgia and Alabama, while the western end of the panhandle is adjacent to Alabama. It stands out as the only U.S. state with coastlines along both the Atlantic Ocean and the Gulf of Mexico. Florida is also the southernmost of the 48 contiguous states, with only Hawaii reaching farther south. It is situated to the west of the Bahamas and approximately 90 miles north of Cuba. In terms of land area, Florida is one of the largest states in the eastern part of the country, surpassed in water area only by Alaska and Michigan. The state's water boundary extends 3 nautical miles offshore in the Atlantic Ocean and 9 nautical miles offshore in the Gulf of Mexico.

The highest natural point in Florida is Britton Hill, which stands at an elevation of 345 feet above sea level, making it the lowest highpoint among all U.S. states. A considerable part of the state, especially south of Orlando, is situated at lower elevations compared to the northern regions and generally maintains a fairly flat terrain near sea level. However, some areas like Clearwater have prominent land formations that rise 50 to 100 feet above sea level. In Central and North Florida, which are typically located 25 miles or more away from the coast, the landscape features rolling hills with elevations ranging from 100 to 250 feet. The highest point in peninsular Florida, which is east and south of the Suwannee River, is Sugarloaf Mountain, a 312-foot peak in Lake County. On average, Florida is considered the flattest state in the United States.

Lake Okeechobee, the largest lake in Florida, ranks as the tenth largest natural freshwater lake among the 50 states and the second-largest one entirely within the contiguous 48 states, following Lake Michigan. The St. Johns River, extending for 310 miles, is the longest river in Florida, with a minimal drop in elevation from its source in South Florida to its mouth in Jacksonville, measuring less than 30 feet.

Florida is home to over 500 non-native animal species and over 1,000 non-native insects that have established themselves throughout the state. Among these exotic species are the Burmese python, green iguana, veiled chameleon, Argentine black and white tegu, peacock bass, mayan cichlid, lionfish, White-nosed coati, rhesus macaque, vervet monkey, Cuban tree frog, cane toad, Indian peafowl, monk parakeet, tui parakeet, and more. While some of these non-native species coexist peacefully with native wildlife, others pose a threat to Florida's indigenous species by preying on them.

Florida boasts over 26,000 square miles (67,000 km2) of forests, covering about half of the state's total land area.

The state also hosts a remarkable diversity of wildflowers, with around 3,000 different types found in Florida. This makes Florida the third-most diverse state in the United States, trailing behind only California and Texas, both of which are larger in size. Wild populations of coconut palms can be found along the state's East Coast, extending from Key West to Jupiter Inlet, and along the West Coast, from Marco Island to Sarasota. Many of the smallest coral islands in the Florida Keys have coconut palms sprouting from coconuts deposited by ocean currents. Coconut palms are cultivated in northern South Florida, reaching approximately Cocoa Beach on the East Coast and the Tampa Bay Area on the West Coast.

On Florida's east coast, mangroves typically dominate the coast from Cocoa Beach southward, while salt marshes are prevalent from St. Augustine northward. The balance between these two ecosystems fluctuates between St. Augustine and Cocoa Beach, depending on annual weather conditions. All three mangrove species in Florida flower in the spring and early summer, with propagules falling from late summer through early autumn. In 1981, it was estimated that mangrove plant communities covered between 430,000 and 540,000 acres in Florida, with the majority (90%) in southern Florida, spanning Collier, Lee, Miami-Dade, and Monroe Counties.

Florida's natural beauty extends underwater with the Florida Reef, the only living coral barrier reef in the continental United States. This reef system is the third-largest in the world, following the Great Barrier Reef and the Belize Barrier Reef. The Florida Reef is located just off the coast of the Florida Keys and is a prominent feature of John Pennekamp Coral Reef State Park, the first underwater park in the United States. The park is teeming with tropical vegetation, marine life, and seabirds. The Florida Reef also extends into other protected areas, including Dry Tortugas National Park, Biscayne National Park, and the Florida Keys National Marine Sanctuary. This delicate ecosystem supports nearly 1,400 species of marine plants and animals, including over 40 species of stony corals and 500 species of fish. However, the Florida Reef, like other coral reefs, faces numerous threats, such as overfishing, plastic pollution in the ocean, coral bleaching, rising sea levels, and changes in sea surface temperature.

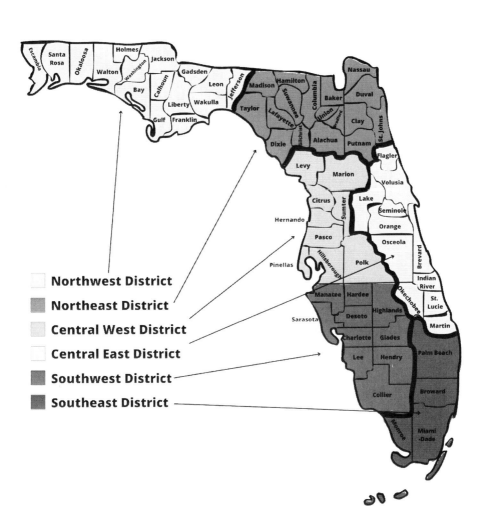

Northwest District

Northeast District

Central West District

Central East District

Southwest District

Southeast District

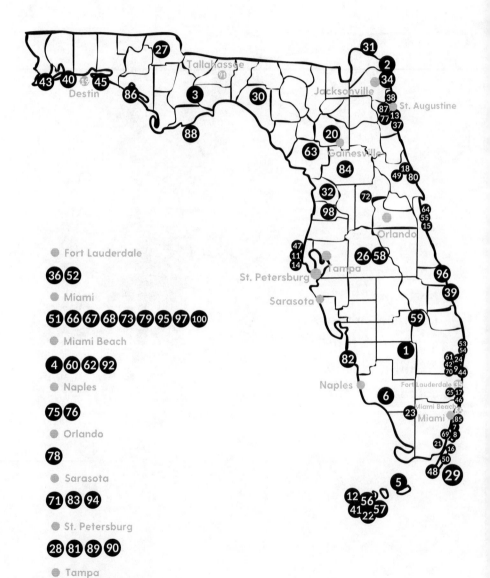

1. Ah-Tah-Thi-Ki Museum
2. Amelia Island
3. Apalachicola National Forest
4. Art Deco Historic District
5. Bahia Honda State Park
6. Big Cypress National Preserve
7. Bill Baggs Cape Florida State Park
8. Biscayne National Park
9. Boca Raton Museum of Art
10. Busch Gardens Tampa Bay
11. Caladesi Island State Park
12. Captain Tony's Saloon
13. Castillo de San Marcos
14. Clearwater Beach
15. Cocoa Beach
16. Dagny Johnson Key Largo Hammock Botanical State Park
17. Dania Beach
18. Daytona International Speedway
19. Destin
20. Devil's Millhopper Geological State Park
21. Dry Tortugas National Park
22. Ernest Hemingway Home and Museum
23. Everglades National Park
24. Flagler Museum
25. Flamingo Gardens
26. Florida Air Museum
27. Florida Caverns State Park
28. Florida Holocaust Museum
29. Florida Keys
30. Forest Capital Museum State Park
31. Fort Clinch State Park
32. Fort Cooper State Park
33. Fort Foster State Historic Site
34. Fort George Island Cultural State Park
35. Fort Lauderdale
36. Fort Lauderdale Swap Shop
37. Fort Matanzas National Monument
38. Fort Mose Historic State Park
39. Fort Pierce Inlet State Park
40. Fort Walton Beach
41. Fort Zachary Taylor Historic State Park
42. Green Cay Nature Center and Wetlands
43. Gulf Islands National Seashore
44. Gumbo Limbo Nature Center
45. Henderson Beach State Park
46. Hollywood
47. Honeymoon Island State Park
48. Islamorada
49. John B. Stetson House
50. John Pennekamp Coral Reef State Park
51. Jungle Island
52. Jungle Queen Riverboat
53. Jupiter
54. Jupiter Inlet Lighthouse and Museum
55. Kennedy Space Center
56. Key West
57. Key West Butterfly and Nature Conservatory
58. Lake Kissimmee State Park
59. Lake Okeechobee
60. Lincoln Road
61. Lion Country Safari
62. Lummus Park
63. Manatee Springs State Park
64. Merritt Island National Wildlife Refuge

65 Miami Beach

66 Miami Children's Museum

67 Miami Design District

68 Miami Seaquarium

69 Monkey Jungle

70 Morikami Museum and Japanese Gardens

71 Mote Marine Laboratory & Aquarium

72 Mount Dora

73 Museum of Contemporary Art North Miami

74 Museum of Science and Industry

75 Naples Pier

76 Naples Zoo at Caribbean Gardens

77 Oldest Wooden School House

78 Orlando Museum of Art

79 Phillip and Patricia Frost Museum of Science

80 Ponce de Leon Inlet Lighthouse

81 Salvador Dali Museum

82 Sanibel Island

83 Siesta Beach

84 Silver Springs State Park

85 South Beach

86 St. Andrews State Park

87 St. Augustine Town Plan Historic District

88 St. George Island

89 St. Petersburg Pier

90 Sunken Gardens

91 Tallahassee

92 The Bass Museum of Art

93 The Florida Aquarium

94 The Ringling

95 Venetian Pool

96 Vero Beach

97 Vizcaya Museum and Gardens

98 Weeki Wachee Springs State Park

99 Ybor City

100 Zoo Miami

PLACE NAME	REGION	COUNTY	VISITED
Ah-Tah-Thi-Ki Museum	Southwest District	Hendry	
Amelia Island	Northeast District	Nassau	
Apalachicola National Forest	Northwest District	Franklin, Leon, Liberty, Wakulla	
Art Deco Historic District	Southeast District	Miami-Dade	
Bahia Honda State Park	Southeast District	Monroe	
Big Cypress National Preserve	Southwest District	Collier	
Bill Baggs Cape Florida State Park	Southeast District	Miami-Dade	
Biscayne National Park	Southeast District	Miami-Dade	
Boca Raton Museum of Art	Southeast District	Palm Beach	
Busch Gardens Tampa Bay	Central West District	Hillsborough	
Caladesi Island State Park	Central West District	Pinellas	
Captain Tony's Saloon	Southeast District	Monroe	
Castillo de San Marcos	Northeast District	St. Johns	
Clearwater Beach	Central West District	Pinellas	
Cocoa Beach	Central East District	Brevard	
Dagny Johnson Key Largo Hammock Botanical State Park	Southeast District	Monroe	
Dania Beach	Southeast District	Broward	
Daytona International Speedway	Central East District	Volusia	
Destin	Northwest District	Okaloosa	
Devil's Millhopper Geological State Park	Northeast District	Alachua	
Dry Tortugas National Park	Southeast District	Monroe	
Ernest Hemingway Home and Museum	Southeast District	Monroe	
Everglades National Park	Southwest District, Southeast District	Collier, Miami-Dade, Monroe	
Flagler Museum	Southeast District	Palm Beach	
Flamingo Gardens	Southeast District	Broward	
Florida Air Museum	Central West District	Polk	
Florida Caverns State Park	Northwest District	Jackson	
Florida Holocaust Museum	Central West District	Pinellas	

PLACE NAME	REGION	COUNTY	VISITED
Florida Keys	Southeast District	Miami-Dade, Monroe	
Forest Capital Museum State Park	Northeast District	Taylor	
Fort Clinch State Park	Northeast District	Nassau	
Fort Cooper State Park	Central West District	Citrus	
Fort Foster State Historic Site	Central West District	Hillsborough	
Fort George Island Cultural State Park	Northeast District	Duval	
Fort Lauderdale	Southeast District	Broward	
Fort Lauderdale Swap Shop	Southeast District	Broward	
Fort Matanzas National Monument	Northeast District	St. Johns	
Fort Mose Historic State Park	Northeast District	St. Johns	
Fort Pierce Inlet State Park	Central East District	St. Lucie	
Fort Walton Beach	Northwest District	Okaloosa	
Fort Zachary Taylor Historic State Park	Southeast District	Monroe	
Green Cay Nature Center and Wetlands	Southeast District	Palm Beach	
Gulf Islands National Seashore	Northwest District	Escambia	
Gumbo Limbo Nature Center	Southeast District	Palm Beach	
Henderson Beach State Park	Northwest District	Okaloosa	
Hollywood	Southeast District	Broward	
Honeymoon Island State Park	Central West District	Pinellas	
Islamorada	Southeast District	Monroe	
John B. Stetson House	Central East District	Volusia	
John Pennekamp Coral Reef State Park	Southeast District	Monroe	
Jungle Island	Southeast District	Miami-Dade	
Jungle Queen Riverboat	Southeast District	Broward	
Jupiter	Southeast District	Palm Beach	
Jupiter Inlet Lighthouse and Museum	Southeast District	Palm Beach	
Kennedy Space Center	Central East District	Brevard	
Key West	Southeast District	Monroe	

PLACE NAME	REGION	COUNTY	VISITED
Key West Butterfly and Nature Conservatory	Southeast District	Monroe	
Lake Kissimmee State Park	Central West District	Polk	
Lake Okeechobee	Central East District, Southwest District, Southeast District	Glades, Okeechobee, Martin, Palm Beach, Hendry	
Lincoln Road	Southeast District	Miami-Dade	
Lion Country Safari	Southeast District	Palm Beach	
Lummus Park	Southeast District	Miami-Dade	
Manatee Springs State Park	Central West District	Levy	
Merritt Island National Wildlife Refuge	Central East District	Brevard	
Miami Beach	Southeast District	Miami-Dade	
Miami Children's Museum	Southeast District	Miami-Dade	
Miami Design District	Southeast District	Miami-Dade	
Miami Seaquarium	Southeast District	Miami-Dade	
Monkey Jungle	Southeast District	Miami-Dade	
Morikami Museum and Japanese Gardens	Southeast District	Palm Beach	
Mote Marine Laboratory & Aquarium	Southwest District	Sarasota	
Mount Dora	Central East District	Lake	
Museum of Contemporary Art North Miami	Southeast District	Miami-Dade	
Museum of Science and Industry	Central West District	Hillsborough	
Naples Pier	Southwest District	Collier	
Naples Zoo at Caribbean Gardens	Southwest District	Collier	
Oldest Wooden School House	Northeast District	St. Johns	
Orlando Museum of Art	Central East District	Orange	
Phillip and Patricia Frost Museum of Science	Southeast District	Miami-Dade	
Ponce de Leon Inlet Lighthouse	Central East District	Volusia	
Salvador Dali Museum	Central West District	Pinellas	
Sanibel Island	Southwest District	Lee	
Siesta Beach	Southwest District	Sarasota	
Silver Springs State Park	Central West District	Marion	

PLACE NAME	REGION	COUNTY	VISITED
South Beach	Southeast District	Miami-Dade	
St. Andrews State Park	Northwest District	Bay	
St. Augustine Town Plan Historic District	Northeast District	St. Johns	
St. George Island	Northwest District	Franklin	
St. Petersburg Pier	Central West District	Pinellas	
Sunken Gardens	Central West District	Pinellas	
Tallahassee	Northwest District	Leon	
The Bass Museum of Art	Southeast District	Miami-Dade	
The Florida Aquarium	Central West District	Hillsborough	
The Ringling	Southwest District	Sarasota	
Venetian Pool	Southeast District	Miami-Dade	
Vero Beach	Central East District	Indian River	
Vizcaya Museum and Gardens	Southeast District	Miami-Dade	
Weeki Wachee Springs State Park	Central West District	Hernando	
Ybor City	Central West District	Hillsborough	
Zoo Miami	Southeast District	Miami-Dade	

REGION	COUNTY	PLACE NAME	VISITED
Northwest District	Bay	St. Andrews State Park	
Northwest District	Escambia	Gulf Islands National Seashore	
Northwest District	Franklin	St. George Island	
Northwest District	Franklin, Leon, Liberty, Wakulla	Apalachicola National Forest	
Northwest District	Jackson	Florida Caverns State Park	
Northwest District	Leon	Tallahassee	
Northwest District	Okaloosa	Destin	
Northwest District	Okaloosa	Fort Walton Beach	
Northwest District	Okaloosa	Henderson Beach State Park	
Northeast District	Alachua	Devil's Millhopper Geological State Park	
Northeast District	Duval	Fort George Island Cultural State Park	
Northeast District	Nassau	Amelia Island	
Northeast District	Nassau	Fort Clinch State Park	
Northeast District	St. Johns	Castillo de San Marcos	
Northeast District	St. Johns	Fort Matanzas National Monument	
Northeast District	St. Johns	Fort Mose Historic State Park	
Northeast District	St. Johns	Oldest Wooden School House	
Northeast District	St. Johns	St. Augustine Town Plan Historic District	
Northeast District	Taylor	Forest Capital Museum State Park	
Central West District	Citrus	Fort Cooper State Park	
Central West District	Hernando	Weeki Wachee Springs State Park	
Central West District	Hillsborough	Busch Gardens Tampa Bay	
Central West District	Hillsborough	Fort Foster State Historic Site	
Central West District	Hillsborough	Museum of Science and Industry	
Central West District	Hillsborough	The Florida Aquarium	
Central West District	Hillsborough	Ybor City	
Central West District	Levy	Manatee Springs State Park	
Central West District	Marion	Silver Springs State Park	

REGION	COUNTY	PLACE NAME	VISITED
Central West District	Pinellas	Caladesi Island State Park	
Central West District	Pinellas	Clearwater Beach	
Central West District	Pinellas	Florida Holocaust Museum	
Central West District	Pinellas	Honeymoon Island State Park	
Central West District	Pinellas	Salvador Dali Museum	
Central West District	Pinellas	St. Petersburg Pier	
Central West District	Pinellas	Sunken Gardens	
Central West District	Polk	Florida Air Museum	
Central West District	Polk	Lake Kissimmee State Park	
Central East District	Brevard	Cocoa Beach	
Central East District	Brevard	Kennedy Space Center	
Central East District	Brevard	Merritt Island National Wildlife Refuge	
Central East District	Indian River	Vero Beach	
Central East District	Lake	Mount Dora	
Central East District	Orange	Orlando Museum of Art	
Central East District	St. Lucie	Fort Pierce Inlet State Park	
Central East District	Volusia	Daytona International Speedway	
Central East District	Volusia	John B. Stetson House	
Central East District	Volusia	Ponce de Leon Inlet Lighthouse	
Central East District, Southwest District, Southeast District	Glades, Okeechobee, Martin, Palm Beach, Hendry	Lake Okeechobee	
Southwest District	Collier	Big Cypress National Preserve	
Southwest District	Collier	Naples Pier	
Southwest District	Collier	Naples Zoo at Caribbean Gardens	
Southwest District	Collier, Miami-Dade, Monroe	Everglades National Park	
Southwest District	Hendry	Ah-Tah-Thi-Ki Museum	
Southwest District	Lee	Sanibel Island	
Southwest District	Sarasota	Mote Marine Laboratory & Aquarium	
Southwest District	Sarasota	Siesta Beach	

REGION	COUNTY	PLACE NAME	VISITED
Southwest District	Sarasota	The Ringling	
Southeast District	Broward	Dania Beach	
Southeast District	Broward	Flamingo Gardens	
Southeast District	Broward	Fort Lauderdale	
Southeast District	Broward	Fort Lauderdale Swap Shop	
Southeast District	Broward	Hollywood	
Southeast District	Broward	Jungle Queen Riverboat	
Southeast District	Miami-Dade	Art Deco Historic District	
Southeast District	Miami-Dade	Bill Baggs Cape Florida State Park	
Southeast District	Miami-Dade	Biscayne National Park	
Southeast District	Miami-Dade	Jungle Island	
Southeast District	Miami-Dade	Lincoln Road	
Southeast District	Miami-Dade	Lummus Park	
Southeast District	Miami-Dade	Miami Beach	
Southeast District	Miami-Dade	Miami Children's Museum	
Southeast District	Miami-Dade	Miami Design District	
Southeast District	Miami-Dade	Miami Seaquarium	
Southeast District	Miami-Dade	Monkey Jungle	
Southeast District	Miami-Dade	Museum of Contemporary Art North Miami	
Southeast District	Miami-Dade	Phillip and Patricia Frost Museum of Science	
Southeast District	Miami-Dade	South Beach	
Southeast District	Miami-Dade	The Bass Museum of Art	
Southeast District	Miami-Dade	Venetian Pool	
Southeast District	Miami-Dade	Vizcaya Museum and Gardens	
Southeast District	Miami-Dade	Zoo Miami	
Southeast District	Miami-Dade, Monroe	Florida Keys	
Southeast District	Monroe	Bahia Honda State Park	
Southeast District	Monroe	Captain Tony's Saloon	

REGION	COUNTY	PLACE NAME	VISITED
Southwest District	Monroe	Dagny Johnson Key Largo Hammock Botanical State Park	
Southeast District	Monroe	Dry Tortugas National Park	
Southeast District	Monroe	Ernest Hemingway Home and Museum	
Southeast District	Monroe	Fort Zachary Taylor Historic State Park	
Southeast District	Monroe	Islamorada	
Southeast District	Monroe	John Pennekamp Coral Reef State Park	
Southeast District	Monroe	Key West	
Southeast District	Monroe	Key West Butterfly and Nature Conservatory	
Southeast District	Palm Beach	Boca Raton Museum of Art	
Southeast District	Palm Beach	Flagler Museum	
Southeast District	Palm Beach	Green Cay Nature Center and Wetlands	
Southeast District	Palm Beach	Gumbo Limbo Nature Center	
Southeast District	Palm Beach	Jupiter	
Southeast District	Palm Beach	Jupiter Inlet Lighthouse and Museum	
Southeast District	Palm Beach	Lion Country Safari	
Southeast District	Palm Beach	Morikami Museum and Japanese Gardens	

AH-TAH-THI-KI MUSEUM

REGION: SOUTHWEST DISTRICT   **COUNTY:** HENDRY   **CITY:** CLEWISTON

DATE VISITED: **WHO I WENT WITH:**

RATING: ☆ ☆ ☆ ☆ ☆   **WILL I RETURN?** YES / NO

Situated in the heart of the Everglades on the Big Cypress Seminole Indian Reservation, the Ah-Tah-Thi-Ki Museum houses an impressive collection of over 200,000 unique artifacts and archival items. It invites visitors to explore and learn about the Seminole people, their rich cultural heritage, and deep historical connections to the Southeast and Florida, where they have resided in Big Cypress since ancient times.

The Ah-Tah-Thi-Ki Museum was first conceived in 1989 and officially opened to the public on August 21, 1997, coinciding with the 40th anniversary of federal recognition of the Seminole Tribe of Florida. The museum extended its reach with a smaller satellite facility in the Seminole Paradise area of the Seminole Hard Rock Hotel and Casino in Hollywood. However, the Hollywood location closed its doors in October 2009.

In 2004, the Big Cypress facility expanded with a second building dedicated to curatorial and conservation needs. The museum showcases artifacts, some of which are on loan from the Smithsonian Institution, and actively shares its collection through traveling exhibits and artifact loans to select community institutions.

Whether you are a lifelong resident of Florida, a recent arrival, or just visiting, the Ah-Tah-Thi-Ki Museum offers an educational and captivating experience. As you drive through the scenic roads and lush vegetation of the Big Cypress Reservation, you'll feel immersed in the natural beauty of the Florida Everglades.

Upon reaching the museum, an engaging five-screen orientation film sets the stage for your journey through the galleries. The exhibits feature rare artifacts and life-sized depictions of traditional Seminole practices in 1890s Florida. Additionally, the museum hosts temporary exhibits that delve into topics relevant to both the past and present Seminole life.

Beyond the indoor galleries, visitors can explore a mile-long boardwalk that winds through a natural cypress dome. Along the way, you'll encounter the Ceremonial Grounds and Living Village, a modern interpretation of historic tourist camps from the early 20th century. Here, you might meet talented Seminole artisans who create and sell world-renowned beadwork, basketry, wood carvings, and patchwork. Educational placards in English, Mikasuki, and Creek (the two Seminole languages) dentify 67 plant species and their traditional uses by the Tribe. Signage also highlights native wildlife species one might encounter in the Everglades. The boardwalk leads to a recreated Living Village where Tribal artisans demonstrate traditional arts and crafts such as woodcarving, beadwork, basketry, and Seminole patchwork.

The Ah-Tah-Thi-Ki Museum aims to leave you with a deeper understanding and appreciation of the unique history and culture of the Seminoles. It highlights their thriving culture within the boundaries of the six Seminole Tribe of Florida reservations and beyond.

While the museum is designed for self-guided tours, they also offer Guide by Cell audio tours to enrich your experience along the boardwalk. For group visits, it's important to note that groups are limited to 10 or fewer individuals, and guided tours and additional activities should be scheduled in advance.

Before you leave, be sure to visit the Museum Store, conveniently located near the admissions desk. The store offers a range of books, DVDs, clothing, and authentic hand-crafted items by Seminole and other Native American artisans.

The museum is open 7 days a week from 9 a.m. to 5 p.m.

AMELIA ISLAND

REGION: NORTHEAST DISTRICT   **COUNTY:** NASSAU   **CITY:** HENDRY

DATE VISITED: **WHO I WENT WITH:**

RATING: ☆ ☆ ☆ ☆ ☆   **WILL I RETURN?** YES / NO

Amelia Island, the southernmost gem in the barrier island chain, invites visitors with its 13 miles of unspoiled Atlantic beach, adorned with the natural beauty of majestic oak trees draped in Spanish moss that create a captivating maritime forest canopy. Covering just over 18 square miles, equivalent to the size and shape of Manhattan, it holds the distinction of being the only place in the United States that has experienced the rule of eight different flags throughout history. Over the years, the island has attracted a colorful array of characters, including adventurers, pirates, princesses, wealthy entrepreneurs, and artists of all kinds. Its allure has remained strong over centuries, and a visit to this small island will reveal why.

Amelia Island boasts historical landmarks such as Civil War-era Fort Clinch, the historically significant American Beach that served as a refuge from segregation, and a thriving 50-block National Historic District in downtown Fernandina Beach, teeming with diverse shops and restaurants. The island's shrimping industry originated here, and to taste the authentic flavor, one can savor wild-caught shrimp available in various Amelia Island eateries and grocery stores.

Whether you seek a family vacation, a romantic escape, a memorable wedding, or simply an opportunity to reconnect amidst the beach and live oak trees, Amelia Island guarantees a plethora of cherished memories. Just like the sea turtles that hatch on its shores during summer nights, you'll find yourself irresistibly drawn back to this enchanting island time and time again.

While exploring these areas, visitors may be lucky enough to encounter some of the local wildlife, including gopher tortoises, deer, raccoons, bobcats, and a diverse array of birds and reptiles.

Amelia Island is highly cherished for its extensive quiet beaches, breathtaking natural scenery, fascinating history, and delightful seaport ambiance. It consistently earns top rankings and numerous awards, both for the island itself and its affiliated partners.

The island's name, Amelia Island, originated from Princess Amelia, the daughter of King George II of Great Britain. Over the course of history, the island changed hands multiple times between various colonial powers. It is believed that a total of eight flags flew over Amelia Island throughout its history, representing the French, Spanish, British, Floridian/Patriot, Green Cross, Mexican, Confederate, and United States.

Early European settlement on the island dates back to around 1000 when American

Indian bands associated with the Timucua people inhabited it, calling it Napoyca. French explorer Jean Ribault was the first recorded European visitor in 1562, naming it Île de Mai. Subsequently, Spanish forces led by Pedro Menendez de Aviles drove out the French in 1565, leading to the establishment of the Santa María de Sena mission on the island.

During British rule, the island was briefly known as Egmont Isle, named after Lord Egmont who owned a vast plantation there. After the American Revolutionary War, Spain regained possession of Florida in 1783, and Amelia Island became an embarkation point for Loyalists leaving the colony.

Following the Second Treaty of Paris in 1783, Florida was returned to Spain, and British inhabitants had to leave or pledge allegiance to Spain. In 1795, American rebels led by Richard Lang attacked the Spanish garrison on Amelia Island, but the Spanish forces ultimately drove them away across the St. Marys River to Georgia.

In 1811, surveyor George J. F. Clarke platted the town of Fernandina, named in honor of King Ferdinand VII of Spain by Enrique White, the governor of the Spanish province of East Florida.

On March 16, 1812, Amelia Island was invaded and seized by insurgents from the United States calling themselves the "Patriots of Amelia Island," under the command of General George Mathews, a former governor of Georgia. This action was tacitly approved by President James Madison. General Mathews moved into a house at St. Marys, Georgia, just nine miles across Cumberland Sound from Fernandina on the northwest end of the island.

That same day, nine American gunboats under the command of Commodore Hugh Campbell formed a line in the harbor and aimed their guns at the town. From Point Peter, General Mathews ordered Colonel Lodowick Ashley to send a flag to Don Justo Lopez, commandant of the fort and Amelia Island, and demand his surrender. Lopez acknowledged the superior force and surrendered the port and the town. John H. McIntosh, George J. F. Clarke, Justo Lopez, and others signed the articles of capitulation; the Patriots raised their own standard. The next day, March 17, a detachment of 250 regular United States troops were brought from Point Peter, and the newly constituted Patriot government surrendered the town to General Matthews. He took formal possession in the name of the United States, ordering the Patriot flag struck and the flag of the United States to be raised immediately.

This was part of a plan by General Mathews and President Madison to annex East Florida, but Congress became alarmed at the possibility of being drawn into war with Spain while engaged in the War of 1812 against Great Britain. The effort fell apart when Secretary of State James Monroe was forced to relieve Matthews of his commission. Negotiations began for the withdrawal of U.S. troops early in 1813. On May 6, the army lowered the flag at Fernandina and took its remaining troops across the St. Marys River to Georgia. Spain seized the redoubt and regained control of the island. In 1816 the Spanish completed construction of the new Fort San Carlos to guard Fernandina.

The unrest and filibuster activities persisted. Gregor MacGregor, a Scottish-born adventurer, led an army of 150 men, which included recruits from Charleston and Savannah, some veterans of the War of 1812, and 55 musketeers. On June 29, 1817, they launched an attack on Fort San Carlos. The commander of the fort, Francisco Morales, surrendered and fled, allowing MacGregor to raise his flag, the "Green Cross of Florida," a green cross on a white background, over the fort. He proclaimed the establishment of the "Republic of the Floridas." However, faced with the threat of Spanish retaliation and lacking sufficient funds and reinforcements, MacGregor abandoned his plans to conquer Florida. He and most of his officers left Fernandina for the Bahamas, leaving a small detachment at Fort San Carlos. The Spanish forces attempted to reassert their authority, but the garrison, along with American irregulars organized by Bram Yasho and former Pennsylvania congressman Jared Irwin, successfully repelled them.

The Battle of Amelia Island began on September 13 when the Spaniards set up a battery of four brass cannons on McLure's Hill east of the fort. They had about 300 men supported by two gunboats, and they shelled Fernandina. Irwin's forces, which included ninety-four men, the privateer ships Morgiana and St. Joseph, and the armed schooner Jupiter, responded to the attack. Spanish gunboats started firing at 3:30 pm, and the battery on the hill joined in the cannonade. The guns of Fort San Carlos and those of the St. Joseph defended Amelia Island. During the battle, cannonballs killed two Spanish soldiers and wounded others. The Spanish commander realized capturing the island was unlikely, leading to the withdrawal of their forces.

Later on, Hubbard and Irwin joined forces with French-born pirate Louis-Michel Aury, who claimed Amelia Island on behalf of the revolutionary Republic of Mexico. Aury had previously been associated with MacGregor in filibuster adventures in South America. Aury had also been a prominent figure among a group of buccaneers based on Galveston Island, Texas. Aury assumed control of Amelia Island and established the "Supreme Council of the Floridas." He even had his secretaries draft a constitution and invited all of Florida to join in resisting Spanish rule. For a few months under Aury's control, the flag of the revolutionary Republic of Mexico was flown on Amelia Island. It's important to note that Aury's "clients," referring to the revolutionary forces in Mexico, were still engaged in their struggle for independence against the Spanish at that time.

The United States had plans to annex Florida and, on December 23, 1817, a naval force captured Amelia Island. Louis-Michel Aury surrendered the island to Commodore J.D. Henley and Major James Bankhead's U.S. forces on the same day. Aury was unwelcome and stayed on the island for over two months. Meanwhile, Major Bankhead occupied Fernandina, and President James Monroe declared that the United States would hold the island "in trust for Spain." This event became known as the Amelia Island Affair.

Despite Spain's anger over U.S. interference at Fort San Carlos, they eventually ceded Florida. The Adams-Onis Treaty officially transferred East Florida and what remained of Spanish claims in West Florida to the United States on February 22, 1821, two years after the treaty was signed in 1819. This was also the year when Mexico gained independence from Spain.

Before the American Civil War, Confederate sympathizers, identifying as the Third Regiment of Florida Volunteers, took control of Fort Clinch on January 8, 1861, just two days before Florida seceded from the Union. The fort was located on the north end of Amelia Island and had been under construction. Federal workers abandoned the site, and Confederate General Robert E. Lee visited Fort Clinch in November 1861 and again in January 1862 to survey coastal fortifications.

Union forces regained control of the island on March 3, 1862, with 28 gunboats under the command of Commodore Samuel Dupont. The island became a refuge for escaped slaves who sought freedom within Union lines. By 1863, there were approximately 1200 freedmen and their children, along with 200 whites living on Amelia Island. This was one of the locations where freedmen gathered near Union forces.

In 1862, Secretary of War Edward M. Stanton appealed to northern abolitionists for aid in supporting the thousands of freedmen who camped near Union forces in South Carolina and Florida. Samuel J. May of Syracuse, New York, responded by organizing a "Freedman's Relief Association" in the city. Funds were raised to support two teachers, including Chloe Merrick from Syracuse, who went to Amelia Island to educate the freedmen. She established a school and orphanage in 1863 and continued to receive support from Syracuse for clothing and supplies for the island's poor. She later married Governor Harrison Reed of Florida in 1869 and continued her support for education and welfare throughout the state. By 1872, around one-quarter of school-age children were attending new public schools on the island.

Amelia Island is the venue for various annual events and festivals, attracting thousands of visitors each year. Some notable events include the Isle of Eight Flags Shrimp Festival, the Amelia Island Jazz Festival, the Amelia Island Chamber Music Festival, the Amelia Island Film Festival, the Amelia Island Concours d'Elegance (a charitable automotive event), and the Amelia Island Blues Festival. The island has also served as a filming location for movies such as the 2002 film Sunshine State and The New Adventures of Pippi Longstocking in 1988.

In the past, Amelia Island hosted a Women's Tennis Association tournament called the Bausch & Lomb Championships from 1987 to 2008, spanning 28 years. Since 2009, the island has been the venue for the annual Pétanque America Open, featuring the game of pétanque, a form of boules.

For golf enthusiasts, Amelia Island offers five golf courses: Oak Marsh Course, Long Point Course (at The Amelia Island Club), Golf Club of Amelia Island, Amelia River Golf Club, and Fernandina Beach Golf Club.

Amelia Island Lighthouse

The Amelia Island Lighthouse has a rich and fascinating history, making it one of Florida's most remarkable structures. It was built in 1820 on Cumberland Island under Spanish rule to guide vessels into the St. Mary's River and along the Atlantic Coast. In 1821, when the United States took over Florida from Spain, the lighthouse was moved brick by brick to the northern end of Amelia Island due to changes in the channel.

During the Civil War, the lighthouse was briefly taken out of service but quickly resumed its operation. In 1903, the oil lamps were replaced with a third-order Fresnel lens, which remains in use today. The tower was electrified in the 1930s, allowing for automation. The Coast Guard took over responsibility for maintaining the lighthouse and continued to operate it until the final keeper retired in 1970.

Throughout the years, the lighthouse witnessed the transition from old sailing ships to modern freighters and fishing boats. Yet, its beacon continued to shine, guiding seafarers toward Fernandina Harbor. Today, the lighthouse offers tours twice a month, and an Augmented Reality app allows people to explore its history from their mobile devices.

Amelia Island Welcome Center

In the late 1800s, the train depot at Centre Street's foot opened, welcoming travelers to the grandeur of Historic Downtown Fernandina Beach during the Gilded Age. It served as a passenger depot until the 1930s. When the railroad no longer needed it, the depot was given to the local historical society and then to the City of Fernandina Beach, with the condition that it be used to promote history. The building's historical significance earned it a place in the National Park Service's Historic American Buildings Survey. On June 8th, 2015, the Amelia Island Welcome Center had a grand re-opening in this little brick building, reviving its historical legacy.

Today, the Welcome Center offers a blend of period charm and modern technology, showcasing the activities and experiences Amelia Island has to offer. Stepping inside, you're surrounded by history, represented by the eight flags that have flown over Amelia Island and the story of David Yulee, whose statue outside the Welcome Center is a popular spot for photos. Interactive map tables and displays provide the latest information.

One place to delve into the island's rich past is the Amelia Island Museum of History, housed in the former Nassau County Jailhouse. This museum is known for being Florida's first spoken-word museum. Notably, the infamous pirate Luis Aury once took over the island, raising the flag of the Mexican Republic in 1817. Aury faced severe punishment for his numerous crimes and was sentenced to hang. On the night before his execution, he tried to avoid humiliation by attempting to slit his own throat. However, he was discovered and hastily stitched up by a surgeon to keep him alive. The following day, Aury was hanged on the gallows at the back of the jail. The museum is located at 233 S 3rd Street.

The Williams House, situated in Fernandina Beach, holds a rich history as one of the oldest and most historic homes in the area. Acquired by Marcellus A. Williams in 1858, the house became a sanctuary for the Williams family during the Civil War when Union troops occupied it. After the war, Williams, who had emancipated his slaves, actively participated in the Underground Railroad, providing a safe haven for escaped slaves. The house features a hidden room near the dining area, which was used to conceal the slaves until they could safely continue their journey. The Williams House is located at 103 S 9th Street.

Bosque Bello Cemetery, aptly known as "Beautiful Woods," is one of Florida's most beautiful and oldest cemeteries. The burial ground is home to the resting places of various individuals from the 19th century, including Spanish residents, Amelia Island Lighthouse keepers, boat captains, politicians, nuns, and veterans from different wars. Bosque Bello Cemetery is situated on North 14th Street, one mile north of Atlantic Avenue.

In the heart of the island lies the Egan's Creek Greenway, a protected 300-acre marsh landscape oasis with walking and bike trails, providing ample opportunities to view wildlife. Legend has it that a pirate buried a substantial treasure in this area in 1900 and then murdered his fellow accomplices, using a chain hanging from a large oak tree as a marker for the hidden loot. As the pirate was covering his tracks, a fatal rattlesnake bite sealed his fate, making the pit his final resting place. If you ever come across the remnants of a rusty chain hanging from a tree during your stroll, it is advised to leave the "money tree" undisturbed. You can access the Greenway from various points, such as the Atlantic Recreation Center, Jasmine St., Sadler Rd., Jean Lafitte Blvd., and Citrona Drive extensions of Beech and Hickory Streets. Parking is available behind the Atlantic Recreation Center, along Jasmine Street's right-of-way, and at the Residence Inn on Sadler Road.

Built in 1857, the Florida House was originally intended as a boarding house for railroad employees. However, during the Civil War, it served as accommodation for Union officers. After the war, Major Leddy, one of the officers, purchased the building and transformed it into a hotel, which he operated with his wife. The Florida House became a popular destination for prominent guests such as the Carnegies, Rockefellers, Ulysses S. Grant, Jose Marti, Henry Ford, and early film stars like Mary Pickford, Laurel, and Hardy. The Florida House is located at 22 S 3rd Street.

Fort Clinch, one of the most well-preserved 19th-century forts in the United States, has a history as a garrison during the Civil and Spanish-American wars, despite never experiencing an actual battle. The fort, once abandoned, began its preservation in the 1930s and officially became a part of the state park system in 1935. Fort Clinch is located at 2601 Atlantic Avenue.

Long before the arrival of Europeans, Timucua Indians settled the site of the original town of Fernandina over a thousand years ago. Throughout the subsequent centuries, this riverfront area, now known as "Old Town," has seen a Spanish fort, the home of a witch named Felipa, known for her love potions, and the well-preserved Captain's House from the 1880s, which was featured in a Pippi Longstocking movie filmed in the 1980s. To reach Old Town, turn onto North 14th Street at the traffic light from historic Centre Street and follow the road until you see Old Town on the left, just before the 14th Street bridge

The Palace, known as the oldest bar in Florida, boasts a rich history filled with stories of ghostly encounters. According to the establishment, spirits from the past ten decades gather In Its rooms to Join In the merriment of drinking to your health. A legendary bartender named Charlie Beresford presided over the bar from 1906 to 1960 and devised a unique bar game to make some extra money. He challenged customers to flip a quarter onto the décolletages of the carved mahogany ladies behind the bar and keep the coin balanced there. At the end of his shift, Charlie would collect the quarters he found on the floor, filling his pockets with the winnings. To this day, current bartenders have felt a cold hand on their shoulders when attempting to revive this particular game.

The Palace holds more eerie occurrences, with sounds of music, glasses clinking, and conversations heard in the early hours of the morning, even when the bar is completely empty. Interestingly, an electric player piano, though unplugged, has been known to start playing a tune at the most peculiar times. The bar's haunted reputation is so well-known that there is even a video of "Uncle Charlie's Ghost" for those interested in seeing the paranormal for themselves. The Palace is located at 117 Centre Street.

Embark on a memorable escape from the ordinary with a range of experiences waiting for you on Amelia Island. Whether you prefer an action-packed adventure or a relaxing day on the water, this island has it all. Here are just a few examples of what you can do:

On the Water:

Discover the beauty of Amelia Island and its surroundings, including neighboring Cumberland Island, on an Amelia River Cruise or one of the many sightseeing charters available. Boat Club & Rentals: Enjoy fishing, cruising, or sightseeing on the water with Amelia Boat Club & Rentals, where you can choose to have a captain or take control yourself. Fishing Charters: Create your own fish story with one of the 40 fishing charters available. The Amelia Island Charter Boat Association and Amelia Island Guides

Association can help you find the perfect fit for your fishing adventure. Kayaking and SUP Boarding: Get up close and personal with nature in the natural backwaters by exploring on a kayak or a stand-up paddleboard (SUP). There are nearly a dozen expert, local tour guide companies to choose from for an unforgettable experience. Catamaran Excursion: Experience a two-person catamaran adventure starting from Egans Creek, passing by Historic Fort Clinch, and ending at Cumberland Island with Backwater Cat Adventures or Riptide Watersports. Sunset Sailing: Treat yourself to a private sunset sail with Windward Sailing or Dream Sailing, where you can relax and enjoy the beautiful views as the sun sets over the horizon.

Explore the wonders of Amelia Island on land with a variety of exciting activities and experiences:

Immerse yourself in the island's history by visiting the Amelia Island Museum of History, located in the old county jail, and the Shrimping Museum on the harborfront. Discover the rich heritage of American Beach and the A.L. Lewis Museum, celebrating the African-American community. Experience the Artrageous Artwalk on the second Saturday evening of each month, where over a dozen galleries open their doors to art enthusiasts in downtown Fernandina Beach and throughout the island. Join one of the diverse tours offered year-round, such as the ones by Anchor Trolley, Coast One Tours, Amelia Island History Tours, and ghost tours led by the Amelia Island Museum of History and Amelia Island Ghost Tours. Savor the incredible foodie experiences on the island, including themed farm-to-table dinners at Omni Amelia Island Resort's Sprouting Project and live Chef's Theatre demonstrations at The Ritz-Carlton, Amelia Island. Also, explore the local cuisine on walking and tasting tours by Amelia Island Downtown Tasting Tours. Tee off at the golf links of Amelia Island, offering 99 holes of championship golf, along with the Little Sandy short course for Omni Amelia Island Resort guests. Take a horseback ride on the beach with Happy Trails Walking Horses, Kelly Seahorse Ranch, or Amelia Island Horseback Riding. Enjoy nature on the trails of Fort Clinch State Park and the Egans Creek Greenway, where you can spot birds and other wildlife. Have active outdoor fun at Pirate Playground, Egans Creek Park, Simmons Road Park, or Central Park. Cycle along the Amelia Island Trail, a scenic coastal path winding past moss-laden live oaks and waterways. Join an eco-tour with Amelia Shark Tooth Adventures to learn how to spot even the tiniest sharks' teeth. Treat yourself to relaxation and rejuvenation at a luxury resort spa, providing the perfect escape to unwind and pamper yourself.

APALACHICOLA NATIONAL FOREST

REGION: NORTHWEST DISTRICT   **COUNTY:** FRANKLIN, LEON, LIBERTY, WAKULLA   **CITY:** TALLAHASSEE

DATE VISITED: **WHO I WENT WITH:**

RATING: ☆ ☆ ☆ ☆ ☆   **WILL I RETURN?**   YES / NO

The Apalachicola National Forest boasts a rich and diverse ecosystem, making it a haven for unique animal and plant species. This vast forest, established in 1936, covers about 574,000 acres, making it the largest national forest in Florida. Located in the Florida Panhandle, southwest of Tallahassee, it offers a range of safe and family-friendly activities, including fishing, hunting, hiking, and trail riding, all amidst serene and varied environments.

One of the forest's highlights is its remarkable biodiversity, making it one of the most biodiverse forests in the country. The landscape of the Apalachicola National Forest is characterized by mostly flat terrain with various features such as bays, sinkholes, and swamps scattered throughout. The soil types vary, with some being excessively drained and others poorly drained. The largest natural forest area is dominated by longleaf pine and slash pine, with an understory consisting of palmetto, gallberry, and wiregrass. In the Munson Sandhills south of Tallahassee, you can find turkey oak and bluejack oak, which thrive in the deep, well-drained sandy soil, along with pine.

Geological sinks in the region are surrounded by mesic hardwood forests. The Apalachicola Savannas in the southwestern part of the forest have sandy ridges with longleaf pine, but they also feature large treeless concave areas with a diverse wetland herbaceous community. Throughout the forest, there are many seepage bogs and swamps filled with bay, cypress, gum, and titi trees, where black gum, red maple, and wax myrtle are commonly found. Additionally, the forest houses the endangered Harper's beauty plant.

The Apalachicola National Forest is home to several endangered species listed under the Endangered Species Act by the U.S. Fish and Wildlife Service. These include the gray bat, wood stork, and four mollusks. Notably, it houses the largest recovered population of endangered red-cockaded woodpeckers worldwide. The Apalachicola's delicate savannahs are open wet, grassy areas that provide a refuge for an unusual combination of grasses, delicate orchids, and carnivorous pitcher plants.

The forest also harbors threatened species, including the bald eagle, eastern indigo snake, flatwoods salamander, Gulf sturgeon, and purple bankclimber mussel. Among the threatened plants are white birds-in-a-nest, Godfrey's butterwort, and the Florida skullcap. The Forest Service closely monitors these species, as well as others like the black bear and gopher tortoise, whose populations are considered sensitive and vital to the ecosystem.

Alligators are present in the Apalachicola National Forest and play a significant role in Florida's ecology. They can be found wherever there is a body of water. While they naturally fear humans, they may lose this fear if they are fed or frequently exposed to people. When this happens, alligators can become dangerous. It is essential not to feed or disturb alligators in any way to avoid potential risks.

Visitors can indulge in numerous recreational opportunities on the forest's waterways and trails, including exploring the 67 linear miles of the Leon Sinks, a unique geological area filled with caverns and sinkholes, and the Apalachee Savannahs, which boast stunning wildflower displays in open prairies near the Apalachicola River.

Visitors to the Apalachicola National Forest can also explore the Fort Gadsden Historic Site, which holds significance in African-American history as the former Negro Fort, where 300 individuals, many of them escaped slaves, lost their lives in 1816 due to an American shell hitting an open magazine. The site, located along scenic Route 65 near Eastpoint, south of Wright Lake campground, features an interpretive center, picnic areas, and tranquil views of the Apalachicola River.

Camping is a year-round activity in the Apalachicola National Forest, although summer camping would require braving the heat without air conditioning. The campgrounds in the forest do not offer hookups, and generator use is not allowed after 10 pm. It's important to be aware that during certain times of the year, open fires may not be permitted due to high fire danger. Visitors are allowed to stay for a maximum of 14 days in one location within a 30-day period, except during hunting season. Campsites are available on a first-come, first-served basis, and reservations are not accepted. Pets are allowed but must be restrained or on a leash.

The forest provides both developed and dispersed camping options. Only the developed campgrounds have fees, and there are no group campgrounds or cabins within the Apalachicola National Forest. There are five designated campgrounds with fees:

Camel Lake Recreation Area Campground in Liberty County offers 10 campsites with views of Camel Lake. Each site includes a picnic table, grill, and fire ring. Drinking water is available, and a bathhouse with flush toilets and hot showers is provided. It is wheelchair-accessible, and a volunteer host lives on-site. Activities like picnicking, swimming, boating, fishing, and hiking are also available. Alcohol is not allowed on the premises. Hickory Landing Boat Ramp & Hunt Campground in Franklin County has 12 campsites. Each site includes a picnic table with a grill or fire ring. Drinking water is available, and vault toilets are provided. A volunteer host resides on-site. The campground has a concrete boat ramp. Mack Landing Boat Ramp & Hunt Campground in Wakulla County offers 10 campsites. Each site includes a picnic table with a grill or fire ring. Drinking water is available, and vault toilets are provided. The campground also has a concrete boat ramp. Whitehead Landing Boat Ramp & Hunt Campground in Liberty County provides 6 campsites. Each site includes a picnic table with a grill or fire ring.

Drinking water is available, and vault toilets are provided. The campground has a concrete boat ramp. Wright Lake Recreation Area Campground in Franklin County has 20 campsites. Each site includes a picnic table, grill, and fire ring. Drinking water is available, and the bathhouse offers flush toilets and hot showers. The campground includes a dump station for RVs. It is wheelchair-accessible, and a volunteer host lives on-site. Activities like picnicking, swimming, boating, fishing, and hiking are also available. Alcohol is not allowed on the premises.

For backcountry camping, outside of developed recreation areas, visitors may camp anywhere on the forest (except during general gun hunting season) for a maximum of 14 days within a 30-day period in one location. Campers are reminded to practice Leave No Trace principles by removing all garbage and trash, preserving vegetation, and protecting water systems to maintain the natural state of the area and prevent overuse.

The Apalachicola National Forest offers six day-use areas, four of which require a fee for entry. Each fee area operates on a self-service basis, accepting exact change or checks made out to the USDA Forest Service. Alcoholic beverages are not permitted in any of the day-use areas. These locations are home to abundant wildlife, including various bird species and alligators. The day-use areas are open from 8 AM to 8 PM from May to September and from 8 AM to 6 PM from October to April.

The specific day-use areas within the Apalachicola National Forest are as follows:

Camel Lake Recreation Area: This area in Liberty County features a designated swim area with a beautiful white sand beach on Camel Lake. A bathhouse with flush toilets and outdoor showers is available. Picnic tables and grills are scattered throughout the area, and one medium-sized shelter is offered on a first-come basis. Visitors can enjoy a small boat ramp, and the site is wheelchair accessible. There are three nearby trails: the Florida National Scenic Trail, the Trail of Lakes, and the Camel Lake Interpretive Trail. *Fort Gadsden Historical Site*: Located in Franklin County, this site is home to a historic fort and has interpretive exhibits and artifacts displayed along the banks of the Apalachicola River. Picnic tables, drinking water, and vault toilets are provided, and access by boat is possible. *Leon Sinks Geological Area*: Found in Leon County, this designated Geological Area offers interpretive signs and views of sinkholes from boardwalks and trails. Picnic tables, a kiosk, a water fountain, and flush toilets are available. Swimming, diving, and motor vehicles are prohibited in the sinks to protect their unique and fragile nature. Lost Lake *Recreation Area*: Located in Leon County, this area offers picnicking by a small lake. Restrooms and drinking water are not provided, and swimming is no longer maintained at the lake. *Silver Lake Recreation Area*: Found in Leon County, this area has a designated swim area with a white sand beach on Silver Lake. A bathhouse with flush toilets and hot showers is nearby, and picnic tables and grills are scattered around the area. Three picnic shelters are available on a first-come basis. The site is wheelchair accessible, and a small boat ramp is provided. Motorized boat use is limited to electric trolling motors. A one-mile interpretive trail winds around the lake. *Silver Lake Recreation Area*: Found in Leon County, this area has a designated swim area with a white sand beach on Silver Lake. A bathhouse with flush toilets and hot showers is nearby, and picnic tables and grills are scattered around the area. Three picnic shelters are available on a first-come basis. The site is wheelchair accessible, and a small boat ramp is provided. Motorized boat use is limited to electric trolling motors. A one-mile interpretive trail winds around the lake. *Wright Lake Recreation Area*: Located in Franklin County, this area offers a designated swim area with a small white sand beach on Wright Lake. A bathhouse with flush toilets and hot showers is nearby, and picnic tables and grills are available among the trees. The site is wheelchair accessible, and a 5-mile interpretive trail circles the lake.

The Apalachicola National Forest features several special interest areas, such as the Bradwell Tract, Lake Bradford Tract, Leon Sinks, Morrison Hammock, River Sinks, and Rocky Bluff. Each area offers unique natural features and diverse habitats for exploration and observation. Moreover, the Apalachee Savannahs Scenic Byway extends 31 miles through the western end of the forest, offering picturesque views of the flat, grassy savannahs, diverse wildflowers, oak and cypress forests, and wildlife, including the endangered red-cockaded woodpecker. The Apalachicola National Forest offers hundreds of miles of waterways for slow and scenic canoe and kayak rides. The Ochlockonee River is a popular option for adventurous paddlers to spend a three-day weekend with campsites available at places like Mack and Wood Lake landings. For shorter canoe and kayak excursions, the New River, Lost Creek, Owl Creek, Kennedy Creek, River Styx, and the Upper Sopchoppy River offer enticing options. Additionally, the forest provides over 80 miles of designated backpacking trails for hikers, with one of the most adventurous stretches meandering through the 39-square-mile Bradwell Bay Wilderness Area. For those seeking shorter hikes, there are six interpretive trails to explore, including the five-mile trail to Leon Sinks and the nine-mile Trail of Lakes, although hikers should be prepared for wet conditions. The Apalachicola National Forest provides opportunities for both mountain biking and road cycling enthusiasts. For mountain biking, there are two designated trails: the Munson Hills Off-Road Bike Trail, which features a natural surface, and the Georgia, Florida, and Alabama (GF&A) Rail Trail, which is paved. Additionally, mountain bikers are welcome to ride on numbered roads and the OHV (Off-Highway Vehicle) trails within the forest. For road cyclists, there are two paved trails to enjoy: the Georgia, Florida, and Alabama (GF&A) Rail Trail, which is still being developed between Tallahassee and Sopchoppy, with some portions completed at both ends, and the St. Marks Rail Trail, following an old rail line from Tallahassee to St. Marks. Moreover, forest roads are open for cycling as well. The specific areas within the Apalachicola National Forest where you can indulge in mountain biking are the GF&A Trail, Munson Hills Mountain Bike Trail, Trailhead, Log Landing Trailhead, and Trout Pond Trailhead. As for road cycling, you can explore the Apalachee Savannahs Scenic Byway and the GF&A Trail, among other forest roads.

ART DECO HISTORIC DISTRICT

REGION: SOUTHEAST DISTRICT   **COUNTY:** MIAMI-DADE   **CITY:** MIAMI

DATE VISITED: **WHO I WENT WITH:**

RATING: ☆ ☆ ☆ ☆ ☆   **WILL I RETURN?**   YES / NO

Art Deco Historic District, also known as the Miami Art Deco District or Old Miami Beach Historic District, is a designated historic area in the South Beach neighborhood of Miami Beach. It was recognized as a historic district on May 14, 1979. The district is famous for being the place where the renowned fashion designer Gianni Versace lived and tragically lost his life when he was assassinated by Andrew Cunanan in a mansion on Ocean Drive. The boundaries of the district are the Atlantic Ocean to the east, Sixth Street to the south, Alton Road to the west, and the Collins Canal and Dade Boulevard to the north. Within this area, you can find 960 historic buildings. Thanks to the efforts of Barbara Baer Capitman, a passionate historic preservationist, the Miami Design Preservation League was established as a non-profit organization with the mission of safeguarding and promoting the visual appeal and authenticity of the Miami Beach Architectural Historic District.

Through Barbara's dedication and perseverance, the Art Deco movement in Miami gained national protection, inspiring designers and developers to revive the district's Art Deco elements and restore its boutique hotels to their original pastel-hued splendor.

This district boasts the largest collection of Art Deco buildings worldwide, featuring various styles like "Streamline," "Tropical," and "Med-deco." These buildings were predominantly constructed between the Great Depression and the early 1940s. The architectural movement reached Miami after the city's real estate market experienced a decline in 1925, followed by the devastating "Great Miami Hurricane" in 1926, which left thousands homeless in the Miami region.

Art Deco architecture reached its peak popularity during the early 1920s and 1930s, presenting a contemporary reinterpretation of neoclassical elements while retaining a sense of history, nostalgia, and sophistication. Originating in Paris in 1925, this style is characterized by its vibrant and eye-catching colors, ranging from soft pastel blues and pinks to bold oranges, lively yellows, greens, and more.

Buildings designed in the Art Deco style often incorporate motifs inspired by exotic plants and animals, creating an atmosphere of uniqueness and fascination. Additionally, these structures boast remarkable architectural details, such as geometric fountains and statues. The whimsical pastel-colored buildings are adorned with glamorous features, including porthole windows, sleek curves, glass blocks, shiny chrome accents, and elegant terrazzo floors.

The designs of these buildings are often associated with a sense of technological modernity, resilience, and optimism. This style was driven by the belief that better times would come and was influenced by the optimistic futurism showcased at American World Fairs in the 1930s.

Situated between 5th Street and 23rd Street, the Art Deco Historic District spans along Ocean Drive, Collins Avenue, and Washington Avenue. Starting from the intersection of 5th Street and Ocean Drive and heading north, visitors are greeted with charming buildings featuring distinctive porthole windows, curved metal rails, and flags reminiscent of ocean liners that once docked at the Port of Miami in the 1930s. The hotels along Ocean Drive, facing the ocean and spanning from 5th to 15th Streets, overlook Lummus Park and the beach. Many of these hotels exhibit influences from the Moderne Style, which was showcased at international expositions such as the Chicago World's Fair of 1933 and the New York World's Fair of 1939. Notable landmarks in this area include The Celino South Beach hotel, a delightful Art Deco gem once frequented by Hollywood stars like Clark Gable, Carole Lombard, and Rita Hayworth, as well as the Beacon South Beach Hotel and the Colony Hotel, both adorned with striking neon accents and prominent signs. Continuing the journey northward to 23rd Street, other remarkable Art Deco highlights await discovery, such as the vibrant Clevelander Hotel on Ocean Drive, known for its lively atmosphere. Visitors can also find The Villa Casa Casaurina, a 1930s Spanish-style mansion where Gianni Versace once resided, and the beautifully restored National Hotel with its two-story lobby and a 205-foot-long pool, the longest in Miami Beach. Not far away lies the renowned Delano South Beach, a former Miami Beach skyscraper now frequented by celebrities and socialites seeking relaxation and luxury. Finally, at the outer edges of the Art Deco Historic District, you'll encounter Lincoln Road, a bustling pedestrian-only promenade and outdoor mall adorned with restaurants, shops, and bars, each displaying Art Deco influences on their facades.

To explore this district, you have the option of taking formal walking tours provided by the Miami Design Preservation League. However, if you prefer to explore on your own, you can do so simply on foot or by bicycle. Note that parking can be difficult, especially on popular streets such as Ocean Drive, Collins Avenue and Washington Avenue.

The Art Deco Welcome Center, situated at Ocean Drive and 10th Street, serves as the headquarters for the Miami Design Preservation League. It plays a vital role in preserving and promoting Miami's Art Deco heritage. Established in 1976 with the primary purpose of saving the area's neglected hotels from destruction, the center has evolved into a comprehensive Visitor Center. Inside the Art Deco Welcome Center, visitors can find a collection of books and brochures about the area, making it a valuable resource for those interested in exploring Miami's Art Deco past. It also serves as the starting point for guided tours that offer a deeper understanding of the city's architectural treasures. Beyond guided tours, the center hosts a range of enriching activities, including lectures,

film screenings, exhibits, and other events related to Art Deco and Miami's cultural scene. The center houses a museum and an onsite gift store where visitors can find unique souvenirs and memorabilia. Moreover, the Art Deco Welcome Center assists visitors in accessing information about Miami's performing arts attractions, national parks, monuments, museums, and public transit options, making it a hub for local tourism. The center's operational hours are seven days a week, from 9 a.m. to 5 p.m. For those interested in the official guided tours, they depart daily at 10:30 a.m. During open hours, visitors can also opt for self-guided audio tours. Additionally, private tours can be arranged upon request. It's essential to note that the center does not offer tours on specific holidays, including New Year's Day, Martin Luther King Jr. Day, Presidents' Day, Memorial Day, Independence Day (July 4), Labor Day, Thanksgiving, and Christmas Day. In addition to the regular tours, the center offers several specialized tours, such as the Gay & Lesbian Walking Tour, Jewish Miami Beach Tour, Lincoln Road Tour, Mediterranean Architecture Tour, MiMo Tour, South Beach Scandals Tour, and Private Art Deco Tours. These private tours can be arranged based on specific interests and preferences.

5

BAHIA HONDA STATE PARK

REGION: SOUTHEAST DISTRICT   **COUNTY:** MONROE   **CITY:** MARATHON

DATE VISITED: **WHO I WENT WITH:**

　　　　　RATING: ☆ ☆ ☆ ☆ ☆   **WILL I RETURN?** YES / NO

Henry Flagler's valiant effort to build a railroad to Key West in the early 20th century turned the remote island of Bahia Honda Key into a tropical destination. You can rent kayaks and snorkeling gear on site, and take a boat trip to the reef. You can bring your own kayak or canoe and launch it from the Loggerhead parking lot on the ocean side of the boat dock on the bay side. Bahia Honda has some of the best nearshore snorkeling spots in the Florida Keys. You can see a variety of marine life just a few hundred feet from shore. Because of the shallow water (4 to 6 feet), snorkeling is good for beginners.

The park is a great place for wading and shorebird watching. Marine life is quite abundant in the waters surrounding the island. Just off the beach, divers can spot many species of small reef fish, as well as stingrays, barracudas, and even the occasional small nurse shark. Several species of wading birds can be seen in the park, including white herons, blue herons, tricolored herons, gray herons, snowy egrets, and white ibises. The Sand and Sea Nature Center features displays about local sea and shore life, including corals, shells, crabs, sea urchins, drift seeds, sea sponges, and sea turtles.

Bicycling is a popular recreational activity in the park. You can take a leisurely ride on the paved road in the park. Helmets are recommended for all cyclists, and Florida law requires helmets to be worn by cyclists 16 years of age and younger. Biking and rollerblading are available on the park's 5.6-mile paved road, and there are several fishing and picnic areas in the area. The Calusa area is located on the southwest corner of the park and has two small pavilions with grills, including one accessible grill and pavilion. There are also picnic tables with grills throughout the area.

There is one nature trail in the park. It is located on the southwest end of the island, in the Calusa area, and leads to the top of the Old Bahia Honda Bridge. You can walk along the trail, which used to be U.S. 1, leading to the bridge. The view is spectacular - you can see the entire island from the top of the bridge. You may see large stingrays or jumping fish. If the water is calm, you may see fish and sea turtles swimming below the surface.

Campsites (primitive and fully hooked up) and vacation homes are available. Boat slips are available for overnight rental and include water, electricity, and full use of park facilities (bathhouse, showers, trash disposal, and pump-out). The marina includes 19 boat slips in a protected basin. Sailing is very popular in Bahia Honda because boaters have access to the Gulf of Mexico and the Atlantic Ocean. All fishing within the park must conform to regulations concerning size, number, method of capture, and season. A fishing license may be required.

BIG CYPRESS NATIONAL PRESERVE

REGION: SOUTHWEST DISTRICT   **COUNTY:** COLLIER   **CITY:** OCHOPEE

DATE VISITED: **WHO I WENT WITH:**

RATING: ☆ ☆ ☆ ☆ ☆   **WILL I RETURN?** YES / NO

Big Cypress National Preserve offers a diverse and unique landscape, where visitors can experience a variety of natural wonders, such as cypress and mangroves, encounter alligators, and even spot panther tracks all in a single day. Unlike traditional national parks, this preserve allows for a wide range of activities to be enjoyed within its boundaries.

The establishment of Big Cypress National Preserve dates back to the 1960s when plans for the world's largest Jetport in south Florida's Greater Everglades were announced. To protect the vast and wild Big Cypress Swamp from potential development, various groups including conservationists, environmentalists, sportsmen, Seminoles, Miccosukees, and others joined forces, setting aside their differences. Their collective efforts led to the creation of Big Cypress National Preserve on October 11, 1974, becoming the nation's first national preserve.

The concept of a national preserve emerged as a compromise. While everyone recognized the importance of protecting the swamp, many opposed simply adding it to nearby Everglades National Park, fearing it would lead to restrictive management and limited access. As a result, the concept of a national preserve was born, offering protection while allowing specific activities defined by Congress in the preserve's legislation.

Before its designation as a national preserve, a variety of traditional, consumptive, and recreational activities were already taking place in Big Cypress. These activities included hunting, oil and gas extraction, operation of off-road vehicles, private land ownership, traditional use by the Miccosukee and Seminole Tribes, and cattle grazing. These activities were permitted through the preserve's enabling legislation, setting it apart from conventional national parks.

Even after becoming a national preserve, many individuals continued to live and engage in recreational activities within the swamp. Those who legally owned land before the preserve's establishment and met specific criteria were exempt from federal acquisition. This ensured their right to land ownership, and as a result, numerous residences and primitive camps can still be found scattered throughout the preserve, some accessible only by off-road vehicles or airboats.

In order to access private lands, hunting locations, or explore the remote areas of Big Cypress, specialized transportation is often required. Swamp buggies and airboats, customized four-wheel drive vehicles, serve as essential means of passage through the challenging terrain of the preserve's vast 729,000 acres. Exploring the network of off-road vehicle trails in the preserve necessitates obtaining permits and undergoing vehicle inspections.

The Miccosukee and Seminole Tribes have a long-standing connection to Big Cypress and the Everglades, and they continue to call this region their home. These tribes maintain their traditional way of life by accessing resources in ways that have been passed down through generations. They use timber to construct traditional shelters known as "chickees" and harvest plants and animals for personal use. The creation of Big Cypress National Preserve has secured the legacy and traditional practices of the Miccosukee and Seminole Tribes.

The Sunniland Formation beneath Big Cypress holds one of Florida's only two reserves of oil. Since its initial discovery in 1943, oil extraction has been ongoing in areas that are now part of the preserve, specifically in Raccoon Point and Bear Island. Private companies hold leases for the mineral rights, and both the state and National Park Service closely monitor and oversee the oil extraction operations.

While there are currently no active leases for cattle grazing in Big Cypress, the cattle industry remains vibrant in southern Florida. In the past, ranchers known as "crackers" worked with cattle on the land, using bullwhips and dogs instead of lassos, which earned them the nickname "cracker." They also used a smaller breed of cattle, called "scrub cows," to graze the dense brush in Big Cypress. When the preserve was established, the legislation included provisions to preserve this traditional use of the land.

Hunting has been a long-standing recreational activity at Big Cypress National Preserve, and it continues to be allowed today. The main species of interest for hunters are whitetail deer during the fall season, turkey during the spring season, and feral hogs. To engage in hunting activities, individuals must possess a valid Florida hunting license, and certain special permits may also be required.

Apart from hunting, fishing and frogging are permitted year-round at Big Cypress with a Florida freshwater fishing license. Unlike many other National Park Service units, Big Cypress National Preserve accommodates a wide range of activities. Visitors can enjoy hiking, fishing, canoeing, off-road vehicle (ORV) riding, or simply relaxing amidst the diverse landscape. The preserve provides various opportunities for the public to explore and appreciate the richness of this unique and varied environment.

Big Cypress National Preserve welcomes public use throughout the year, 24 hours a day. Visitors have the flexibility to enter or exit the preserve at any time. If planning an overnight stay, it is necessary to use designated campground sites or obtain a valid permit for backcountry camping. Occasionally, the superintendent may implement area closures to protect specific resources or ensure the safety of visitors. Park rangers have the authority to issue citations to individuals who violate these closure terms.

While Big Cypress National Preserve itself does not have lodging options, there are various nearby communities that offer a diverse range of accommodations to cater to your preferences. The town of Everglades City, located close to the preserve, provides options such as motels, hotels, cabins, and rental properties for visitors. If you prefer to stay a bit further away and take day trips to the preserve, cities like Miami, Homestead, and Naples offer numerous lodging choices to help you find the perfect place for your stay.

The campgrounds at Big Cypress National Preserve may have seasonal closures, temporary closures for repairs, or closures due to resource concerns. For up-to-date information about campground closures, visitors can check the reservation website or contact the Nathaniel P. Reed Visitor Center at 239-695-4758. To secure a camping spot at any of the campgrounds, reservations can be made through the website www.recreation.gov. However, for Pink Jeep and Gator Head campgrounds, access is limited to permitted off-road vehicles, biking, or hiking, and visitors must possess a valid backcountry permit. In addition to the designated campgrounds, backcountry camping is also an option for visitors at Big Cypress National Preserve.

Bear Island Campground: This primitive campground has no water, but it offers vault toilets. There are forty designated sites available. To access the Bear Island Campground, visitors need to travel along a 20-mile secondary gravel road. Nearby, you can find Gator Head Campground and Pink Jeep Campground. *Burns Lake*: This is another primitive camping area without water, but it provides vault toilets. It also offers a day use picnic area and backcountry access parking. There are 15 designated RV/tent sites available for camping. *Gator Head Campground*: This is a primitive campground with nine campsites, but no water facilities. Vault toilets are available for use. Nearby, you can find Bear Island Campground and Pink Jeep Campground. *Midway Campground*: This campground is equipped with electric hookups for RV sites, a dump station, flush toilets, and water. Each RV campsite has a picnic table and hibachi-style grill. Covered picnic areas are available around the lake for day use. *Mitchell's Landing*: This is a primitive campground with no water facilities, but vault toilets are available. There are eleven sites available for camping, and access to the Mitchell Landing Campground is along a secondary gravel road. *Monument Lake*: The campground offers restrooms, drinking water, and 26 designated RV sites along with 10 tent sites. However, there are no hookups for electricity, sewer, or water available at this campground. *Pinecrest Campground*: This campground is reserved for group camping only. There are four sites, each accommodating eight tents with 15 people in each group. There is no water available at this campground, and access is through a secondary gravel road. The stay limits are 10 days from January 1 to April 30 and 14 days from May 1 to December 31. The maximum total length of stay for any camping activity within the national preserve is 180 days in a

12-month period. *Pink Jeep Campground*: This primitive campground has nine campsites, but no water facilities. Vault toilets are available for use. It is located nearby Bear Island Campground and Gator Head Campground. Unless specifically allowed in certain areas during hunting seasons, camping gear cannot be left unattended in the backcountry of Big Cypress National Preserve when the user is not actively camping and staying overnight at the campsite. Backcountry camping is only permitted at designated campsites in the Bear Island Unit, such as Gator Head and Pink Jeep Trail, during the specific hunting season. Campers who leave their equipment at the designated campgrounds in the Bear Island Unit will be required to pay the daily camping fee for the days their equipment occupies the site. In Zone 4, airboat users must camp only in designated campsites (1-17), and backcountry camping is allowed in other areas of Zone 4, except the seaside sparrow closure area, as long as access is gained by foot or non-motorized vessel. However, no personal property, such as tents, grills, cookware, tables, bedding, etc., can be left in the backcountry of Zone 4 when the user is not actively camping and staying overnight at the campsite. Tent camping is allowed in established campgrounds and non-developed areas throughout the preserve, except as restricted in the Bear Island Unit and Zone 4. However, in non-developed areas, backcountry camping is not allowed within ½ mile of any developed area or established county or state roads. Once the daily camping limit has been reached for each time period, no person, party, or organization can use another designated area for the remainder of that season. Additionally, no individual shall be allowed to camp in the Preserve's backcountry for more than a total of 30 days per year.

Exploring Big Cypress through hiking can be done on designated trails or by navigating through unmarked areas using orienteering techniques. Hikers should be mindful of the season and be prepared for varying conditions. The dry season offers the most comfortable hiking experience, while the wet season presents unique challenges, including the possibility of wading through waist-deep water in certain areas. Regardless of the season, hikers can enjoy numerous rewards, such as observing otters eating fish, feeling the breeze through their hair, encountering tropical blooms, or coming across bear tracks. Before entering the backcountry, each group should obtain a backcountry permit. Additionally, during hunting seasons, it is advisable for all individuals venturing into the Preserve's backcountry to wear a lightweight, blaze orange vest for safety. These vests can be purchased at local sporting goods stores.

The Nathaniel P. Reed Visitor Center is accessible seven days a week, from 9:00 am to 4:30 pm, except on December 25th when it remains closed. Meanwhile, the Oasis Visitor Center operates on Fridays, Saturdays, and Sundays, also from 9:00 am to 4:30 pm. The Off-road Vehicle Permit Office has been relocated to the Nathaniel P. Reed Visitor Center and operates on Fridays, Saturdays, Sundays, and Mondays from 9:00 am to 1:30 pm. For administrative matters, the Preserve Headquarters Office, situated in Ochopee, operates from Monday to Friday, from 8:00 am to 4:30 pm. The office remains closed on all federal holidays.

BILL BAGGS CAPE FLORIDA STATE PARK

REGION: SOUTHEAST DISTRICT   **COUNTY:** MIAMI-DADE   **CITY:** KEY BISCAYNE

DATE VISITED: **WHO I WENT WITH:**

RATING: ☆ ☆ ☆ ☆ ☆   **WILL I RETURN?**   YES / NO

Cape Florida, or "the Cape of Florida," was named by explorer Ponce de Leon during the first Spanish expedition to Florida in 1513. The park offers breathtaking views of the Atlantic Ocean and Biscayne Bay from the top of the historic 1825 Cape Florida Lighthouse. Visitors can delve into history on guided tours of the lighthouse or explore the park on foot, by bike, or by boat or kayak.

The park has a 1.5-mile paved bike path and unpaved access roads that are easy to ride on. You can ride several miles in a loop, navigating various paths and roads. You can rent individual bikes or quad bikes from the park's concession located a few steps from the Lighthouse Cafe. Helmets are highly recommended for all cyclists and Florida law requires helmets for cyclists aged 16 and under. The terrain is completely flat. Nature trails are located on the west side of the park. The park has more than a mile of sandy Atlantic beachfront, where snorkeling and swimming is possible.

Besides the beach and tours of the lighthouse and keeper's quarters, activities include fishing from the seawall along Biscayne Bay, hiking, and wildlife viewing. Birds may be seen along the sea wall and the nature trails, depending on the season, weather, and migration patterns. The park is home to the Cape Florida Banding Station (CFBS). The park has such amenities as picnicking areas and youth camping. It also has a visitor center and a museum with interpretive exhibits and concessions. Visitors can anchor overnight in No Name Harbor. The park also has a free pump-out facility for all boats and covered picnic tables. Eighteen covered pavilions allow for picnicking in the shade overlooking the Atlantic Ocean and Biscayne Bay, and picnic tables and grills are located throughout the picnic area. Mooring to the seawall is not permitted from 11 p.m. to 8 a.m., and no more than two boats can be moored together within the harbor. Some of the best shoreline fishing in the region is available from the seawall located along Biscayne Bay. All fishing within the park must conform to regulations concerning size, number, method of capture, and season.

BISCAYNE NATIONAL PARK

REGION: SOUTHEAST DISTRICT   **COUNTY:** MIAMI-DADE   **CITY:** MIAMI

DATE VISITED: **WHO I WENT WITH:**

RATING: ☆ ☆ ☆ ☆ ☆   **WILL I RETURN?** YES / NO

Biscayne National Park safeguards one of the world's most extensive coral reef systems. What sets this park apart from many other national parks in the United States is that it comprises 95% water. Consequently, the most effective way to discover its wonders is by boat, rendering it remarkably distinct. Boat enables you to access the offshore reefs, known for excellent snorkeling and diving spots, as well as the keys and the Jones Lagoon mangrove swamp.

Biscayne's warm subtropical waters offer an aquatic haven for activities such as canoeing, kayaking, motorboating, sailing, scuba diving, snorkeling, fishing, and paddleboarding. However, the adventure is not confined to underwater experiences. As a stop on the Atlantic Flyway, the park also ranks among the best birdwatching spots.

Situated in southern Florida, Biscayne National Park lies just a mere 15 miles away from bustling Miami, yet it transports visitors to an entirely distinct realm. Despite its proximity to one of the largest urban centers in the nation, the pristine condition of Biscayne National Park's untamed waters, islands, and mangroves remains surprisingly intact. Despite efforts in the 1960s to convert the area into an extensive waterfront residential community, the park thrives today.

This park serves as a protector of Biscayne Bay, the barrier reefs that extend offshore, and the northernmost stretch of the Florida Keys. Dominated by water, the park encompasses more than 250 square miles, leaving little room for land.

The term "key" derives from the Spanish word "cayo," signifying a "small island." Keys are formed atop the surface of coral reefs. Spanning 180 miles and extending from Biscayne Bay to Dry Tortugas National Park, the Florida Keys encompass over 800 of these islands.

Within Biscayne National Park, four distinctive ecosystems thrive: the coral limestone keys, the mangrove swamps lining the shoreline, the offshore Florida reef, and the shallow waters of Biscayne Bay.

For the best vistas within the park, the 65-foot-high Boca Chita Lighthouse, constructed in 1938, provides a remarkable view of the Miami skyline. This lighthouse, located on Boca Chita Key, can only be accessed by boat. The Biscayne National Park Institute (BNPI) offers eco-friendly packages that include visits to the key and lighthouse, such as a half-day heritage cruise and a full-day sailing and snorkeling adventure.

Regarding hikes, the Black Point Jetty Trail and the Spite Highway Trail offer opportunities for exploration. The former, starting at the south end of SW 8th Avenue, provides the better experience of the park's two mainland trails. The latter, a seven-mile trail on Elliott Key, allows a chance to spot the rare Schaus swallowtail butterfly. This path was originally carved in the 1960s by disgruntled developers who used bulldozers to protest national park authorities taking over the land. The Convoy Point Jetty Trail, a brief 0.8-mile round trip mostly on a wooden boardwalk, offers an easy walk suitable for kids of all ages and parents with strollers. At the Dante Fascell Visitor Center, there's a "touch table" where visitors can handle corals, animal bones, and sponges, gaining insights into the park's ecosystems.

For children aged eight and older, BNPI organizes various guided activities, including small-group snorkeling sessions and outings that combine snorkeling with sailing and paddling, along with island visits. Some activities, like the snorkel and paddle eco-adventure, are available for kids aged 12 and older.

Accommodation options in Biscayne National Park include tent camping on Elliott Key or Boca Chita Key. Since there are no roads to these islands, access is restricted to private boats. The campsites on both islands are on a first-come, first-served basis, and reservations are made through recreation.gov. Facilities on the islands include boat docks, restrooms, and grills. Elliott Key offers additional amenities like showers, picnic tables, and potable water. For indoor accommodations, Homestead is the nearest option, with several hotels located a 15-minute drive from the park's visitor center at the intersection of Campbell Drive and the turnpike.

Additional information to consider includes fishing regulations, as anglers aged 16 and above need a Florida Fish & Wildlife Conservation Commission (FWC) license to fish in the park's waters. Boating guidelines are essential due to low tides and sensitive coral areas; it's recommended to review these rules, along with marina details, safety measures, and tide predictions before visiting.

Visitors without a vehicle can access the park via the Homestead National Parks Trolley (available on weekends from late November to April), which connects with Miami-Dade municipal bus services from various parts of the metro area.

For those planning a visit, it's important to note that due to its boat-accessible nature, trips to Biscayne National Park often require advance planning, such as booking boat tours or island camping reservations. During the summer, packing insect repellent is essential as the park's mosquitoes are known for their aggressiveness. Additionally, using reef-friendly sunscreens (containing zinc oxide and titanium dioxide) is highly recommended for anyone entering the water for swimming, scuba diving, or snorkeling.

Water enthusiasts can explore various routes, including the Elliott Key Paddling Trail and the Crocodile Creek Paddling Trail, both suitable for canoeing and kayaking. Additionally, snorkelers and divers can delve into the Biscayne Maritime Heritage Trail, which connects six shipwrecks within the park boundary.

Biscayne National Park is a haven for diverse wildlife, from sea turtles and the elusive American crocodile to manatees, bottlenose dolphins, over 600 native fish species, and a myriad of bird species.

The area was inhabited by the Glades people around 10,000 years ago. In the 1500s, the Spanish arrived and took control of the region. The treacherous coral reefs and shallow waters near the Florida coast led to frequent shipwrecks. During the 1800s, the first settlements emerged on Elliott Key, where crops like pineapples and key limes were cultivated. In the early 1900s, the Cocolobo Cay Club was established on Adams Key. Dignitaries like John F. Kennedy, Richard Nixon, and Lyndon Johnson graced Adams Key with their visits in the mid-1900s. Elliott Key even played a role in CIA training activities after the Cuban Revolution of 1959. In 1968, this area was designated as a national monument, and it officially attained national park status on June 28, 1980. In 2022, the park welcomed 700,000 visitors seeking to explore its unique offerings.

Service animals are welcome within Biscayne National Park. However, regular pets are permitted only in specific areas, such as Convoy Point grounds (excluding the Dante Fascell Visitor Center) and on Elliott Key. Boca Chita Key does not allow pets, even on docked boats. All pets must remain on a leash no longer than six feet and under the control of their owners at all times. Owners are responsible for cleaning up after their pets and properly disposing of waste. The complete pet policy for Biscayne National Park, including the definition of service animals, can be found on the park's official website.

Regarding accessibility, there are designated accessible parking spots near the visitor center, and the Homestead National Parks Trolley provides free and wheelchair-accessible transportation. This trolley is also service animal-friendly and operates from various locations within the city of South Florida.

The Dante Fascell Visitor Center ensures accessibility with features such as ramp and elevator access, ADA-compliant restrooms, Braille information brochures, wheelchair-accessible picnic tables, and a theater equipped with accessible seating for viewing videos. The Convoy Point Jetty Trail is wheelchair-accessible, allowing mobility devices to traverse it comfortably. Additionally, some boat tours within the park are designed to be accessible as well. Further information, including a map of the Jetty Trail, can be found on the park's website.

BOCA RATON MUSEUM OF ART

REGION: SOUTHEAST DISTRICT	COUNTY: PALM BEACH	CITY: BOCA RATON

DATE VISITED:	WHO I WENT WITH:

RATING: ☆ ☆ ☆ ☆ ☆   WILL I RETURN?   YES / NO

Established by a group of artists, the inception of the Boca Raton Museum of Art dates back to 1950 when it took shape as the Art Guild of Boca Raton. Over time, this organization has evolved into a comprehensive entity comprising an Art School, Guild, Store, and Museum. The museum boasts permanent collections encompassing contemporary art, photography, non-western art, glass, and sculpture, all complemented by an eclectic array of special exhibitions. Situated within Mizner Park at 501 Plaza Real, Boca Raton, Florida, the museum is a prominent cultural hub in the area.

The Boca Museum of Art offers a diverse blend of traveling exhibitions and enduring collections that encompass both established and emerging artists, showcasing an array of artworks including those by renowned masters. The institution's offerings extend to encompass educational programs, artist talks, film screenings, children's classes, and various events. Every year, it draws over 200,000 visitors, solidifying its role as a pivotal cultural institution in and around Boca Raton. The museum actively encourages visitors to sketch within its galleries and even provides essential tools such as clipboards, sketchbooks, and pencils available at the front desk.

The Boca Raton Museum of Art constitutes a dynamic creative hub encompassing both the Museum in Mizner Park and the Art School. Over the span of seven decades, this institution has been an unwavering source of cultural enrichment and artistic inspiration for both the local community and visitors hailing from all corners of the globe. Within the Museum's walls, a diverse array of interactive engagements awaits visitors, whether they are exploring the Museum itself or seeking creative encounters from the comfort of their homes. These captivating In-Gallery items are conveniently stationed at the Visitors Service desk in the welcoming front lobby.

The vibrant tapestry of events presented by the Museum and Art School, orchestrated by Education Department, is a testament to commitment to offering a sweeping spectrum of in-person experiences. From soul-stirring musical performances and enlightening demonstrations to thought-provoking lectures and compelling film screenings, the aim is to mesmerize, provoke thought, and infuse a personalized dimension into events that can be cherished by individuals, couples, and families alike. Nurturing a love for learning that endures a lifetime and fostering a heightened awareness of the world are core missions of the Museum. To this end, an assortment of educational programs has been meticulously designed to complement various curricula, catering to all fields of study and grade levels. Teachers and students alike can refine their visual literacy, establish connections to their academic syllabi, and channel their creativity in response to artwork —whether they engage from their homes, classrooms, or within the Museum's inspiring walls.

Discover a rich tapestry of programs dedicated to art and the humanities, thoughtfully curated for adults, families, and children. Crafted to cater to a wide spectrum of interests, these offerings provide a platform for forging connections through illuminating discussions, spirited performances, cinematic experiences, and captivating interactive sessions.

Operating as an extension of the museum, the Art School at the Boca Raton Museum of Art provides a diverse array of classes. Situated at the museum's original location on Palmetto Park Road, the art school caters to individuals at all skill levels. The spectrum of offerings spans across various artistic domains including photography, weaving, ceramics, and jewelry making. This wide array ensures that both beginners and seasoned artists can find classes suited to their interests. Additionally, the art school hosts a summer art camp tailored for children aged five to twelve.

Functioning as a supplementary component of the Boca Raton Museum of Art, the Artists' Guild was established in 1984 under the guidance of the museum's board of trustees. With a mandate to promote art, the guild orchestrates over twenty exhibitions annually. The proceeds generated from the sales of artworks during these exhibitions are directed towards supporting the museum's initiatives. The Artists' Guild extends its membership to both artists and enthusiasts, fostering a community of individuals who are actively involved in or passionate about the arts.

The Boca Raton Museum of Art proudly participates as a Blue Star museum, which signifies that it grants free admission to active-duty military personnel and their families during the period spanning Memorial Day to Labor Day. With accreditation from the American Alliance of Museums, the museum stands as a credible and esteemed institution.

The Art School's location is on West Palmetto Park Road, situated a mile to the east of I-95.

BUSCH GARDENS TAMPA BAY

| REGION: CENTRAL WEST DISTRICT | COUNTY: HILLSBOROUGH | CITY: TAMPA |

DATE VISITED: _____ WHO I WENT WITH: _____

RATING: ☆ ☆ ☆ ☆ ☆   WILL I RETURN?   YES / NO

Busch Gardens Tampa Bay was established in 1959. This esteemed park has been renowned for its beautiful gardens and abundant landscaping for a long time. However, it has now gained additional praise for its exhilarating roller coasters, impressive animal exhibits featuring truly wild animals, captivating shows, delectable food options, and various other attractions.

Whether you're an avid coaster enthusiast or looking for fun for the whole family, this theme park offers a wide selection of the best roller coasters and thrill rides in the state. Experience the adrenaline rush of a triple-launch coaster, enjoy a family spin coaster that offers a unique ride every time, and take on epic coaster legends that will leave you exhilarated. With a variety of thrilling attractions, Busch Gardens is the ultimate destination for anyone seeking excitement and adventure in Tampa Bay.

Park attractions:

The Serengeti Flyer is a thrilling ride at Busch Gardens Tampa Bay, and it holds the title of being the tallest and fastest ride of its kind in the world. As riders swing back and forth, they will be taken to great heights above the park's vast 65-acre Serengeti Plain, providing them with breathtaking views. During the ride, guests will experience multiple moments of weightlessness, known as negative-G moments, before plunging back towards the ground. The Serengeti Flyer is designed with twin dueling arms that progressively elevate riders to higher points, reaching speeds of up to 68 mph and a maximum height of 135 feet at its peak. Seating on the ride consists of back-to-back rows of 10 across two gondolas, allowing up to 40 guests to enjoy the exhilarating experience simultaneously.

Iron Gwazi is an adrenaline-pumping roller coaster at Busch Gardens that takes thrills to new heights. Riders will be taken on a breathtaking journey as they plunge from a 206-foot-tall peak into a steep 91-degree drop, reaching top speeds of 76 miles per hour. The coaster offers a total of twelve airtime moments, including three inversions, giving riders the feeling of sinking their teeth into crocodile-inspired thrills. Iron Gwazi is a hybrid coaster design that combines the innovation of a steel coaster with the nostalgic charm of a wooden coaster. While incorporating elements from the classic wooden coaster Gwazi, the ride features all-new thrill components and a reimagined track layout, taking the experience to a whole new level.

Tigris is another exhilarating attraction at Busch Gardens that offers an innovative experience for riders. The coaster catapults guests through a series of looping twists with forward and backward motion, heart-pounding drops, a skyward surge of 150 feet, and an inverted heartline roll, all at speeds exceeding 60 miles per hour. With over 1,800 feet of steel track designed to mimic the agility of a tiger, Tigris showcases the awe-inspiring abilities of this powerful cat.

Cheetah Hunt, Tampa Bay's longest roller coaster, is a thrilling triple-launch ride that celebrates the fastest land animal. The coaster takes riders high above the park, then dashes along the ground through a rocky gorge, covering a length of 4,400 feet. This attraction has quickly become a favorite among coaster enthusiasts for its exhilarating experience.

Cobra's Curse, Florida's first family spin roller coaster ride, offers a unique experience with every ride. This one-of-a-kind coaster features a 30,000-pound snake king and a 70-foot vertical lift, bringing riders within inches of its massive eyes and fangs. During the three-and-a-half-minute ride, coaster trains speed along 2,100 feet of serpentine-like track, traveling backward, forward, and spinning freely. Each ride on Cobra's Curse is different as the trains spin randomly, influenced by the rider's weight distribution. The coaster's air-conditioned queue adds to the excitement, immersing guests in a themed experience with a state-of-the-art snake exhibit.

Height restrictions apply to these attractions, ensuring rider safety. For Iron Gwazi, riders must be 48 inches tall to ride alone, while those 42 inches tall can ride with a responsible person aged 14 or older.

SheiKra is an extreme roller coaster at Busch Gardens that offers a heart-pounding experience for thrill-seekers. The ride starts by climbing 200 feet into the air, leading to a 90-degree drop that stops just at the edge before plunging straight down. Riders will experience a 70 mph roller coaster whirlwind that includes an Immelmann loop, a second dive into an underground tunnel, and a splashdown finale that splashes water on the waiting fans.

Montu is a favorite inverted roller coaster among coaster enthusiasts in Florida. The ride begins with a high climb, followed by a twisting drop, a 60-foot vertical loop, an Immelmann loop, and a weightless roll. With seven inversions, including a unique Batwing inversion, Montu is known for its intense thrills and smooth steel track.

Kumba, named after the distant roar of the king of the jungle, is a legendary roller coaster with thrilling features. After a 135-foot drop, riders experience a diving loop and 3 seconds of weightlessness while spiraling 360 degrees. The coaster boasts one of the world's largest vertical loops and has been voted one of the world's best roller coasters by enthusiasts.

Falcon's Fury takes riders to a height of 300 feet, offering stunning views of Tampa and Busch Gardens. The unique feature of this ride is that the seats pivot 90 degrees before dropping riders face-first at 60 mph. It provides an exhilarating experience, inspired by skydiving, as riders feel the intense thrill of the drop.

Congo River Rapids is a thrilling whitewater rafting expedition that takes riders down a racing river through the Congo. The ride features plunges, waterfalls, and a mysterious water cave, giving riders a refreshing splash or a serious soaking. Onlookers along the banks of the Congo River Rapids add to the excitement by firing water spray jets at the adventurers on the ride.

Serengeti Railway is a relaxing train ride that offers the opportunity to take in the breathtaking beauty of Busch Garden's Serengeti Plain. The train stops in Nairobi and Stanleyville, providing passengers with a close view of free-roaming herds of African animals, including giraffes, zebras, antelopes, and ostriches.

Scorpion is a unique roller coaster with a 360-degree vertical loop, providing an exhilarating experience of being upside down. It is one of the only three roller coasters of its kind left in the world, and it still delivers thrills with every twist and turn. The ride features a 360-degree loop and reaches speeds of 50 miles per hour. Guests between 48" and 54" must be accompanied by a supervising companion who is at least 14 years old and at least 54" tall.

Air Grover is a kids' ride located in the Sesame Street Safari of Fun play area. It offers a junior coaster experience for young children who may be riding their first roller coaster. Parents can accompany their little ones on this children's ride to add to the excitement.

Grand Caravan Carousel, located in Pantopia, is a classic family attraction. Riders under 42" must be accompanied by a responsible person who is at least 14 years old.

Ubanga-Banga Bumper Cars provide timeless family fun and have been a favorite among amusement park rides for generations. Riders must be at least 42" tall to ride, and guests between 42" and 52" must be accompanied by a supervising companion.

Gwazi Gliders is a fun aerial ride designed for kids. Young ones can enjoy floating up and down on this thrilling aerial ride, making it a great attraction for junior thrill-seekers. Guests must be 56" or less to ride, and handheld infants are not permitted.

Stanley Falls is a family-favorite wild water ride. This log flume ride takes guests through a lush jungle and ends with a thrilling 40-foot splashdown. It's a perfect way to cool off on a hot day and is suitable for younger guests who are looking for a fun water adventure.

CALADESI ISLAND STATE PARK

REGION: CENTRAL WEST DISTRICT   **COUNTY:** PINELLAS   **CITY:** DUNEDIN

DATE VISITED: **WHO I WENT WITH:**

RATING: ☆ ☆ ☆ ☆ ☆   **WILL I RETURN?** YES / NO

The park is accessible by passenger ferry or private boat. Attractions include a 3-mile nature trail, marina, picnic pavilions, bathhouses, and beach. The park allows activities such as boating, kayaking and canoeing, fishing, picnicking, swimming and snorkeling, bird watching, and other wildlife. Boaters can use the 108-slip marina on the bay or anchor offshore in calm weather. Enjoy over three miles of paddling through the majestic mangrove tunnels of Caladesi Island.

Caladesi Island State Park features a marina with floating docks with 30-amp electric and water connections. A covered pavilion with a grill is available for picnicking. The marina has a snack bar and gift store. Three sites are handicapped accessible. Fishing is permitted in designated areas. All fishing within the park must comply with regulations regarding size, number, method of fishing, and season. A fishing license may be required. Hiking the nature trails, including the Beach Loop and Hammock Loop, is a great way to experience the flora and fauna of Caladesi Island. The terrain is mostly flat and in some places sandy.

Beachcombing or shelling is a popular activity for many visitors. Collectors can find a multitude of shells including conchs, whelks, and olives. Plan your shelling around the low phase of the tide which exposes most of the beach area.

CAPTAIN TONY'S SALOON

REGION: SOUTHEAST DISTRICT   **COUNTY:** MONROE   **CITY:** KEY WEST

DATE VISITED: **WHO I WENT WITH:**

RATING: ☆ ☆ ☆ ☆ ☆   **WILL I RETURN?**   YES / NO

Captain Tony's Saloon stands as a renowned bar situated in Key West, Florida, specifically at 428 Greene Street.

Over the years, this establishment has been a favored haunt for numerous celebrated artists, writers, and notable figures. A distinctive tradition here involves the addition of a painted barstool whenever a celebrity visits, bearing their name. The bar is adorned with stools commemorating individuals like Ernest Hemingway, Truman Capote, Jimmy Buffett, Shel Silverstein, John Prine, John F. Kennedy, Harry Truman, Mike Leach, among others.

A distinctive feature adorning the exterior sign is a large Jewfish, caught by Captain Tony and meticulously preserved. Legend has it that dropping a quarter into the fish's mouth grants good luck that accompanies you until you depart the island.

Tony Tarracino, affectionately known as Captain Tony, lends his name to the establishment. He was a pivotal figure in Key West, renowned not only as a saloonkeeper but also as a boat captain, politician, gambler, and captivating storyteller. Often referred to as "the conscience of Key West," Captain Tony's vibrant persona added to the unique atmosphere of the bar.

Amidst its four walls resides a tapestry of history and culture, interwoven with the narratives of notable individuals who have graced its doors. Captain Tony's Saloon remains an enduring testament to the rich and dynamic legacy of Key West, making it a cherished haven of living history.

The building housing Captain Tony's Saloon has a rich history that mirrors the vibrant character of Key West itself. Originally constructed in 1852, it served as an ice house and city morgue. In the 1890s, it transformed into a wireless telegraph station, becoming especially significant during the Spanish-American War in 1898, relaying the news of the battleship Maine's destruction. Throughout its existence, the building fulfilled various roles—housing a cigar factory in 1912, serving as a brothel and a Navy-favored bar, and transitioning through multiple speakeasies, the last being The Blind Pig, renowned for gambling, women, and bootleg rum. Observant visitors will notice a large tree inside the bar, which was originally the gallows tree in the open courtyard used for executions. The building was later constructed around this tree. At least 75 people, including pirates and other wrongdoers, were hanged here. Surprisingly, the tree is still alive, with a portion of it extending through the roof. Although Hurricane Irma damaged its top, about six inches of the tree still protrudes from the building. Strangely, it continues to grow twigs and leaves inside the dimly lit bar. By the 1930s, a local named Josie Russell purchased the establishment, turning it into Sloppy Joe's Bar. Ernest Hemingway frequented this spot between 1933 and 1937. In 1938, facing a rent increase, Russell and patrons transported the entire bar to Sloppy Joe's current location. The bar underwent numerous changes and closures until it came into David Wolkowsky's possession in 1962. Renamed "The Oldest Bar," it was eventually acquired by Tony Tarracino (Captain Tony) in 1968, who christened it Captain Tony's Saloon. Notably, Jimmy Buffett's journey began in Key West with appearances at Captain Tony's during the early 1970s, often compensated in tequila. He immortalized the bar and Captain Tony in his song "Last Mango in Paris." Bob Dylan, who released the song "Key West (Philosopher Pirate)" in 2020, also frequented the establishment over the years, leading to his name being painted on a barstool. During a renovation project in the 1980s, the floorboards were removed, revealing the remains of approximately 15 to 18 individuals. Among these remains was a tombstone belonging to a young woman named Elvira Drew. Elvira, who was married and in her mid-teens, was married to an abusive, alcoholic man in his fifties. She met her end in 1822 at the age of 19 when she was hanged on the winter solstice, nearly two centuries ago, for killing her husband. Unfortunately, self-defense was not a valid argument at that time. Elvira's tombstone now rests beside the pool table, seemingly for eternity, or at least until the bar undergoes another round of renovations. Another tombstone found in the bar, positioned beneath the ancient hanging tree, belongs to Reba I. Sawyer, a native of Key West who lived from 1900 to 1950. Upon her death, her husband stumbled upon scandalous letters exchanged between his wife and another man. These letters revealed their secret liaisons and plans to rendezvous at Captain Tony's Saloon. In response, the widowed husband transported his cheating wife's tombstone from the cemetery into the bar, positioning it under the tree, declaring, "This is where she wanted to be, so this is where she will stay." Interestingly, there are more bodies buried beneath the bar's floor than there are tombstones to mark them. Some graves are level with the current floor, while others lie beneath it. Consequently, wherever you step in the bar, you are walking on someone's final resting place. And before you depart, don't forget to bid farewell to the resident skeleton, now artfully dressed and displayed inside the bar. Tarracino sold the bar in 1989 but remained a regular presence until his passing in 2008, greeting patrons and fans on Thursdays.

CASTILLO DE SAN MARCOS

REGION: NORTHEAST DISTRICT   **COUNTY:** ST. JOHNS   **CITY:** ST. AUGUSTINE

DATE VISITED: **WHO I WENT WITH:**

RATING: ☆ ☆ ☆ ☆ ☆   **WILL I RETURN?**   YES / NO

The Castillo de San Marcos, which translates to "St. Mark's Castle" in Spanish, holds the distinction of being the oldest masonry fort in the continental United States. Situated on the western shoreline of Matanzas Bay within the city of St. Augustine, Florida, this fort has a rich history.

Its design was conceived by the Spanish engineer Ignacio Daza, and construction began in 1672. This commencement of construction occurred 107 years after the city itself was founded by the Spanish Admiral and conquistador Pedro Menéndez de Avilés, during the period when Florida was under Spanish rule. The decision to build the fort came after a raid by the English privateer Robert Searles in 1668, which had caused significant destruction in St. Augustine and inflicted damage upon the existing wooden fort. Governor Francisco de la Guerra y de la Vega initiated the fort's construction, and it continued under the leadership of his successor, Manuel de Cendoya, in 1671. The first coquina stones, distinctive to the fort's architecture, were laid in 1672. While the core of the fortress was completed in 1695, it underwent numerous modifications and renovations in the subsequent centuries. In 1763, when Britain took control of Florida as a result of the Treaty of Paris, St. Augustine became the capital of British East Florida, and the fort was renamed Fort St. Mark. However, in 1783, with the signing of the Peace of Paris, Florida was returned to Spanish rule, and the fort reverted to its original name. In 1819, Spain signed the Adams–Onís Treaty, ceding Florida to the United States in 1821. Consequently, the fort was repurposed as a United States Army base and renamed Fort Marion, in honor of the American Revolutionary War hero Francis Marion. In 1924, the fort was designated a National Monument, and after 251 years of continuous military use, it was deactivated in 1933. The 20.48-acre site was subsequently transferred to the United States National Park Service. Finally, in 1942, an Act of Congress restored the fort's original name, Castillo de San Marcos. The Castillo de San Marcos faced multiple attacks and was subjected to two sieges during its history. The first siege occurred in 1702 when English colonial forces led by Carolina Colony Governor James Moore targeted the fort. The second siege took place in 1740, led by English Georgia colonial Governor James Oglethorpe. Interestingly, the ownership of the fort changed hands five times, all through peaceful means, among four different governments. These periods included Spanish control from 1695 to 1763 and again from 1783 to 1821, followed by the Kingdom of Great Britain from 1763 to 1783. Finally, the United States took possession in 1821 and maintained control until the present day, with the exception of the period during the American Civil War when the Confederate States of America briefly controlled it. This fort's strategic placement of cannons and its unique star-shaped design meant that it was never breached or taken by force throughout its various periods of ownership. During its time under United States control, the fort served as a military prison, incarcerating members of Native American tribes, including the famous war chief Osceola during the Second Seminole War, as well as members of western tribes such as Geronimo's band of Chiricahua Apache. It's worth noting that the Native American art form known as Ledger Art had its beginnings at the fort, particularly during the imprisonment of Plains tribes' members like Howling Wolf of the southern Cheyenne. Despite being partly constructed by African slaves under Spanish ownership, the fort later played a significant role as one of the first entry points for fugitive slaves escaping from British North America into Spanish Florida, where they were granted freedom by colonial authorities. This contributed to the establishment of the first free Black settlement in what would become the United States, known as Fort Mose, situated just north of St. Augustine. In 1933, ownership of the Castillo was transferred to the National Park Service, and together with the nearby St. Augustine Historic District, it has become a popular tourist destination that continues to attract visitors to this day.

There are various activities and ways to make the most of your visit to the fort, tailored to suit your interests, schedule, and preferences. Here's a selection of opportunities to enhance your experience at the park:

Engage with Park Rangers: Knowledgeable rangers and volunteers are available to answer your questions and offer insights into the park's history and culture. You can attend formal presentations, which typically last 15-20 minutes and delve into specific themes. Alternatively, there are informal stations where you can interact directly with cultural artifacts, ask questions, and spend as much time as you'd like. The topics, locations, and schedules for these programs may vary depending on the season, weather, and visitor numbers. You can inquire with the park staff upon your arrival or look for signs in the courtyard area to find out about upcoming opportunities.

Experience Living History: Throughout the fort, you'll encounter rangers and volunteers dressed in period attire. They are available for photographs, can answer your inquiries, and share stories about the daily lives and experiences of the colonial inhabitants.

Historic Weapon Demonstrations: Witness engaging musket and cannon demonstrations, typically held on weekends. These demonstrations occur on Saturdays and Sundays at various times: 10:30 AM, 11:30 AM, 1:30 PM, 2:30 PM, and 3:30 PM.

Explore the Fortress: Take a leisurely stroll through the fort's casements and explore the exhibits within. Brochures and maps are available to guide you as you navigate the site. Additionally, you can access a self-guided tour on your mobile device by downloading the Castillo's park app, compatible with Android and iOS.

Become a Junior Ranger: Young visitors can participate in the Junior Ranger program and earn a badge.

Be Inspired: Take a moment to relax and contemplate while enjoying the best view of the city from the gun deck. The fort's green area provides ample space for recreation, whether you prefer a picnic or a peaceful nap in the shade.

To reach Castillo de San Marcos, you have a few travel options depending on your starting point:

If you're coming from the center of Florida, you can drive to the site, which is approximately a 3.5-hour journey. You would typically take the I-4 E highway and then transition onto US-27 N roads.

If you're starting from downtown Orlando, the drive is shorter, taking around 1 hour and 45 minutes. You'd follow the I-4 E highway, and then connect to the I-95 N roads.

An alternative option is to take the 'Greyhound' bus from central Orlando, which has a stop in St. Augustine. Once you arrive in St. Augustine, the monument is just a 2-minute walk from the bus stop.

CLEARWATER BEACH

| REGION: CENTRAL WEST DISTRICT | COUNTY: PINELLAS | CITY: CLEARWATER |

DATE VISITED: WHO I WENT WITH:

RATING: ☆ ☆ ☆ ☆ ☆   WILL I RETURN?   YES / NO

Clearwater Beach is a popular destination located on a barrier island in Pinellas County, Florida. It is situated on the Gulf of Mexico's west-central coast, and it consists of both a resort area and a residential neighborhood. To access Clearwater Beach from the main city of Clearwater, you can cross the Intracoastal Waterway using the Clearwater Memorial Causeway.

This stunning beach is renowned for its pristine white sand that stretches along the Gulf for 2.5 miles (4 km). It boasts a full marina on the side facing the Intracoastal Waterway. On the south, it is connected to another barrier island called Sand Key, where Sand Key Park is located.

Clearwater Beach offers a variety of amenities and activities for visitors to enjoy, including shopping, dining at restaurants, and engaging in exciting activities like parasailing, jet ski rentals, boat tours (often featuring dolphin sightings in the Gulf waters), miniature golf, fishing charters, and adventurous "pirate ship" cruises.

This beach has received numerous accolades and recognition, frequently being ranked among the best beaches in the United States. The Sandpearl resort located here has been named one of the best beach resorts in the U.S. In January 2013, Clearwater Beach was honored with the title of Florida's Best Beach Town in a USA Today reader poll, competing with ten other Florida beach destinations. Moreover, in February 2019, TripAdvisor named Clearwater Beach as the best beach in the United States and the sixth-best beach in the world.

The area has two main airports: St. Pete-Clearwater International Airport and Tampa International Airport. While both serve the region, most visitors choose to fly into Tampa International Airport, even though it's a bit farther from Clearwater and St. Pete (approximately a 45-minute drive). The reason for this preference is that flights to Tampa International Airport are often cheaper than those to St. Pete-Clearwater International Airport.

If you land at Tampa International Airport and need to get to Clearwater or St. Pete, you have a few transportation options. Taxis are available, but they can be a bit pricey. Another option is to rent a car, which can be more cost-effective and gives you the freedom to explore the area at your own pace. Having a car can also be convenient for getting around during your stay. For transportation along the beach, visitors can utilize the Clearwater Jolley Trolley, which has been operating since 1982. The trolley route covers North Clearwater Beach and goes down to Sand Key, including Island Estates. The main thoroughfare on the north end of the beach is Mandalay Avenue, while Gulfview Boulevard serves as the main road on the south end. Both areas offer a diverse selection of businesses, restaurants, and shops.

At Pier 60, named after State Road 60, which ends at Clearwater Beach, visitors can enjoy various amenities. The area features a playground, a snack bar with an attached souvenir shop, and a long fishing pier. The pier hosts daily performances by professional entertainers and children's acts. Every evening, a special event called "Sunsets at Pier 60" takes place, featuring street performers and musical acts. On the pier itself, local artisans set up nightly displays of their handmade goods, including jewelry, candles, and other gifts.

Beach Walk is a beautification project that has significantly improved the beach's appeal in recent years. Located just south of Pier 60, Beach Walk features a compact pedestrian zone adorned with high-end hotels and condos. The area is equipped with drinking fountains, shower nozzles for rinsing off sand, and bicycle racks. The beachfront also underwent "renourishment" efforts, including dune restoration, enhancing the natural beauty along a wide curving sidewalk. The Clearwater Municipal Marina, situated directly across from the pier, offers deep sea fishing and boating activities for visitors. A highlight of the area's nightlife scene is Shephard's Beach Resort and the Palm Pavilion Inn. Visitors can also find various Frenchy's restaurant locations and retail stores, such as Surf Style and Ron Jon Surf Shop.

For outdoor enthusiasts, a paved bicycle trail flanked by mangrove trees runs parallel to the Clearwater Memorial Causeway leading to the city. Just a short distance from the beach, in the Island Estates area, visitors can explore the Clearwater Marine Aquarium, home to Winter, the famous bottlenose dolphin featured in the movie "Dolphin Tale."

If you're planning a vacation to Clearwater Beach, remember that the dress code on the barrier island is cool and casual. It's common to wear bathing suits, shorts, and flip flops. Even though water temperatures can be a bit chilly at around 68°F in the winter, it's still a good idea to pack your bathing suit since the year-round sunshine makes sunbathing possible even if swimming is not ideal. During the summer months, which are Clearwater Beach's warmest, you'll need to be prepared to beat the Florida heat. In January, the coolest month, the temperature averages in the low 70s, providing pleasant weather for outdoor activities. However, in August, there's typically a higher average rainfall, and you should be cautious of afternoon thunderstorms, especially if you're on the beach, as lightning can pose a serious risk. Thankfully, Clearwater Beach has not experienced a major hurricane in the last decade. If you're traveling during the Atlantic Hurricane Season from June 1 to November 30, it's essential to monitor the tropics and be aware of potential weather hazards.

Looking for accommodations in Clearwater Beach and St. Petersburg that cater to families? Here are some options:

Sheraton Sand Key Resort is a lovely beachside retreat situated right next to Sand Key Park in Clearwater Beach. Clearwater Beach Marriott Suites on Sand Key is a fantastic choice for families, as it offers spacious suites and amenities like a kiddie pool, playground, and Lisa's Klubhouse, which hosts activities for children aged 5 to 12. There are also exciting activities available for teenagers. If you prefer staying in St. Pete Beach on Florida's Gulf Coast, consider the Tradewinds Island Grand Resort. This family-friendly resort offers suites with kitchen facilities, making it convenient for families. Kids will enjoy the inflatable slide on the white-sand beach, beach cabanas, water-trikes, and five pools. The resort also features a kids club and a meandering river with paddle boats for added fun.

There are numerous exciting activities in Clearwater Beach and St. Petersburg that can easily fill a week-long family vacation, and you might even find yourself wanting to return for more. Here are some things to do:

Experience the high seas: Take advantage of the water activities, whether it's going on a fishing charter, embarking on a dolphin-watching trip, or simply enjoying a leisurely boat ride. *Enjoy a beach day*: Even if your accommodation isn't directly on the beach, there are plenty of fantastic public beaches to visit, such as Sand Key Park, Fort De Soto Park, and Pass-a-Grille Beach. *Visit the Clearwater Marine Aquarium*: This well-known aquarium is famous for Winter, the dolphin who inspired the movie Dolphin Tale. The focus here is on rescuing, rehabilitating, and releasing sick and injured animals. *Get an adrenaline rush at Busch Gardens Tampa Bay*: Located in Tampa Bay, this theme park offers an array of high-thrill rides, from roller coasters to water slides. *Set sail on a pirate cruise*: Captain Memo's Pirate Cruise in Clearwater Beach is a popular choice. This vibrant red pirate ship sails multiple times a day and features costumed performers, treasure hunts, dancing, face painting, and more. *Explore the Suncoast Seabird Sanctuary*: If your kids love nature, head to this sanctuary, home to hundreds of rescued birds, making it an excellent spot for birdwatching. *Take a leisurely stroll on the piers*: The St. Petersburg Pier extends a mile from the mainland and houses The Pier Aquarium, shops, restaurants, and various attractions. In Clearwater Beach, Pier 60 and its surrounding park host a free daily Sunset Festival with artists, street performers, and evening movie screenings. *Discover the Salvador Dalí Museum*: St. Pete boasts many museums, including the Salvador Dali Museum, which offers family-friendly programming like storytelling, kid-friendly tours, and arts and crafts workshops. *Plan a day trip to Disney World or Universal Studios in Orlando*: If you're feeling adventurous, take a two-hour drive to Orlando, where you can explore the famous theme parks for a day of magical experiences.

15

COCOA BEACH

REGION: CENTRAL EAST DISTRICT   **COUNTY:** BREVARD   **CITY:** COCOA BEACH

DATE VISITED: **WHO I WENT WITH:**

RATING: ☆ ☆ ☆ ☆ ☆   **WILL I RETURN?** YES / NO

Cocoa Beach, located an hour's drive to the east of Orlando on Florida's Space Coast, is often described as the quintessential beach town. It provides a wide range of recreational and leisure activities, making it an ideal destination for various types of travelers, whether you're on a family beach vacation, a business trip, a weekend getaway, or just a day at the beach.

This coastal area is known for its affordability while offering an abundance of exciting attractions and experiences. In addition to enjoying the sun and the beach, visitors to the Space Coast can engage in thrilling activities such as deep-sea fishing and eco-tours, which include kayak adventures and airboat rides, allowing for up-close encounters with Florida's diverse wildlife. The Kennedy Space Center, with the possibility of witnessing a rocket launch into space, is a notable local attraction. There are also opportunities to explore the region's rich history through museum visits and historic site tours or to indulge in beachside shopping for unique treasures. Golf enthusiasts can savor the outdoors on exceptional golf courses, while water sports enthusiasts can revel in wind and watersports. Moreover, the proximity to Orlando's attractions allows for convenient day trips, followed by delightful beachfront dining options, ranging from elegant restaurants to casual spots with a sandy vibe. After sunset, Cocoa Beach offers a laid-back beach-style nightlife, from cool jazz clubs to beachside cafes. To top it off, visitors can enjoy an overnight stay in a perfect hotel room and wake up to breathtaking sunrise views on the beach.

In addition to its many offerings, Cocoa Beach holds the distinction of being the closest beach to Orlando and is conveniently located near Port Canaveral, Florida's rapidly growing port. Travelers can embark on affordable cruises to exotic destinations from Port Canaveral's world-class cruise terminals, with cruise lines like Disney Cruise Line, Carnival, and Royal Caribbean making it their home port.

Cocoa Beach, Florida, saw its initial settlement efforts following the Civil War when a family of newly emancipated slaves started a settlement. Unfortunately, a devastating hurricane in 1885 discouraged further settlement in the area. However, in 1888, a group of individuals from Cocoa purchased the entire tract of land. This land remained largely undeveloped until the arrival of Gus Edwards, an attorney who bought Cocoa Beach and began its development. The City of Cocoa Beach was officially established on June 5, 1925, and it gained city status on June 29, 1957.

Cocoa Beach's significant growth occurred during the 1960s, coinciding with America's space program. The John F. Kennedy Space Center, located approximately 15 miles away, played a pivotal role in this growth. Many young families moved to Cocoa Beach during this period, as one or both parents worked in various capacities within the space program. Children raised in this community were sometimes affectionately referred to as "Cape Brats." The town experienced such a surge in population that schools had to accommodate the overflow of students by setting up portable classrooms. It wasn't uncommon to have as many as 45 children in a single classroom. Following manned space flights, the community celebrated with astronaut parades. Long before the emergence of Silicon Valley, Cocoa Beach and neighboring towns were hubs for the most talented and skilled technical professionals. Today, many workers from the Kennedy Space Center still call Cocoa Beach their home.

Additionally, Cocoa Beach gained television fame as the setting for the 1960s sitcom "I Dream of Jeannie," although only one episode was actually filmed in the area, specifically Jeannie's wedding scene.

Cocoa Beach and the entire Space Coast of Florida are a paradise for outdoor enthusiasts. This region boasts remarkable natural beauty, including pristine sandy beaches that serve as nesting grounds for turtles, vibrant lagoon waters, and a multitude of nature parks that offer exceptional opportunities for outdoor activities, exploration, and relaxation. During your visit to the Space Coast, you can embark on exciting adventures such as observing dolphins and the endangered Florida Manatee while peacefully kayaking through the stunning Thousand Islands in Cocoa Beach. Alternatively, you can marvel at majestic cranes and wading birds while traversing the Blackpoint Wildlife Drive at the Merritt Island National Wildlife Refuge. For those seeking a thrill, you can go on an exhilarating airboat ride on the St. Johns River to spot alligators. If hiking is more your style, you can explore the breathtaking hammocks featuring a blend of tropical and temperate vegetation by taking a stroll through a captivating Nature Trail.

The beaches are open 24/7, year-round, offering warm Southern waters and an average daytime temperature of 73°F, ensuring there's something for everyone to enjoy.

If you're particularly keen on catching some impressive waves, you'll be thrilled to know that the Space Coast boasts over 100 of the finest surfing spots on the East Coast. As a fun fact, did you know that the 11-time ASP World Champion surfer, Kelly Slater, hails from Cocoa Beach, Florida? This is where his incredible surfing journey began. So, whether you're a seasoned pro or a novice surfer, you're sure to discover an amazing spot to ride the waves and showcase your skills.

Aside from the oceanfront parks, the City of Cocoa Beach provides "stub-end" streets that lead to the Atlantic Ocean. Each of these streets offers access to the beach, complete with dune crossovers, parking spaces (some metered), and litter barrels for your convenience. However, please remember not to bring bottles or pets onto the beach and be sure to dispose of your trash in the provided litter barrels when you depart.

The restaurant scene in the Cocoa Beach area is characterized by a wealth of options, stunning settings, and diverse menus. Whether you're craving impeccably prepared, locally sourced Florida seafood, a delectable flame-grilled prime American beef steak, mouthwatering slow-cooked Southern barbecue, or genuine international cuisine, you'll find a restaurant in the Cocoa Beach area that will not only meet but exceed your culinary expectations, leaving your taste buds thoroughly delighted.

Cocoa Beach and the entire Space Coast of Florida offer a treasure trove of exceptional golfing experiences. Whether you're looking to tee off for a round of golf, hone your skills at the driving range, peruse the offerings at the pro shops, or simply unwind in supremely comfortable surroundings, you'll find a wealth of golfing opportunities to indulge in.

Cocoa Beach is situated in Brevard County, Florida, which is conveniently located halfway between Jacksonville and Miami. Brevard County is known for its extraordinary length, spanning over 70 miles from north to south, while maintaining close proximity to the coastline, with only a short distance from the seacoast at any given point. In fact, the county boasts an impressive 8,000 miles of waterfront due to its unique geography. One of the defining features of Brevard County is the presence of the John F. Kennedy Space Center, earning it the well-deserved moniker of the "Space Coast."

The Space Coast enjoys a subtropical climate characterized by distinct wet and dry seasons. The dry season typically spans from December through May, while the wet season occurs from June to November. January stands as the coldest month, with an average low temperature of 50.7 degrees Fahrenheit and an average high of 71 degrees Fahrenheit. On the other hand, the warmest months are July and August, with average highs reaching 90 degrees Fahrenheit and average lows at 72.2 degrees Fahrenheit. The driest month in the region is April, with an average rainfall of 1.6 inches, whereas September is the wettest month, receiving an average of 6.6 inches of rainfall.

If you're planning to drive into Florida, here are the driving directions to reach Cocoa Beach:

From the North (I-95): Head south on I-95. Take Exit 205A, which leads to Route 528 (Beachline) East. After crossing the IntraCoastal Waterways, you'll arrive at Port Canaveral. The Beachline will transition into A1A, guiding you directly into the heart of Cocoa Beach. *From Orlando International Airport (MCO):* Upon leaving the airport, take the Beachline Expressway (SR 528) heading east. Once you pass the IntraCoastal Waterways, you'll reach Port Canaveral. The Beachline then becomes A1A, leading you directly into the central area of Cocoa Beach. *From Melbourne International Airport (MLB): Drive south on Airport Blvd. until you reach New Haven Avenue (US 192). Turn east onto US 192. Continue east on US 192 until you reach A1A. Head north on A1A for* approximately 20 miles, and you will arrive in Cocoa Beach.

DAGNY JOHNSON KEY LARGO HAMMOCK BOTANICAL SP

REGION: SOUTHEAST DISTRICT	COUNTY: MONROE	CITY: KEY LARGO

DATE VISITED: **WHO I WENT WITH:**

RATING: ☆ ☆ ☆ ☆ ☆   **WILL I RETURN?** YES / NO

This park is located on County Road 905, half-mile north of the intersection with U.S. Highway 1 at Mile Marker 106. The park's name refers to Dagny Johnson, a local environmental activist. The park contains one of the largest tracts of West Indian tropical hardwood hammock in the United States. This park is located on County Road 905, half-mile north of the intersection with U.S. Highway 1 at Mile Marker 106.

The park is home to 84 protected plant and animal species, including wild cottonwood, mahogany mistletoe, and American crocodile. More than 6 miles of nature trails provide plenty of opportunities for birdwatchers and photographers. Most of the park's trails are paved making them suitable for cyclists. Bicycling is easy along the main paved half-mile boulevard. The extended Port Bougainville (Port B) trail is either gravel or a leaf-littered coral rock substrate, with a loop choice of 1 or 2 miles. Some areas are suitable for both thin and fat tire bicycles, but fat tires are recommended for other areas. Helmets are strongly recommended for all cyclists, and Florida law requires helmets to be worn by cyclists 16 years of age and younger. Signs along the self-guided nature trail provide information about the park's ecosystem and wildlife. Guided tours are also available. Many species of tropical birds reside here, including the white-winged pigeon, mangrove cuckoo, and black-throated vireo. Tropical vagrants such as the thick-billed vireo and La Sagra flycatcher are common in the park. Visitors can hike a nature trail that leads through a tropical hardwood hammock and includes a native butterfly garden.

DANIA BEACH

REGION: SOUTHEAST DISTRICT   **COUNTY:** BROWARD   **CITY:** DANIA BEACH

DATE VISITED: **WHO I WENT WITH:**

RATING: ☆ ☆ ☆ ☆ ☆   **WILL I RETURN?**   YES / NO

Dania Beach, formerly known simply as Dania until 1998, is a city situated in Broward County, Florida, within the United States. It is part of the South Florida metropolitan area. Dania Beach is notable for hosting one of the largest jai alai frontons in the United States, known as The Casino at Dania Beach. Jai-Alai is a popular sport in Latin American countries and the Philippines, primarily due to Spanish influences. The game likely originated in the Basque Country and may have a tradition dating back up to 500 years. In the United States, it is considered the fastest game in the world, and it's no wonder, as the ball made of goat skin, weighing 120 to 140 grams, can reach speeds of 300 kilometers per hour. Jai-Alai is played in Miami, Tampa, and Dania Beach, and nowhere else in the United States.

Dania Beach is also a place where you will find an entertainment center called Boomers!, formerly known as Grand Prix Race-O-Rama. In this amusement park, you can forget about the outside world and indulge in fun and entertainment. Boomers! is part of a network of family entertainment centers where you can find carousels, swings, mini-golf courses, rocking boats, go-karts, and roller coasters. In the Dania Beach complex, you will encounter the wooden roller coaster known as Dania Beach Hurricane.

Dania Beach is also home to Pirate's World Amusement Park. This themed amusement park opened in 1967 on a 100-acre site. As the name suggests, the park's theme revolves around pirates. Here, you can enjoy a ride on a pirate ship and even participate in cannon-shooting activities.

Additionally, it's worth mentioning that Dania Beach is home to the IGFA Fishing Hall of Fame and Museum. IGFA stands for the International Game Fish Association, which is a leading authority in the world of fishing. Interestingly, the rules established by IGFA are universally respected and adhered to by all anglers. The IGFA Fishing Hall of Fame and Museum is the world's largest complex and collection of exhibits and information related to sport fishing. Exhibitions, educational activities, and interactive virtual reality shows are just a part of what you will encounter in the museum, which spans over sixty thousand square feet of space. Here, you will find information about 170 species of caught fish, as well as records of the largest fish caught and the rarest ones encountered.

The area's history traces back to the late 19th century when it was initially established as a neighborhood named Modello. In November 1904, it was officially incorporated as the town of Dania, primarily due to the Danish ancestry of most of its 35 residents at the time. On January 4, 1926, Dania voted to annex itself into the City of Hollywood. However, following the devastating impact of the September 1926 Miami hurricane on

Hollywood's fortunes, a significant portion of Dania chose to secede from the City of Hollywood and reincorporate as an independent city. This decision led to the creation of Dania's current city boundaries, which are not continuous. In November 1998, the city formally changed its name to Dania Beach, though the name Dania is still commonly used to refer to the city. In 2001, Dania Beach expanded its territory by annexing several unincorporated areas of Broward County, resulting in an increase of approximately 3,600 residents. Historically, the city was renowned as the "Tomato Capital of the World" during its agricultural phase, but as it evolved into an urban center, it earned the title of the "Antique Capital of the South." This new designation came about due to the proliferation of antique shops, particularly along Federal Highway, which is recognized as the city's "Antique Row."

Dania Beach is located in close proximity to Fort Lauderdale-Hollywood International Airport and major transportation routes. This makes Dania Beach an excellent starting point for many tourists because everything is conveniently close, yet it is not an expensive, world-famous resort. Dania Beach is connected to Fort Lauderdale-Hollywood Airport by Broward County Transit bus lines and suburban Tri-Rail train lines that connect all the major cities in the southern part of Florida.

Dania Beach also offers interesting events. An annual event, attracting not only tourists but also residents of neighboring towns, is the Dania Beach Arts and Seafood Celebration. This event spans two days of craft and art, music, contests, magnificent sand sculptures that are truly breathtaking, marine art and craftsmanship, as well as delicious food from local eateries, including fresh, delightful seafood.The main collaborating hotel with the festival is Sheraton Hotels and Resorts. If you find the attractions and events in Dania Beach insufficient, and you get tired of sunbathing on the beach or splashing in the crystal-clear waters, you can take advantage of the proximity to Hollywood or Fort Lauderdale and embark on numerous interesting excursions. Fort Lauderdale will welcome you with open arms if you are a fan of diving or sunbathingon larger beaches. Alternatively, you can head straight to downtown Fort Lauderdale and Las Olas Boulevard, filled with bars, nightclubs, elegant boutiques, modern shops, as well as interesting restaurants and pubs.

As you can see, if you find yourself in Dania Beach, you will have plenty to do, from amusement parks to the Dania Beach Arts and Seafood Celebration festival. However, if you prefer to use Dania Beach as a base, it may turn out to be a great choice.

DAYTONA INTERNATIONAL SPEEDWAY

REGION: CENTRAL EAST DISTRICT   **COUNTY:** VOLUSIA   **CITY:** DAYTONA BEACH

DATE VISITED: **WHO I WENT WITH:**

RATING: ☆ ☆ ☆ ☆ ☆   **WILL I RETURN?**   YES / NO

The history of Daytona International Speedway commenced in 1953 when Bill France Sr. recognized that racing on the beach was becoming less feasible due to the expanding land usage driven by a rapidly growing population and the immense race crowds. On April 4, 1953, France initiated his vision for the future of racing in Daytona Beach, Florida, by proposing the construction of a permanent speedway facility. Subsequently, on August 16, 1954, France entered into a contract with the City of Daytona Beach and Volusia County officials to build what would later become known as Daytona International Speedway, often referred to as the "World Center of Racing."

In 1957, the land was cleared to prepare for the construction of the Speedway. Notably, the track was designed with its famous 31-degree high-banked turns, which allowed for higher speeds and improved visibility for spectators as cars raced around the 2.5-mile tri-oval. The banking was created by using dirt from the infield, resulting in the formation of a 29-acre body of water known as Lake Lloyd.

The transition from racing on the beach-road course to Daytona International Speedway took place in 1959, and the inaugural DAYTONA 500 occurred on February 22 of that year, drawing a crowd of over 41,000 spectators. The car entries for this race included both hardtop and convertible cars (it was the only DAYTONA 500 to feature convertibles). The finish of the first DAYTONA 500 was so close that it was initially inconclusive. Johnny Beauchamp was celebrated as the victor, but after 61 hours, Lee Petty was declared the official winner following the examination of newsreel footage, which showed that Petty had edged out Beauchamp at the finish line by a margin of approximately two feet.

In 1961, the DAYTONA 200 motorcycle race was relocated from the beach to Daytona International Speedway (DIS). The subsequent year marked the debut of what is now recognized as the Rolex 24 At DAYTONA, the most prestigious sports car race in North America. Initially, this race was a three-hour event, and it evolved into the 24-hour endurance race that we know today in 1966.

A significant transformation of DIS commenced on July 5, 2013, with the groundbreaking of the $400 million DAYTONA Rising frontstretch renovation project. This initiative aimed to modernize the historic speedway into a cutting-edge motorsports facility. As a result, the Speedway now boasts approximately 101,500 permanent seats that are wider and more comfortable, 40 escalators, 17 elevators, a doubled number of restrooms, three times as many concession stands, and three concourse levels extending across the nearly mile-long frontstretch. Furthermore, the Speedway features over 60 luxury suites offering trackside views and an entirely revamped hospitality experience for corporate guests. The project was successfully completed in January 2016 and earned the prestigious Sports Business Award for Sports Facility of the Year from the SportsBusiness Journal.

The approximately 500-acre motorsports complex hosts a diverse schedule of racing events unparalleled anywhere in the world. In addition to at least nine major event weekends, the Speedway grounds are utilized extensively for various activities such as concerts, civic and social gatherings, car exhibitions, photo shoots, production vehicle testing, and police motorcycle training. Moreover, Daytona International Speedway offers daily track tours and serves as the home to the champion DAYTONA 500 car and the Motorsports Hall of Fame of America.

DESTIN

REGION: NORTHWEST DISTRICT   **COUNTY:** OKALOOSA   **CITY:** DESTIN

DATE VISITED: **WHO I WENT WITH:**

RATING: ☆ ☆ ☆ ☆ ☆   **WILL I RETURN?**   YES / NO

Destin is a city situated in Okaloosa County, Florida, within the United States. It serves as one of the principal cities within the Crestview–Fort Walton Beach–Destin metropolitan area.

Nestled along Florida's Emerald Coast, Destin is renowned for its pristine white beaches and the stunning emerald green waters of the Gulf of Mexico. Originally established as a humble fishing village, Destin has evolved into a highly sought-after tourist destination. According to the Florida Department of Environmental Protection, more than 80 percent of the Emerald Coast's annual 4.5 million visitors choose to explore Destin. The city proudly bears the moniker "The World's Luckiest Fishing Village" and boasts of having the largest fleet of fishing vessels in the state of Florida.

Destin's geographical location places it on a narrow peninsula that separates the Gulf of Mexico from Choctawhatchee Bay. This peninsula was initially a barrier island, but over time, it became connected to the mainland due to the effects of hurricanes and changes in sea level. In the 1940s, it regained its status as an island with the completion of the Choctawhatchee-West Bay Canal.

Destin derives its name from Leonard Destin, a fishing captain hailing from New London, Connecticut. Captain Leonard Destin settled in the area during the period spanning from 1845 to 1850. He established a New England colonial-style residence at the site where the Moreno Point military reservation was situated. Over subsequent decades, Captain Destin and his descendants became prominent figures in the local fishing industry, with a long-standing presence in the region.

The development of condominiums in Destin commenced in the 1970s, even though the official incorporation of Destin as a municipality didn't occur until 1984. Notably, the city has witnessed rapid growth since the 1980s, transforming from a small fishing community into a thriving coastal city.

Situated on a peninsula that separates the Gulf of Mexico from Choctawhatchee Bay, Destin's geographical location is historically intriguing. This peninsula initially served as an island, but a series of hurricanes and shifts in sea levels gradually connected it to the mainland.

Destin enjoys proximity to several neighboring cities within the region. To the west, Fort Walton Beach lies at the inlet of Santa Rosa Sound into Choctawhatchee Bay. To the north of Destin, across the bay, is Niceville, and these two cities are connected by the

Mid-Bay Bridge. The primary thoroughfare in the city is U.S. Route 98, which runs from west to east. U.S. Route 98 leads eastward to Panama City, spanning a distance of 56 miles, and westward to Pensacola, covering a distance of 48 miles.

Located at the westernmost tip of the peninsula is East Pass, also known as Destin Pass. It serves as the boundary between the peninsula and Santa Rosa Island to the west. East Pass holds the distinction of being the sole outlet from Choctawhatchee Bay into the Gulf of Mexico. Many historical accounts suggest that this pass was initially dug by hand, with a sudden rush of water causing it to widen considerably within a matter of hours. Early maps and surveys conducted by Spanish, French, and English surveyors, such as Thomas Jefferys's 1775 map "The Coast of West Florida and Louisiana," provide evidence of the early existence of this pass. Ongoing dredging efforts are necessary to maintain the navigability of East Pass.

"Crab Island" was originally comprised of two islands formed from sand dredged up by the Army Corps of Engineers from the East Pass. These islands were substantial enough to support sea grass, small shrubs, and nesting seabirds. However, it has since transformed into a significant sandbar that only emerges during low tide. Despite this change, Crab Island has become a popular anchorage spot in the region. The entrance to Destin Harbor, situated as a lagoon between the beachfront and the primary part of the western peninsula, is located just north of the East Pass jetty. This lagoon takes shape due to a sand spit named Holiday Isle, and numerous condominiums have been constructed along the harbor's edge since the 1970s. Additionally, Norriego Point serves as a protective feature for the harbor and was expanded in size to combat coastal erosion.

The stunning white beaches and pristine emerald waters of the Destin area serve as a major attraction for numerous tourists. According to the Florida Department of Environmental Protection, more than 80 percent of the 4.5 million annual visitors to the Emerald Coast choose to travel to Destin as their destination. One of the appealing features for visitors is the opportunity to charter fishing vessels directly from the harbor. Additionally, Destin boasts 12 beach access points throughout the city, including the renowned Henderson Beach State Recreation Area. Another nearby attraction is the Okaloosa Day Use Area, which is part of the Gulf Islands National Seashore and is located just across East Pass on Santa Rosa Island.

What distinguishes Destin's beaches is the extraordinary whiteness of its sand. This unique sand originates from the Appalachian Mountains and is primarily composed of finely ground quartz crystals, lending it the appearance of sugar. This distinctive sand is carried by the Apalachicola River's flow and subsequently deposited into the Gulf of Mexico. Due to prevailing ocean currents, the sand drifts westward along the Gulf Coast, settling from east of Panama City to the coast of Alabama.

Destin hosts several annual events that attract visitors throughout the year. In October, the Destin Fishing Rodeo, which has been a tradition since 1948, lures anglers to the city. Additionally, the Destin Seafood Festival takes place during the same month, offering a weekend filled with fresh seafood and showcasing the works of local artists.

The city offers a range of accommodations, including hotels, motels, and numerous high-rise condominiums. Private vacation rentals are a prominent feature of the real estate landscape in Destin, Florida. These rentals include a variety of options such as condominiums, beachfront homes, townhouses, resorts, studios, cottages, and a few bungalows. Most vacation rental properties are concentrated on the south side of US Hwy 98, near the Gulf of Mexico, while many locals reside on the northern side of US Hwy 98 along the Choctawhatchee Bay.

Destin is surrounded by other popular tourist destinations in its vicinity. To the east, in Walton County, lies Sandestin, a well-known golf and beach resort. Further along the coast, you'll find Seaside, famous as the filming location for the 1998 movie "The Truman Show," as well as Grayton Beach and Rosemary Beach. To the west are Navarre Beach and Pensacola Beach, with the historic Civil War fortification, Fort Pickens, situated at the western tip of Santa Rosa Island. Notably, many celebrities own homes in this area.

DEVIL'S MILLHOPPER GEOLOGICAL STATE PARK

REGION: NORTHEAST DISTRICT   **COUNTY:** ALACHUA   **CITY:** GAINESVILLE

DATE VISITED: **WHO I WENT WITH:**

RATING: ☆ ☆ ☆ ☆ ☆   **WILL I RETURN?** YES / NO

The most prominent feature of the park is a large sinkhole formed by dissolution in the limestone by acidic groundwater over long periods of time. The cut-off limestone sides of the sinkhole provide a highly visible geologic record of the area. Significant fossil deposits include shark teeth, seashells, and the fossilized remains of extinct land animals. Visitors can picnic and learn more about the sinkhole through interpretive displays.

The park is a popular spot for a quick escape from the city for a picnic. A wheelchair accessible table is available. The boardwalk system that descends to the bottom of the Devil's Millhopper is open. A half-mile nature trail winds around the top of the sinkhole. Dogs may be kept on a 6-foot leash.

Squirrels, rabbits, and a variety of reptiles and amphibians can be seen in the park. The visitor center offers exhibits explaining the formation of the Devil's Millhopper. An audiovisual program is also available.

DRY TORTUGAS NATIONAL PARK

REGION: SOUTHEAST DISTRICT   **COUNTY:** MONROE   **CITY:** KEY WEST

DATE VISITED: **WHO I WENT WITH:**

RATING: ☆ ☆ ☆ ☆ ☆   **WILL I RETURN?** YES / NO

Dry Tortugas National Park is located approximately 70 miles (113 km) west of Key West in the Gulf of Mexico. The park preserves Fort Jefferson and several Dry Tortugas islands, which are the westernmost and most isolated among the Florida Keys. The coral reefs in this archipelago are the least disturbed compared to the reefs in the rest of the Florida Keys.

The park is renowned for its abundant marine life, breeding grounds for tropical birds, colorful coral reefs, as well as shipwrecks and sunken treasures. The focal point of the park is Fort Jefferson, an immense yet unfinished coastal fortress. Fort Jefferson holds the distinction of being the largest brick masonry structure in the Western Hemisphere, comprising over 16 million bricks.

Fort Jefferson was constructed with the primary objective of safeguarding one of North America's most strategically important deepwater anchorages. This fortified harbor served as a crucial "advance post" for American ships tasked with patrolling the Gulf of Mexico and the Straits of Florida. Situated amidst the islands and shoals comprising the Dry Tortugas, the harbor provided ships with opportunities to replenish supplies, make repairs, and find shelter during storms. Its location along one of the world's busiest maritime routes was its most significant military advantage. While passing vessels could easily circumvent Fort Jefferson's largest guns, they could not evade the naval vessels that utilized its harbor.

In the hands of an enemy, the Dry Tortugas could have posed a threat to the heavy ship traffic between the Gulf Coast cities (such as New Orleans, Mobile, and Pensacola) and the eastern seaboard of the United States. Additionally, it could have served as a potential staging area for enemy forces, offering them a launching point for attacks along the Gulf Coast.

To defend this valuable harbor, one of the largest forts ever constructed was poised and ready. Although it was never fully completed or armed during its nearly thirty-year construction period (1846-1875), Fort Jefferson played a crucial role. It was a part of a network of coastal forts stretching from Maine to California, with Fort Jefferson being the most sophisticated. As a symbol of American intent to be left undisturbed, the fort was never attacked but served as an effective deterrent. It contributed to safeguarding the peace and prosperity of a young nation.

During the Civil War, Union warships used the harbor for their blockade of Southern shipping. The fort also functioned as a prison, primarily for Union deserters, with its most famous inmate being Dr. Samuel Mudd, who had set the broken leg of John Wilkes Booth.

Abandoned by the Army in 1874, the fort later served as a coaling station for warships. In 1898, the USS Maine embarked on its historic mission to Havana, Cuba, departing from the Dry Tortugas. Although the fort had brief uses during both world wars, its role as the "Guardian of the Gulf" had long since ended.

Dry Tortugas is unique in its blend of a mostly undisturbed tropical ecosystem with significant historical artifacts. Access to the park is only possible by seaplane or boat. Activities include snorkeling, picnicking, birdwatching, camping, scuba diving, saltwater fishing, and kayaking. Overnight camping is restricted to eight primitive campsites at the Garden Key campground, situated just south of Fort Jefferson.

Dry Tortugas National Park is part of the Everglades & Dry Tortugas Biosphere Reserve, designated by UNESCO in 1976 under its Man and the Biosphere Programme.

Over 99 percent of the park's expanse consists of water. In 2007, the northern and western sections of the park, including the central group of islands, were designated as a research natural area spanning 46 square miles (120 km2). Within this area, harvesting marine life and anchoring vessels are strictly prohibited. Vessels wishing to anchor must use specifically designated mooring buoys or docks. Approximately 54 percent of the park is open to fishing. The park is bordered by the Florida Keys National Marine Sanctuary to the east, south, and west, and by the Tortugas Ecological Reserve to the northwest.

The keys within the park are characterized by their low and irregular terrain. Some of them have sparse growths of mangroves and various vegetation, while the smallest islands may have only small patches of grass or no plant life at all. While nominally there are seven islands, there have been as many as eleven in the past two centuries. The islands constantly undergo changes in size and shape, with the number of distinct landmasses varying as water levels expose or cover the lower islands and sandy land bridges between some of them. Certain smaller islands have vanished and reappeared multiple times due to the impact of hurricanes. The primary islands within the park, roughly arranged from west to east, include Loggerhead Key, Garden Key, Bush Key, Long Key, Hospital Key, Middle Key, and East Key.

The Dry Tortugas were first sighted by a European explorer named Juan Ponce de León on June 21, 1513. During his visit, Ponce de León captured 160 sea turtles, which led him to name the islands the "Tortugas," meaning turtles. The term "Dry" was added because these islands lack surface freshwater. Interestingly, this name is the second oldest surviving European place-name in the United States.

The archipelago is notable for its high concentration of historically significant shipwrecks dating from the 17th century onwards. One such event occurred in 1742 when the HMS Tyger wrecked in the Dry Tortugas. The stranded crew survived on Garden Key for 56 days and even engaged in a battle with a Spanish sloop before eventually sailing to Jamaica in several boats.

Florida was acquired by the United States from Spain in 1819, and the Dry Tortugas were recognized as strategically important for controlling the Straits of Florida and the Gulf of Mexico. Construction on a lighthouse began on Garden Key in 1825, and in 1856, work commenced on a more powerful lighthouse on Loggerhead Key to replace the Garden Key light.

Prominent naturalists and scientists also visited the Dry Tortugas in the past. John James Audubon explored the area in 1832, and Louis Agassiz did so in 1858.

Furthermore, the Dry Tortugas hold a wealth of maritime history. In 1989, Seahawk Deep Ocean Technology investigated a shipwreck believed to be part of the 1622 Spanish treasure fleet, located in 1,332 feet (406 meters) of water. This exploration yielded a variety of cultural artifacts, including olive jars, copper, gold, silver, and glass items.

One of the most famous shipwrecks in the area is that of the Nuestra Señora de Atocha, which was wrecked by a severe hurricane on September 6, 1622, near the Dry Tortugas. The wreck was discovered by Mel Fisher and his company on July 20, 1985. The treasure recovered, known as "The Atocha Motherlode," was valued at an estimated $450 million and included 40 tons of gold and silver, thousands of Spanish silver coins (pieces of eight), gold coins, Colombian emeralds, gold and silver artifacts, and 1,000 silver ingots. Additionally, Fisher's company, Salvors Inc., found the remains of several other nearby shipwrecks, including the Atocha's sister galleon, the Santa Margarita, lost in the same year, and the remains of a slave ship known as the Henrietta Marie, lost in 1700.

With less than 1% of Dry Tortugas National Park consisting of dry land, the most immersive way to experience this exceptional national treasure is by venturing into the water.

The park is situated at the southwest corner of the Florida Keys reef system, which ranks as the third largest in the world. Thanks to its remote location and the eastward-flowing Gulf current just south of the park, you're almost guaranteed to encounter a significantly higher abundance of marine life, often in larger sizes than what you'd find elsewhere in the Florida Keys.

It's essential to note that all coral, reef fish, and cultural artifacts are safeguarded within the park. While you don't need to worry about being attacked by marine wildlife, you should remain vigilant to avoid unintentional contact. Brushing against coral can harm it, and you might inadvertently encounter potentially hazardous creatures such as fire coral, jellyfish, sea urchins, or the venomous lionfish.

Dry Tortugas National Park boasts vibrant coral and seagrass communities. To fully enjoy what the park offers, it's crucial to adhere to all rules and regulations.

Here are some important guidelines to keep in mind:

Do not disturb coral or collect shells, as all coral, whether alive or dead, is protected. Shipwrecks and historical artifacts are legally protected. When snorkeling outside the designated area, always display an approved dive flag. For your safety, it's never advisable to snorkel alone; always use the buddy system when entering the water.

Bringing your own boat to Dry Tortugas National Park offers the most extensive opportunities to explore this incredible national gem.

There's a primitive campground located on Garden Key, which is a short distance from the public dock. Here are some important details regarding camping at the park:

Reservations are not available for the 6-person campsites; however, all arriving campers are guaranteed a camping spot. Individual campsites can each accommodate up to three 2-person tents, totaling a maximum of 6 people. These sites are allocated on a first-come, first-served basis. Campers are responsible for bringing all necessary supplies, including tents, fresh water, fuel, ice, and food. Additionally, all trash and garbage must be packed out upon departure. The only fires permitted are those using gas camping stoves or charcoal briquettes placed in campsite BBQ units. (Note: If you plan to arrive via the ferry, please be aware that compressed gas canisters are not allowed onboard, so you should bring charcoal for grilling.) Campsites come equipped with picnic tables, elevated grills for charcoal fires, and hooks to keep items above the ground.

Campground Facilities:

Composting toilets are available within the campground, with a closure period from approximately 10 a.m. to 3 p.m. During these hours, visitors can use the facilities on the commercial ferry boats docked at the harbor. Dry Tortugas does not have public showers. Visitors can use the fresh water rinse on the ferry when it's docked at Garden Key (no soap is permitted). There is no public wifi, cellular service, or electrical hook-ups at the park. Plan to bring battery-powered devices as needed. Transportation options for campers are limited to private vessels, the daily commercial ferry, and authorized tour guides. The seaplane does not provide transportation for campers. Additionally, there's a group site available for 10-20 people, and reservations are required for this group campsite.

Dry Tortugas National Park is an outstanding fishing destination. When one thinks of fishing, words like patience, relaxation, challenge, and cherished memories often come to mind. As you paddle, you'll have the opportunity to peer into the crystal-clear waters, witnessing the diverse marine life that calls the seagrass beds and coral reefs their home.

The park offers various fishing opportunities catering to different levels of experience. You can opt for quick paddles near Garden Key or venture on longer open-water excursions. Bush and Long Key, being the closest to Garden Key, host thousands of nesting birds during the spring season. Typically, a trip around these two islands can be completed in a few hours.

For those seeking more adventure, Loggerhead Key, located 3 miles to the west of Garden Key, presents a more extensive journey that can take several hours to complete. Loggerhead is the largest island in the park and provides excellent snorkeling spots and nearly deserted beaches. However, this trip involves crossing deep, open waters with powerful currents, making it suitable for experienced paddlers.

Starry night skies and natural darkness are invaluable aspects of national parks, as they preserve some of the last remaining areas of true darkness and provide an exceptional opportunity for the public to connect with this increasingly rare resource. Dry Tortugas National Park is deeply committed to safeguarding and sharing its nighttime skies, allowing both present and future generations to revel in this endangered treasure. Camping on Garden Key serves as an ideal means to fully embrace the wonders of the night skies within the Dry Tortugas.

㉒ ERNEST HEMINGWAY HOME AND MUSEUM

REGION: SOUTHEAST DISTRICT	COUNTY: MONROE	CITY: KEY WEST

DATE VISITED:	WHO I WENT WITH:

RATING: ☆ ☆ ☆ ☆ ☆   WILL I RETURN?   YES / NO

The Ernest Hemingway House, located on Key West Island in Florida, was the home of the famous American writer Ernest Hemingway during the 1930s. This historic house can be found at 907 Whitehead Street, right across from the Key West Lighthouse, near the southern shoreline of the island. The house stands at an elevation of 16 feet (4.9 meters) above sea level, making it the second-highest point on the island. Its resilience to tropical storms and hurricanes is reinforced by its robust 18-inch thick limestone walls. Because of its connection to Hemingway, it's the most popular tourist attraction in Key West. It's also renowned for its large population of cats that are known as Hemingway cats.

In 1928, the renowned writer Ernest Hemingway and his wife, Pauline Pfeiffer, relocated to Key West. Over the next three years, they resided in various rented homes, with their final rental being a two-story residence at 1301 Whitehead Street. Initially, when Pauline first saw 907 Whitehead Street while scouting for a house, she referred to it as a "cursed haunted house." At the time, the property was in foreclosure and was in a state of severe disrepair. However, recognizing its potential, she persuaded her affluent Uncle Gus to purchase it for $8,000 as a wedding gift for her and Ernest. Ernest appreciated the privacy that the 1.5-acre plot offered him for his writing. They enlisted the help of unemployed locals (known as Conchs) to restore the entire house. The house was originally built in 1851 in a French Colonial style by a wealthy marine architect and salvager named Asa Tift. From 1931 to 1939, Hemingway and his wife Pauline Pfeiffer lived in the house. They worked on restoring the deteriorating property and made various improvements to it. During their time there, Hemingway wrote some of his most celebrated works, including the non-fiction book "Green Hills of Africa" (1935), the short stories "The Snows of Kilimanjaro" and "The Short Happy Life of Francis Macomber" in 1936, and the novels "To Have and Have Not" (1937) and "Islands in the Stream" (1970).

While most of the interior furnishings were chosen by Pauline, Ernest insisted on including his hunting trophies. Pauline also replaced the house's ceiling fans with chandeliers, even though it reduced air circulation. Additionally, the couple converted the second floor of the carriage house into a writing studio for Ernest and transformed the basement into a wine cellar. One of the most striking and unique features of the Hemingway Home property is its in-ground swimming pool, which was an extraordinary luxury for a residential home in 1930s Key West. The construction of this pool in 1938 came at a final cost of $20,000, a staggering amount for the time. What makes it even more remarkable is the sheer effort involved in excavating a massive hole in solid coral, measuring 24 feet in width, 60 feet in length, 10 feet in depth at the southern end, and 5 feet in depth at the northern end. The Hemingway pool, the only one within a hundred-mile radius in the 1930s, was undoubtedly an impressive architectural achievement.

Interestingly, not many are aware that it was Ernest Hemingway himself who devised the plan for the pool, despite his subsequent complaints about the expense. His duties as a war correspondent during the Spanish Civil War meant that he left the oversight of the project to his wife, Pauline, who managed the construction of the pool from 1937 to 1938. Ernest Hemingway's vocal objections to the rising construction costs are part of a humorous story that tourists can enjoy when visiting the property today. It is said that he, in apparent frustration at the escalating expenses, dramatically tossed a penny onto the partially built flagstone pool patio, exclaiming, "Pauline, you've spent all but my last penny, so you might as well have that!" Whether this anecdote is true or not, there is indeed a penny embedded in the cement at the north end of the pool as a symbolic nod to Ernest's supposed exclamation. The location of the pool was previously occupied by Hemingway's famous boxing ring, where he would engage in sparring sessions with local amateur boxers like Shine Forbes. The construction of the pool necessitated the relocation of the boxing ring to its current site, which is now occupied by the Blue Heaven Restaurant on Petronia Street, a few blocks away. The pool boasts a massive capacity of 80,784 gallons, and during the time of its installation, Key West had no access to fresh running water. To fill the pool, the construction process involved drilling down to the saltwater table and installing a water pump to extract saltwater, as the available freshwater sources were insufficient for such a large pool. Until the 1940s, when Key West finally had a freshwater supply piped in, the maintenance of the pool was quite labor-intensive. Using the saltwater pump, it took two to three days to completely fill the pool. During the hot summer months, the saltwater would remain fresh for only about two to three days. Afterward, the pool needed to be entirely drained, a day or two was spent scrubbing it clean and removing algae and debris, and then the process would repeat. This charming swimming pool undeniably possesses a magical and almost mystical quality. This is vividly illustrated by a comment made by poet Elizabeth Bishop, a friend of Pauline's, who wrote about the famous pool in one of her letters to Robert Lowell: "The swimming pool is wonderful - it is very large, and the water, sourced from deep beneath the reef, is quite salty. It also illuminates at night - I've noticed that each underwater light bulb has a brightness five times that of the lone bulb in the lighthouse across the street, so the pool must be visible from Mars. It's an amazing experience to swim around in this kind of greenish glow, where your friends appear as luminous frogs..."

Hemingway lived in the house for eight years before moving to Cuba in 1939. Following their divorce in 1940, Pauline continued to live in the house until her death in 1951, after which the house remained unoccupied. Ownership of the house remained in Hemingway's name until his suicide in July 1961. In the same year, his three children auctioned off the house for $80,000.

The new owners originally planned to use the Hemingway House as their private residence. However, because of the continuous interest from visitors, they decided to open the house to the public and establish it as a museum in 1964. On November 24, 1968, it was officially designated as a National Historic Landmark. Although Hemingway's family had already taken away a significant portion of the furnishings, the owners still had much of the larger furniture and many of Hemingway's personal belongings. This led to some criticism regarding the museum's authenticity because not all the furniture was original. All of the rooms in the house are accessible to visitors, except for Hemingway's writing room, which can only be viewed through a screen. Despite the debate over authenticity, the property has become the most popular tourist attraction in Key West.

In September 2017, just before Hurricane Irma hit the Florida Keys, the federal government ordered the entire island chain to evacuate. However, the museum's curator, general manager, and a group of employees made the courageous choice to stay behind and not evacuate, even though they were responsible for the care of the cats on the property. Hemingway's granddaughter encouraged them to evacuate, dismissing the house as "just a house." Nonetheless, these employees opted to remain with the cats and the house, and they managed to survive the storm without significant damage.

The Hemingway House and its surrounding grounds are home to numerous cats, often referred to as Hemingway cats. Approximately half of these cats have an unusual characteristic known as polydactyly, which means they have six toes on each paw. These felines are given names of famous celebrities like Humphrey Bogart or Marilyn Monroe, and they even have their own resting place in a cemetery located in the house's garden. Legend has it that all the cats on the property are descendants of a white, six-toed cat named Snow White, which was reportedly given as a gift to the Hemingways by a sea captain. However, both Hemingway's niece, Hilary, and his son, Patrick, have contested this claim, stating that Hemingway did not own cats in Key West. Instead, they suggest that a neighbor owned several polydactyl cats, and these cats might be the ancestors of the Hemingway cats. Adding to the confusion, there is a photograph showing a young Patrick and Gloria (Hemingway's daughter) playing with a white cat in Key West, although Patrick couldn't recall the specific incident. Starting in 2003, the museum became involved in a lengthy legal dispute lasting nine years with the United States Department of Agriculture (USDA). The dispute centered around whether the Animal Welfare Act of 1966, which typically regulates the treatment of animals in zoos and circuses with big cats, applied to the museum's population of six-toed cats. The USDA argued that the Hemingway House was effectively operating as a zoo, with the cats serving as an exhibit. Undercover agents were even sent by the USDA to monitor the cats in 2005 and 2006. The museum's owners challenged these claims in court. An investigator from People for the Ethical Treatment of Animals (PETA) examined the cats in 2005 and concluded that they were "fat, happy, and relaxed." Ultimately, in 2012, the United States Court of Appeals for the 11th Circuit ruled that the Animal Welfare Act applied because the museum used the cats in advertisements and sold merchandise related to the cats.

EVERGLADES NATIONAL PARK

REGION: SOUTHWEST D., SOUTHEAST D. **COUNTY :** COLLIER, MIAMI-DADE, MONROE **CITY:** FORT LAUDERDALE. MIAMI

DATE VISITED:	WHO I WENT WITH:

RATING: ☆ ☆ ☆ ☆ ☆   **WILL I RETURN?** YES / NO

Everglades National Park, the third-largest national park in the United States, is a vast and captivating wilderness area covering a significant portion of the southern tip of the Florida peninsula. Encompassing 1.5 million acres of wetlands, the park is teeming with a diverse array of wildlife, including millions of alligators, turtles, wading birds, fish, and numerous endangered species, with the Florida Panther being an exceptionally rare find. The park's landscape is a mix of various ecosystems, such as pine uplands, sawgrass rivers, hardwood forests, mangrove islands, and boggy marshlands. Access to Everglades National Park is available from three separate entry points, which are located quite a distance from one another. There are no roads that pass through the park's center or connect its different visitor centers.

Visitors to Everglades National Park are almost guaranteed to witness an abundance of wildlife, particularly wading birds and alligators. It offers a unique opportunity to explore and learn about the fragile ecosystem of the largest subtropical wilderness area in the United States. Whether you choose to spend a substantial amount of time delving into the park's depths or just make a brief visit, the untamed nature of the Everglades becomes apparent immediately. This is a place where wildlife and a sometimes harsh environment demand respect and careful consideration.

Everglades National Park offers four visitor centers. Each visitor center provides different activities and opportunities to spot wildlife based on the terrain. *Gulf Coast Visitor Center*: Located in Everglades City, this center grants access to the Ten Thousand Islands, a network of mangrove islands along the west coast. It's popular among families for its calm and shallow waters, making it ideal for birdwatching, dolphin and manatee spotting. Boat rides are available for exploring the islands, but alligators are less likely to be seen here. *Shark Valley Visitor Center*: Situated on US 41, this center offers a 15-mile paved loop road into the "River of Grass." It's known for immediate alligator sightings, along with American crocodiles, aquatic turtles, and various birdlife. Tram rides and bike rentals are available for an easy introduction to the park's ecosystem. *Ernest F. Coe Visitor Center*: Located 50 miles south of Miami on Florida's east coast, this is the largest visitor center surrounded by dense forests and wet prairie. It offers wildlife viewing platforms and up-close animal encounters, with chances of spotting alligators, roseate spoonbills, and more. *Flamingo Visitor Center*: Situated at the end of State Road 9336, this center is remote but well-developed, offering a snack bar, marina store, and other services.

Here, you may spot manatees, dolphins, and flamingos. Boat tours, canoe, kayak, and bike rentals are available.

The accessibility to Everglades National Park depends on which coast of Florida you are located on and which visitor center you intend to visit. If you are on the west coast, the Gulf Coast Visitor Center is conveniently accessible from Fort Myers, Naples, and Marco Island. Fort Myers also has an international airport for easy travel. On the east coast, both the Ernest F. Coe and Flamingo visitor centers are closest to Miami and Miami International Airport. The Shark Valley Visitor Center is situated along US 41, one of the main roads that cuts across the southern end of the state. It is closer to Miami, but visitors from Naples can still plan a day trip to reach this center. To access any of the park's visitor centers, having a car is necessary as they are spread out and not directly connected.

As for accessibility within the park, visitors will be pleased to find that the park visitor centers and bathrooms are wheelchair accessible. Additionally, many of the popular trails within the park are paved, providing ease of access for wheelchair users. While some non-paved trails may have uneven surfaces, they generally have minimal elevation changes. Moreover, for those interested in exploring the park by boat, guided boat tours are also wheelchair accessible, offering an opportunity to experience the natural beauty of Everglades National Park.

Accommodations in the Everglades National Park area include both camping options and hotels. The park provides developed campgrounds at the Flamingo and Ernest F. Coe visitor centers, some of which offer electrical hook-ups for added convenience. For those seeking hotel accommodations, there are recommended options located near the park visitor centers: *Everglades Rod & Gun Club*: This charming establishment features rustic cottages and a historic bar and restaurant. It is conveniently situated in Everglades City, merely one mile away from the Gulf Coast Visitor Center. *Shark Valley Area Hotels*: If you prefer to stay close to the Shark Valley Visitor Center, two options are worth considering. The Comfort Suites Miami-Kendall is located approximately 26 miles away, while the Miccosukee Resort & Gaming, a tribal-owned hotel and casino, is situated around 18 miles away. *Ernest F. Coe Visitor Center Hotels*: In close proximity to the Ernest F. Coe Visitor Center, you'll find several budget to mid-range hotels in Florida City, only 9 miles away. Florida City serves as the last mainland stop before reaching the Florida Keys, making it a convenient base for exploring both the park and the Keys, although the scenery might not be as breathtaking as other locations. Moreover, at the Flamingo Visitor Center, Flamingo Adventures offers unique accommodations, such as houseboat and eco-tent rentals.

In addition to wildlife watching, the park offers fishing, canoeing, kayaking, and biking opportunities. There are also developed campgrounds at Flamingo and Ernest F. Coe visitor centers, along with nearby hotels and motels for lodging options. Remember to bring sunscreen, water, mosquito repellent, and a camera to make the most of your visit to this captivating wilderness area.

Fishing opportunities are available at the Gulf Coast, Flamingo, and Ernest F. Coe visitor centers within Everglades National Park. However, fishing licenses are mandatory for both Florida residents and non-residents, with short-term licenses also offered.

The Shark Valley, Flamingo, and Ernest F. Coe centers offer bike rentals and biking opportunities within the park. Due to the park's unique landscape, with a significant portion submerged and the backcountry largely inaccessible, there are only a few hiking trails available at the visitor centers. These trails are relatively short walks with no significant changes in elevation. Notably, the Gulf Coast Visitor Center does not have any hiking trails. Some of the top hiking trails within the park are as follows:

From the Ernest F. Coe Visitor Center: *Anhinga Trail*: This 0.8-mile trail, accessible from the Royal Palm Nature Center, takes you through a marsh and offers up-close views of wading birds and alligators. *Gumbo Limbo Trail*: A 0.4-mile trail passing through palm and gumbo limbo hammock, providing an excellent spot for orchid and bromeliad enthusiasts.

From the Flamingo Visitor Center: *West Lake Trail*: A half-mile boardwalk suspended over a mangrove swamp, extending into Florida Bay. *Snake Bight Trail*: An unpaved 1.6-mile trail and boardwalk section, offering prime opportunities to spot gopher tortoises, white-tail deer, and raptors.

From the Shark Valley Visitor Center: Park Loop Trail: A 15-mile paved loop, serving as the centerpiece of Shark Valley, providing abundant wildlife viewing opportunities of various species and suitable for walking or biking. *Bobcat Boardwalk*: A half-mile raised boardwalk crossing a sawgrass slough and hardwood hammock, allowing a close-up view of the park's ecosystem.

Although alligators may appear slow and lazy while basking in the sun on dry land, it's crucial not to be tempted to get too close to them. Under no circumstances should anyone try to pick up or approach baby alligators, even if they seem adorable. Mother alligators are always nearby, and their protective nature can be dangerous. Furthermore, it's essential to refrain from feeding or touching any wildlife, including raccoons and birds that may seem accustomed to receiving snacks from humans. Interacting with wild animals can disrupt their natural behavior and may even pose risks to both the animals and humans involved. If you visit the park with a leashed pet, keep in mind that they are allowed on paved vehicular roads and campgrounds. However, pets are not permitted on hiking and biking trails or in any wilderness areas within the park. This measure is in place to protect both the wildlife and the safety of visitors and their pets.

FLAGLER MUSEUM

REGION: SOUTHEAST DISTRICT   **COUNTY:** PALM BEACH   **CITY:** PALM BEACH

DATE VISITED: **WHO I WENT WITH:**

RATING: ☆ ☆ ☆ ☆ ☆   **WILL I RETURN?** YES / NO

Upon its completion in 1902, Whitehall, the Gilded Age estate owned by Henry Flagler in Palm Beach, was hailed by the New York Herald as "more marvelous than any palace in Europe, more opulent and majestic than any other private residence on the planet." Presently, Whitehall holds the status of being a National Historic Landmark and is accessible to the public as the Flagler Museum. It provides opportunities for self-guided tours, hosts changing exhibitions, and offers special programs for visitors.

The primary mission of the Henry Morrison Flagler Museum is to safeguard, study, and elucidate Whitehall, along with its associated collections and any materials linked to the life of Henry Morrison Flagler. These components are regarded as distinctive and significant facets of Florida's history and the Gilded Age in America.

Henry Morrison Flagler was born on January 2, 1830, in Hopewell, New York, to Reverend and Mrs. Isaac Flagler. At the age of 14, after completing the eighth grade, Flagler relocated to Bellevue, Ohio, where he secured employment with his relatives at the grain store of L.G. Harkness and Company. His compensation was $5 per month, along with room and board. In 1852, Henry Flagler became a partner in the newly established D. M. Harkness and Company alongside his half-brother, Dan Harkness. The subsequent year, on November 9, he entered into matrimony with Mary Harkness. Together, they had three children: Jennie Louise, Carrie, and Henry Harkness. Unfortunately, only Henry Harkness survived to have offspring, one of whom would later establish the Flagler Museum. In 1862, Henry Flagler and his brother-in-law, Barney York, established the Flagler and York Salt Company, a business engaged in salt mining in Saginaw, Michigan. However, with the conclusion of the Civil War, the demand for salt, which had been substantial for preservation purposes by the Union Army, significantly declined. Consequently, the Flagler and York Salt Company faced financial collapse. Burdened with heavy debts, Flagler returned to Bellevue, Ohio, where he experienced substantial losses. His initial investment of $50,000 and an additional $50,000 borrowed from his father-in-law and Dan Harkness were entirely lost. In the subsequent year, Flagler re-entered the grain business, this time as a commission merchant, and successfully repaid the money he had borrowed for his previous venture in the salt business. During this period, Flagler became acquainted with John D. Rockefeller, who was employed as a commission agent by Hewitt and Tuttle for the Harkness Grain Company. In the mid-1860s, Cleveland was rapidly emerging as the epicenter of the American oil refining industry, prompting Rockefeller to depart from the grain trade and establish his own oil refinery. In need of capital to launch his new venture, Rockefeller approached Henry Flagler, with whom he had conducted business for several years. Flagler secured $100,000 from a relative under the condition that he be granted a partnership stake of 25% in the newly formed company, Rockefeller, Andrews, and Flagler. On January 10, 1870, the partnership of Rockefeller, Andrews, and Flagler was officially established as a joint-stock corporation called Standard Oil. In just two years, Standard Oil ascended to become the dominant force in the American oil refining industry, churning out 10,000 barrels of oil per day. Five years later, Standard Oil relocated its headquarters to New York City, and the Flaglers also made the move, taking up residence at 509 Fifth Avenue in the city. In 1878, Flagler's wife, Mary, who had long battled health issues, fell seriously ill. Following her physician's advice, she and Flagler ventured to Jacksonville, Florida, for the winter in the hopes of improving her health. Sadly, Mary did not recover, and she passed away on May 18, 1881, at the age of 47, leaving Henry Flagler to raise their young son alone. Two years after Mary's death, Flagler married Ida Alice Shourds. Shortly after their marriage, the couple visited St. Augustine, Florida, a place they found charming but lacking in adequate accommodations and transportation infrastructure. Flagler believed that Florida had the potential to attract a significant number of tourists. While Flagler remained on the Board of Directors of Standard Oil, he stepped back from his day-to-day involvement in the company to pursue his interests in Florida. Flagler returned to St. Augustine in 1885 and embarked on the construction of the Hotel Ponce de Leon, an expansive 540-room establishment. Recognizing the importance of a reliable transportation system to support his hotel ventures, Flagler acquired the Jacksonville, St. Augustine & Halifax Railroad, which eventually became the foundation of the Florida East Coast Railway system. The Hotel Ponce de Leon welcomed its first guests on January 10, 1888, and it enjoyed immediate success. Just two years later, Flagler decided to expand his holdings in Florida by constructing a railroad bridge over the St. Johns River, granting him access to the southern part of the state. Alongside this effort, Flagler began to establish a hotel empire, initially acquiring the Hotel Ormond, located north of Daytona. In 1894, Flagler initiated the construction of the Hotel Royal Poinciana on the shores of Lake Worth in Palm Beach, and he extended his railroad further south to West Palm Beach. The Hotel Royal Poinciana swiftly claimed the title of the world's largest resort. In 1896, Flagler erected the Palm Beach Inn (later renamed The Breakers in 1901), which overlooked the Atlantic Ocean in Palm Beach. Possibly in the late 1880s, Henry Flagler began contemplating the ambitious idea of extending his railroad and hotel network all the way to Key West. However, the urgency of his plans accelerated when the severe freezes of 1894 and 1895 damaged the area around Palm Beach but spared the region that would become Miami, situated about sixty miles to the south. Julia Tuttle, the Florida East Coast Canal and Transportation Company, and the Boston and Florida Atlantic Coast Land Company each offered Flagler land incentives to extend his railroad farther south, prompting him to take immediate action on the project. Flagler's railway, which was renamed the Florida East Coast Railway in 1895, successfully reached Biscayne Bay by 1896. Flagler took significant measures to develop the area, including dredging a channel, constructing streets, establishing the first water and power systems, and even funding the town's inaugural newspaper, the Metropolis. In 1896, when the town was in the process of incorporating, its residents sought to pay tribute to the individual responsible for its rapid growth and initially wanted to name it "Flagler." However,

Flagler declined this honor and encouraged them to choose an old Indian name for the river around which the settlement was built, leading to the adoption of the name "Miami." A year later, in Miami, Flagler unveiled the exclusive Hotel Royal Palm. Unfortunately, Flagler experienced the loss of his second wife, Ida Alice, who had been battling mental illness for an extended period. In 1895, Ida Alice had to be institutionalized. On August 24, 1901, Flagler entered into his third marriage, this time with Mary Lily Kenan. As a gift to Mary Lily, Flagler commissioned the construction of Whitehall in 1902, designed by architects John Carrère and Thomas Hastings. Possibly starting from the late 1880s, Henry Flagler had been contemplating the idea of extending his railway and hotel network all the way to Key West. It wasn't until 1905, with the commencement of the Panama Canal Project by the United States, that Flagler decided the time had come to carry out this ambitious endeavor. This extension to Key West would entail the addition of 156 miles of track, most of which would traverse over water. Flagler aptly named this extension the "Over-Sea Railroad." At that time, Key West held the status of being one of Florida's most populous cities and was poised to become the closest deepwater port in the United States to the Panama Canal. Flagler envisioned capitalizing on the potential for increased trade with Cuba, Latin America, and the western regions that the Panama Canal would facilitate. In 1912, after years of intense effort, the Over-Sea Railroad to Key West was completed. It stood as the most audacious engineering feat ever undertaken by a private individual. On January 22nd, 1912, Henry Flagler arrived in Key West, where he was warmly welcomed by thousands of appreciative citizens and an entire week of festivities ensued. Just a little over a year later, Flagler suffered a serious fall down a staircase at Whitehall. Regrettably, he never fully recovered from the injuries sustained in the accident. On May 20, 1913, at the age of 83, Henry Flagler passed away due to his injuries. He was interred in St. Augustine, alongside his daughters, Jennie Louise and Carrie, as well as his first wife, Mary Harkness. Following an illustrious career as a founding partner, often referred to as "the brains," behind Standard Oil, which remained the world's largest and most profitable corporation for over a century, Henry Flagler redirected his efforts toward the development of Florida. Over the next 25 years, he played a pivotal role in shaping modern Florida. The transportation infrastructure he established, along with the burgeoning tourism and agricultural industries, still form the bedrock of Florida's economy today. Furthermore, the construction of the Over-Sea Railroad stands as the most audacious engineering achievement ever undertaken by a private individual. When Henry Flagler embarked on his work in Florida, the state was arguably one of the poorest in the Union. Presently, largely thanks to the efforts of Henry Flagler, Florida ranks as the third largest state in the United States, boasting an economy larger than that of more than 90% of the world's nations. Undoubtedly, no single individual has exerted a more significant and enduring influence on a state than Henry Flagler has on Florida. On March 30, 1902, an article in the New York Herald hailed Whitehall, the Palm Beach residence of Henry Flagler, as being "more remarkable than any European palace, more majestic and opulent than any other privately owned dwelling on the planet." Flagler, with the intention of gifting it to his wife, Mary Lily Kenan Flagler, undertook the construction of Whitehall, an opulent mansion from the Gilded Age, spanning 75 rooms and over 100,000 square feet. The couple utilized this residence as a winter escape from 1902 until Henry Flagler's passing in 1913, effectively establishing the Palm Beach season as a prestigious destination for the affluent during the Gilded Age. For the design of Whitehall, Flagler enlisted the services of the same architects responsible for his Hotel Ponce de Leon in St. Augustine, namely John Carrere and Thomas Hastings. Both architects received their training at the École des Beaux-Arts in Paris and gained experience at the prominent New York firm of McKim, Mead and White. They were practitioners of the Beaux Arts architectural style, which gained popularity at the 1893 World's Columbian Exposition in Chicago. (You can take a virtual tour of the World's Columbian Exposition here.) Carrère and Hastings collaborated on several other iconic Gilded Age landmarks, including the New York Public Library and the Fifth Avenue mansion of Henry Clay Frick. In their role as architects for Whitehall, Carrère and Hastings oversaw the exterior design, interior layout, and had full control over the marble entrance hall and its grand double staircase. The façade of Whitehall is characterized by imposing marble columns and crowned with a distinctive red barrel-tiled roof. The mansion is organized around a central courtyard and comprises two main floors, an attic, and a basement. Alongside the grand public spaces on the first floor, there are twelve guestrooms, house servants' quarters on the west side of the second floor, and guest servants' accommodations in the attic on the east side. Additionally, the mansion included a pantry, a kitchen, and private offices for Mr. Flagler and his secretary. Whitehall was erected on Brelsford Point, strategically positioned on the eastern shore of Lake Worth, with Flagler's Hotel Royal Poinciana situated to the north and The Breakers Hotel to the east. The mansion is enveloped by an elaborately adorned wrought iron fence, renowned as one of the most impressive fences of its era. The interior design of Whitehall was conceived and executed by the New York firm of Pottier & Stymus. Pottier & Stymus adorned the home's interior with period rooms, showcasing a variety of styles, including Louis XIV, Louis XV, Louis XVI, Italian Renaissance, and Francis I. Throughout the winters spent at Whitehall, the Flaglers played host to a continuous stream of guests and visitors. Following Henry Flagler's passing in 1913, the house remained shuttered until the 1916 season. Mary Lily, now married to Robert Worth Bingham, made only one more visit to the home in 1917. Following Mary Lily's passing later that year, Whitehall passed into the ownership of her niece, Louise Clisby Wise Lewis. Subsequently, Ms. Lewis sold Whitehall to a consortium of investors who added an eleven-story tower on the west side, comprising over 250 bedrooms, and converted the entire structure into a hotel. This hotel operated from 1925 to 1959, during which time the original portion of the house was repurposed for lobbies, card rooms, lounges, a bar, and guest suites. In 1959, the entire building faced the threat of demolition. Henry Flagler's granddaughter, Jean Flagler Matthews, became aware of this impending fate and took the initiative to establish a nonprofit organization, the Henry Morrison Flagler Museum, which acquired the property in 1959. The following year, Whitehall was opened to the public, marked by a grand "Restoration Ball" held on February 6, 1960. Henry Flagler's personal Railcar No. 91 is on prominent display within the Flagler Kenan Pavilion at the Museum. This railcar, originally constructed in 1886 for Flagler's private use, was acquired by the Museum in 1959 to preserve a vital piece of Florida's history and commemorate Flagler's remarkable legacy. In 1967, extensive research efforts were undertaken to meticulously restore Railcar No. 91 to its authentic appearance during Flagler's era. Subsequently, additional information about the railcar's original design surfaced from various sources, including the National Museum of American History, Smithsonian Institution, Delaware State Archives, and the Hagley Museum and Library. These invaluable documents, including the initial shop order for Railcar No. 91, serve as the foundation for its current preservation efforts. Both the interior and exterior of Railcar No. 91 have been faithfully restored to their original 1912 state. This was the year when Flagler embarked on a historic journey using this railcar along the Over-Sea Railroad, celebrating the extraordinary engineering achievement and the completion of the FEC Railway, extending from St. Augustine to Key West.

Presently, the Flagler Museum attracts nearly 100,000 visitors from across the globe each year.

FLAMINGO GARDENS

REGION: SOUTHEAST DISTRICT	**COUNTY:** BROWARD	**CITY:** DAVIE

DATE VISITED: **WHO I WENT WITH:**

RATING: ☆ ☆ ☆ ☆ ☆   **WILL I RETURN?**   YES / NO

Established in 1927, Flamingo Gardens stands as one of the oldest botanical gardens and attractions in South Florida. Initially founded by Floyd L. and Jane Wray as an orange grove, this nonprofit botanical gardens boasts an impressive collection, including 15 "Champion" trees, which are the largest of their species in Florida. Specialized botanical gardens feature some of the most extensive collections of naturalized orchids, cycads, and heliconias & gingers in the contiguous United States. Flamingo Gardens is also home to over 3,000 species of rare & exotic, tropical, subtropical, and native plants and trees.

Flamingo Gardens' botanical gardens span 60 acres of lush tropical paradise. Within the gardens, an impressive arboretum hosts some of Florida's largest trees. Situated on Long Key, Flamingo Gardens is set within a natural oak hammock that was once surrounded by the Everglades, preserving one of South Florida's last untouched hardwood forests, much like when it was inhabited by the ancient Tequesta people.

The Everglades Wildlife Sanctuary at Flamingo Gardens provides a permanent haven for birds and animals that have suffered injuries and cannot be released back into the wild. It boasts the largest collection of Florida native wildlife, featuring residents such as a black bear, bobcats, otters, hawks, and flamingos. The sanctuary is also home to threatened or endangered species like the American alligator, American snapping turtle, Florida burrowing owl, wood stork, bald eagle, and Florida Panther, which serve as educational ambassadors to inform the public about the Everglades and conservation efforts.

The Wray Home Museum, nestled among 200-year-old oak trees, was constructed in 1933 by Floyd L. and Jane Wray as a weekend retreat. It holds the distinction of being the oldest residence in Broward County west of University Drive and is now recognized as a Cultural Landmark. Following restoration efforts, the Wray Home Museum offers visitors to Flamingo Gardens a window into South Florida life during the 1930s. Its exhibits showcase significant items connected to the Wrays and Flamingo Groves, along with other historical artifacts from that era.

Flamingo Gardens originally had its beginnings as "Flamingo Groves," a citrus orchard established in 1927 by Floyd L. and Jane Wray. The Wrays, who arrived in Florida in 1925, were captivated by the horticultural potential of the subtropical region. They acquired 320 acres of land encompassing Long Key in the Everglades, including the surrounding areas. On January 2, 1927, Floyd L. Wray officially incorporated Flamingo Groves, marking the inception of one of South Florida's earliest botanical gardens and tourist attractions.

In its early days, when Floyd Wray and his partner Frank Stirling founded Flamingo Groves in 1927, it predominantly consisted of a naturalized hammock amid reclaimed land from the Everglades. Their initiative led to the planting of the first citrus tree on February 22, eventually expanding the grove to encompass 2,000 acres featuring more than 60 varieties of citrus, complete with a 20-acre citrus laboratory. As the 1930s rolled in, the botanical gardens received exotic plants and seeds from the federal government for experimental cultivation. This endeavor aimed to showcase rare tropical fruits, flowering trees, and shrubs, further enhancing the botanical collection at Flamingo Groves.

The Wrays opened their gardens to the public, inviting visitors to experience the beauty of their horticultural haven. They constructed a weekend residence atop the Live Oak hammock situated within the groves, where annual barbeque events were hosted on the expansive lawn. Daily tours were offered, showcasing the citrus groves, botanical gardens, and the fruit shipping area. Interestingly, it's believed that nesting Flamingos were already present on the property at the time of purchase, and Mrs. Wray introduced Peacocks to the gardens in the 1940s, much to the delight of visitors. Additionally, given the indigenous alligator population in the area, an exhibit was introduced in the 1960s, featuring daily demonstrations and shows with these reptiles.

In 1969, Mrs. Wray established the Floyd L. Wray Memorial Foundation in honor of her late husband. The foundation's mission was to preserve the core property for future generations and emphasize the historical significance of the Florida Everglades. Subsequently, the name was changed to Flamingo Gardens, and the gardens were not only preserved but also expanded. In 1990, the Everglades Wildlife Sanctuary was inaugurated, housing the Bird of Prey Center and later featuring a half-acre Free-flight Aviary that represented the five ecological zones of South Florida. Pioneering the concept in the country, the sanctuary provided a permanent home for injured or non-releasable Florida native wildlife. Over the years, various wildlife displays were introduced, including exhibits featuring alligators, River otters, Bald & Golden eagles, bobcats, tortoises, and Florida panthers.

Flamingo Gardens stands as a testament to natural preservation in South Florida today. It proudly hosts one of the few remaining natural jungle growths in the region, harboring an extensive collection of over 3,000 tropical and subtropical plant and tree species, among which stands the largest tree in Florida. Moreover, Flamingo Gardens is home to the most extensive compilation of State Champion trees, signifying the largest tree of their respective species, as determined by the Florida Forestry Service.

The Everglades Wildlife Sanctuary on the premises shelters more than 90 native species, solidifying its status as the largest collection of Florida native wildlife within the state. Recognizing its historical and cultural significance, the property has achieved Broward Cultural Heritage Landmark status. Furthermore, the Wray Home, a registered Historical Landmark in the state of Florida, serves as a museum that offers visitors a captivating glimpse into life during the 1930s.

26

FLORIDA AIR MUSEUM

REGION: CENTRAL WEST DISTRICT   **COUNTY:** POLK   **CITY:** LAKELAND

DATE VISITED: **WHO I WENT WITH:**

          RATING: ☆ ☆ ☆ ☆ ☆   **WILL I RETURN?**   YES / NO

The Florida Air Museum, formerly known as the International Sport Aviation Museum and the SUN 'n FUN Air Museum, holds the official designation as Florida's "Official Aviation Museum and Education Center." It serves as a showcase for a diverse range of aircraft, encompassing one-of-a-kind designs, classics, ultra-lights, antiques, and warbirds.

Situated on the grounds of the Sun 'n Fun fly-in and expo, the museum is supported primarily by the Sun 'n Fun campus, which contributes significantly to its collections and educational programs. The entire campus is located adjacent to Lakeland Linder International Airport, positioned just to the south of the airport's runways.

The primary museum building houses a substantial portion of the collection, particularly smaller aircraft like the Boeing-Stearman Model 75 famously associated with the Red Baron Pizza aerobatic team. The display floor features an array of unique aircraft designs, homebuilt aircraft, and even a Mercury rocket motor. The collection is complemented by a wide range of engines spanning from World War I to the present day. This building also includes facilities such as a library, offices, a conference room, and a small museum gift shop. Meanwhile, the hangar annex serves as a home for larger aircraft and engines.

Additionally, the campus is home to the Buehler Restoration Center, an 8,000-square-foot facility located in close proximity to the Florida Air Museum at SUN 'n FUN. This center serves as the hub for SUN 'n FUN's year-round aircraft restoration activities and was made possible through a generous $300,000 grant from The Emil Buehler Perpetual Trust, supplemented by support from a State of Florida Cultural Facilities and Historical Grant.

As early as the 1980s, just a few years after the inception of the SUN 'n FUN Fly-In, the founding director Billy Henderson and other visionaries conceived the idea of establishing an aviation museum to serve as an anchor for the campus. This museum would offer year-round educational and historical experiences. In 1983, a dedicated museum committee took shape, undertaking tasks such as interviewing architects, obtaining land from the City of Lakeland, and securing the current location for the Florida Air Museum on the SUN 'n FUN campus.

The first glimpse of a "mini-museum" emerged in 1986 within a corner of Hangar A. In 1988, the SUN 'n FUN Aviation Foundation was established to manage the construction and operation of the SUN 'n FUN Air Museum. By 1989, the entire Hangar A was temporarily transformed into a museum space. Marion Robles, a volunteer curator, used his connections with the National Naval Aviation Museum in Pensacola, Florida, to acquire a loan of various aircraft and aircraft engines. This collection included a Boeing NA-75 (N-25) Stearman and the Lockheed XFV-1 "Vertical Riser" shipboard fighter. For many years, attendees of the SUN 'n FUN Fly-In might recall seeing the "Vertical Riser" prominently displayed on its tail near the main office. Today, visitors can find it fully restored, thanks to the dedicated work of volunteers, beside the Guest Hospitality Center in Southeast Exhibits.

In 1991, the City of Lakeland provided funding for the construction of the present museum building, along with a lease agreement for the adjacent land. Originally conceived as a facility focused on restoration and education, this building now serves as the central hub of the Florida Air Museum, with ongoing and planned expansions in various directions. The formal opening of the main building to the public took place during the April 1992 SUN 'n FUN Fly-In.

During the construction of the museum, Milt Voigt, a dedicated volunteer, established an aviation research library, now situated on the second level of the Florida Air Museum and accessible to visitors by appointment. Mr. Voigt played a pivotal role in persuading the Howard Hughes Corporation that the SUN 'n FUN Museum would be an ideal location to house a substantial collection of aviation memorabilia belonging to Mr. Hughes. This collection stands as one of the museum's most cherished assets, and a rotating selection of artifacts is on display throughout the year.

Subsequently, the museum underwent a name change to become the International Sport Aviation Museum, and it introduced informative exhibits such as the Florida Aviation History Wall, designed to complement the aircraft on display and the Hughes collections. Many of these exhibits are still on view today.

In 1999, a pavilion, originally intended to serve as the structural core for an expanded facility, was completed. This pavilion now hosts evening programs during the SUN 'n FUN Fly-In and various events throughout the year. It includes conference rooms, outdoor seating with a stage, and various support areas.

In 2002, the museum underwent a name change, becoming known as the Florida Air Museum. During that same year, it was granted the esteemed title of the "Official Aviation Museum and Education Center of the State of Florida" by Governor Jeb Bush and the Florida Legislature. The museum takes great pride in this recognition and continually strives to uphold and embody the essence of this honor.

In 2014, the museum realigned its operations with the Aerospace Center for Excellence located on the SUN 'n FUN Expo campus. This strategic alignment aimed to advance the mission of educating, engaging, and fostering the next generation of aerospace professionals. As part of this effort, the museum introduced new interactive STEM exhibits, created a family-friendly discovery area, and integrated the arts into various aspects of its activities.

FLORIDA CAVERNS STATE PARK

REGION: NORTHWEST DISTRICT **COUNTY:** JACKSON **CITY:** MARIANNA

DATE VISITED: **WHO I WENT WITH:**

RATING: ☆ ☆ ☆ ☆ ☆ **WILL I RETURN?** YES / NO

Florida Caverns offers visitors a rarity in the state, an opportunity to explore magnificent caverns. As you move between the large underground rooms, you will see numerous chisel marks made by Civilian Conservation Corps workers from the 1930s. The caves and watercourses are home to blind crayfish, bats, and salamanders. The area was inhabited by Native Americans and is an archeologically significant site.

Other activities at the park include camping, boating, horseback riding, and fishing. The boat pier is located between the park entrance station and the family campground. Due to water levels and possible underwater hazards on the Chipola River, it is recommended that only small boats be launched from this location. Boaters can take a leisurely trip along the river, fishing and watching a variety of wildlife. Canoe rentals on the Chipola River are available daily. There is a visitor center with interpretive exhibits. Sinkhole (1.1 miles, red trail blaze) and Bumpnose (6.8 miles, orange trail blaze) multiuse trails in the back of the park are accessible to cyclists, equestrians (with proof of negative Coggins), and hikers. Visitors wishing to use the multiuse trails should park at the Blue Hole day use area. Keep an eye out for a variety of plants, flowers, and wildlife as you hike through these scenic natural areas that are recovering from the devastation caused by Hurricane Michael. Trail maps are available at the ranger station upon request. All bicyclists and horseback riders are advised to wear helmets. Florida law requires the use of helmets by persons 16 years of age and younger. The park closes at sunset and visitors must exit the park by that time; please plan accordingly. It is recommended to bring water, snacks, insect repellent, a trail map, a whistle, and a cellphone while on the trails.

The park has 38 campsites, for both recreational vehicles and tents. All sites are within a short walk or bike ride to the Blue Hole day-use area. Thirty-two campsites in the Blue Hole camping area are equipped with 30/50-amp electricity, water, sewer hookups, a picnic table, an in-ground grill, and a fire ring. Five picnic areas are located throughout the park for your enjoyment. Tables and grills are available on a first-come, first-served basis.

FLORIDA HOLOCAUST MUSEUM

REGION: CENTRAL WEST DISTRICT   **COUNTY:** PINELLAS   **CITY:** ST. PETERSBURG

DATE VISITED: **WHO I WENT WITH:**

RATING: ☆ ☆ ☆ ☆ ☆   **WILL I RETURN?** YES / NO

The Florida Holocaust Museum, one of the largest Holocaust museums in the United States, stands as a testament to the remarkable journey and vision of Walter P. Loebenberg, a St. Petersburg businessman and philanthropist.

Loebenberg, himself a survivor who escaped Germany in 1939 and served in the U.S. Army during World War II, joined forces with local businesspeople, community leaders, Holocaust survivors, and individuals who had lost relatives to create a living memorial. Their collective goal was to honor the memory of those who suffered and perished during the Holocaust while ensuring that such atrocities would never recur for any group.

This dedicated group garnered community support and engaged internationally renowned Holocaust scholars, including Thomas Keneally, author of "Schindler's List," and Elie Wiesel, who served as Honorary Chairman of the Holocaust Center.

The museum's journey began modestly in 1992 when it rented a space at the Jewish Community Center of Pinellas County in Madeira Beach, Florida. With a single staff member and a small group of volunteers, it quickly surpassed all expectations. The inaugural exhibit, "Anne Frank in the World," drew over 24,000 visitors within the first month, leaving a profound impact on the Tampa Bay community.

Over the subsequent five years, the Holocaust Center continued to grow, welcoming more than 125,000 visitors who came to view internationally acclaimed exhibits and participate in educational programs, lectures, and commemorations. The Center extended its reach by providing study guides, teacher training, and presentations to schools in an eight-county area surrounding Tampa Bay.

Despite operating within a 4,000-square-foot facility not designed for museum or educational purposes, the Tampa Bay Holocaust Memorial Museum and Educational Center became a leading source of Holocaust information in the Southeastern United States and a prominent Holocaust institution nationally.

Recognizing the need for more space, the Board of Directors approved the purchase of a 27,000-square-foot building in downtown St. Petersburg, Florida. Within a year, the renovated facility opened its doors on February 28, 1998, ahead of schedule and under budget. During its first year in the new location, over 65,000 visitors explored the museum's exhibits, including traveling and special exhibitions that delved into Holocaust history and contemporary issues.

In January 1999, the museum officially adopted the name "The Florida Holocaust Museum" to better align with its mission statement and reflect its role as a statewide and national resource. This change enhanced its impact beyond the Tampa Bay area.

The museum also played a pivotal role in shaping legislation that, in 1994, made Florida one of the first states to mandate Holocaust education in public schools from kindergarten through twelfth grade. Collaborating with the Pinellas County School System, the museum developed guidelines for K-12 teachers, offering grade-appropriate instructional goals and bibliographies for Holocaust education.

The Florida Holocaust Museum embodies the mission of preserving the memory of the Holocaust, educating future generations about its horrors, and fostering a future marked by peace, harmony, and the rejection of hatred and intolerance in our neighborhoods, nation, and world.

The primary exhibition at the Museum, titled "History, Heritage, and Hope," occupies the entire first floor. This comprehensive exhibition utilizes a variety of mediums, including original artifacts, video presentations, and photographs, to provide an in-depth exploration of the Holocaust's history. The exhibition commences by delving into the roots of antisemitism and the conditions of life prior to World War II. It subsequently addresses the ascent of Adolf Hitler, the German regime, and the introduction of anti-Jewish laws and regulations.

Furthermore, the exhibition explores the experiences of other victim groups during this period, the establishment of ghettos, and instances of rescue. It culminates in sections dedicated to concentration camps and extermination centers, featuring an actual boxcar that was used during the Holocaust. The exhibition's final segment, titled "Lessons for Today," sheds light on ongoing genocides and contemporary acts of hatred, providing visitors with a thought-provoking perspective on the relevance of the Holocaust in the modern world.

The Florida Holocaust Museum proudly houses one of the few surviving railroad boxcars that the Germans used to transport Jewish individuals and other prisoners to infamous locations such as Auschwitz and Treblinka. Specifically, this significant artifact is Boxcar #113 069-5. Today, it is situated atop authentic tracks from the Treblinka Killing Center, serving as a solemn and poignant tribute to the countless souls who tragically lost their lives during the Holocaust. This boxcar is prominently featured as part of the museum's permanent exhibition, "History, Heritage, and Hope."

During the Holocaust, boxcars played a horrifying role as they often served as the initial site of death for many victims. These stark, freight cars frequently transformed into suffocation chambers, crammed with as many as 100 or more individuals at a time. Those who endured this harrowing journey faced unbearable conditions, including severe overcrowding, hunger, thirst, and abysmal sanitation. Regrettably, numerous deportees, particularly the elderly and children, perished during these horrific trips.

The "Kaddish in Wood" exhibition showcases meticulously crafted wooden sculptures created by Dr. Herbert Savel, a practicing physician residing in Elizabethtown, New York. Dr. Savel has received training in the German woodcarving technique and employs this skill to craft three-dimensional relief sculptures. These sculptures draw inspiration from photographs captured during the Holocaust era, depicting the victims of German persecution. While Dr. Savel has created numerous woodcarvings, this particular exhibition comprises 130 sculptures, with a specific emphasis on depicting French children who were affected by the Holocaust.

Dr. Savel's artistic endeavor is driven by the objective of presenting the Holocaust in a manner that can be comprehended by the human mind. Through his artwork, he endeavors to convey the immense suffering endured by individuals, thereby returning the unfathomable atrocities of the Holocaust to a humanized perspective. In essence, Dr. Savel's art seeks to reestablish the profound impact of the Holocaust on individual lives.

FLORIDA KEYS

REGION: SOUTHEAST DISTRICT   **COUNTY:** MIAMI-DADE, MONROE   **CITY:** VARIOUS CITIES

DATE VISITED: **WHO I WENT WITH:**

RATING: ☆ ☆ ☆ ☆ ☆   **WILL I RETURN?** YES / NO

The Florida Keys is a chain of coral cay islands located off the southern coast of Florida, making up the southernmost part of the contiguous United States. They originate from the southeastern coast of the Florida peninsula, approximately 15 miles (24 km) south of Miami, and extend in a gentle curved path heading south-southwest and then westward, ultimately reaching Key West, which is the westernmost inhabited island. Beyond that, they continue to the uninhabited Dry Tortugas. These islands are situated within the Florida Straits, which separate the Atlantic Ocean to the east from the Gulf of Mexico to the northwest, forming one boundary of Florida Bay. The closest point from the southern part of Key West is a mere 93 miles (150 km) from Cuba. The Florida Keys are positioned between approximately 24.3 and 25.5 degrees North latitude.

Monroe County encompasses over 95% of the land area within the Florida Keys, with a small section extending northeast into Miami-Dade County, including areas like Totten Key. The total land area of the Florida Keys measures 137.3 square miles (356 km2).

The Keys were originally inhabited by indigenous tribes, namely the Calusa and Tequesta peoples, and their presence in the area was documented by Juan Ponce de León during his explorations in 1513. De León named these islands "Los Martires" (meaning "The Martyrs") because, when viewed from a distance, they appeared to resemble suffering figures. The term "Key" itself is derived from the Spanish word "cayo," which means a small island. For a significant period, Key West held the distinction of being the largest town in Florida, and it thrived economically due to revenues generated from shipwrecks. This remote outpost was strategically positioned for trade with neighboring regions like Cuba and the Bahamas, and it lay on the primary trade route originating from New Orleans. However, as navigation techniques improved, resulting in fewer shipwrecks, Key West experienced a decline in the late nineteenth century.

Historically, the Florida Keys were primarily accessible via water routes. This began to change with the completion of Henry Flagler's Overseas Railway in the early 1910s. Henry Flagler, a prominent developer along Florida's Atlantic coast, embarked on an ambitious project to extend his Florida East Coast Railway all the way to Key West, connecting the previously isolated Keys to the mainland. To achieve this, Flagler oversaw the construction of a series of railroad trestles that stretched over the sea.

The Overseas Highway, a remarkable 110-mile scenic route, stands as one of the most unique road trips in the United States. This captivating journey features breathtaking ocean views, traverses 42 bridges, showcases natural wonders, and immerses travelers in a rich historical experience like no other. Each segment of the Florida Keys, connected by this highway, possesses its own distinct character, worlds apart from the hustle and bustle of major cities and theme parks.

Key Largo, the initial and longest island in this chain, is approximately a 60-minute drive from Miami International Airport. Bordered by Florida Bay and the expansive Everglades National Park backcountry to the west, and the crystal-clear waters of the Gulf Stream in the Atlantic Ocean to the east, Key Largo offers a splendid blend of coastal attractions. Visitors can indulge in a range of activities that celebrate its deep connection to the sea, including scuba diving, snorkeling, accommodations in an underwater hotel, sport fishing, eco-tours, idyllic beaches, and engaging dolphin encounter programs.

Key Largo holds a special place in cinematic history as the location where Humphrey Bogart and Lauren Bacall faced off against Edward G. Robinson and a menacing hurricane in the iconic 1948 gangster movie, "Key Largo." Today, visitors can embark on a tour aboard "The African Queen," the very boat featured in the 1951 film of the same name starring Bogart and Katharine Hepburn, albeit set in World War I Africa.

Beyond its maritime allure, Key Largo boasts a wealth of on-shore attractions, including nature trails and a rehabilitation center dedicated to wild birds. However, the crowning jewel is the John Pennekamp Coral Reef State Park, recognized as the United States' inaugural underwater preserve. Remarkably, this park is encompassed within the Florida Keys National Marine Sanctuary, further enhancing its ecological significance.

Islamorada, a charming village comprised of a cluster of cozy islands, encompasses Windley Key, Upper Matecumbe Key, and Lower Matecumbe Key. Additionally, there are two offshore islands, accessible solely by boat, each with a unique historical significance: Indian Key, a site where early settlers endured attacks by raiding Indians, and Lignumvitae Key, an ancient patch of land adorned with tropical hardwood trees, most notably the lignumvitae.

This locale in Islamorada offers a delightful playground for adults, featuring a wide array of attractions such as eco-tours, water sports equipment rentals, tennis facilities, scenic bicycle trails, and captivating historic hikes. Visitors can relish the breathtaking romantic views overlooking both the Atlantic Ocean and Florida Bay. When it comes to dining, options range from upscale continental cuisine and freshly caught seafood to casual and delightfully eccentric eateries.

Renowned as the "Sport-Fishing Capital of the World," Islamorada boasts a remarkable diversity of angling opportunities. It proudly houses the Florida Keys' largest fleet of offshore charter boats and shallow-water "backcountry" vessels, all captained by tournament-grade experts.

Just south of Islamorada, adventure-seekers can explore pristine tropical forests at Long Key State Park. Continuing further along Grassy Key, the Dolphin Research Center offers an extraordinary chance for intimate encounters with these highly intelligent marine mammals.

Marathon, situated at the midpoint of the Florida Keys, encompasses a cluster of keys, including Boot, Knights, Hog, Vaca, Stirrup, Crawl, and Little Crawl keys, along with East and West Sister's Island, Deer and Fat Deer keys, Long Pine and Grassy keys. In 1999, it officially became the City of Marathon, quickly establishing itself as a family-friendly destination within the Florida Keys. The area offers a plethora of activities suitable for all ages, including golf, world-class diving and snorkeling, boating, opportunities for dolphin encounters, leisurely walks along the pristine white sands of Sombrero Beach, and a wide range of water sports such as kayaking and standup paddling.

Marathon boasts several environmental and natural attractions, including the hardwood hammock and rainforest areas of Crane Point Hammock, a 64-acre reserve located on historically and archaeologically significant land in the Keys. Pre-Columbian artifacts have been unearthed here, and the site is home to both the Museum of Natural History of The Florida Keys and the Children's Museum.

Just offshore lies Pigeon Key, a site with historical significance as it once housed the laborers who constructed Flagler's railroad in the early 1900s. Today, visitors can embark on a tour of this island, offering a glimpse into life during the early 20th century, all within the backdrop of stunning and tranquil scenery.

Following the Seven Mile Bridge, one of the world's longest segmental bridges, travelers can enjoy panoramic vistas of the Straits of Florida and the Gulf of Mexico from Bahia Honda Bridge. A visit to the state park here provides an opportunity to experience a beach frequently ranked as one of the most beautiful in the United States.

Big Pine Key and the Lower Keys, spanning from the western end of the Seven Mile Bridge to just outside Key West, have been at the forefront of advocating responsible utilization and preservation of the region's abundant terrestrial and marine wildlife for several decades. This commitment to conservation has earned this area the moniker of the "Natural Keys."

To escape the hustle and bustle and fully immerse oneself in the tranquility of the Keys' natural beauty, many opt for the popular nature tours offered in the Lower Keys, often conducted by kayak. These tours provide unforgettable opportunities to observe migratory and wading birds, as well as the unique flora and fauna found in this serene natural enclave of the Keys.

Big Pine serves as a launching point for Looe Key, a shallow coral formation renowned as one of the most breathtaking shallow water dive sites. Additionally, Big Pine is the habitat of the diminutive Key deer, a subspecies of the white-tailed deer. To safeguard and maintain wildlife habitats, the National Key Deer Refuge was established in 1957.

For those seeking a deeper connection with nature and an authentic experience, camping has become an increasingly popular choice among Keys visitors. The Lower Keys offer an array of campsites, allowing nature enthusiasts to fully appreciate the natural wonders of the area.

Key West, the final destination along the Overseas Highway, holds the distinction of being the southernmost city in the United States, and it's actually closer to Havana, Cuba, than it is to Miami.

Exploring Key West reveals a unique blend of historic charm and tropical allure. Meandering through the streets, you'll encounter quaint, colorfully-restored homes that once housed thousands of cigar workers in the 19th century. On the flip side, grand mansions constructed by influential business figures and city leaders have been transformed into guest houses and inns, complete with modern amenities, swimming pools, and lush tropical gardens.

Engage in conversations with the locals, many of whom are native-born Key Westers known as Conchs. Their childhood memories often involve playing amidst tropical fruit trees in their backyards and harvesting the eponymous shellfish from nearby shallow waters.

The island's vibrant history has inspired renowned figures like novelist Ernest Hemingway. Hemingway's residence, a pre-Civil War mansion on Whitehead Street, is now a museum and an attraction for thousands of visitors annually.

Key West also became home to treasure hunter Mel Fisher, who recovered millions of dollars' worth of gold and silver from the ship Nuestra Señora de Atocha, a 17th-century Spanish galleon that sank 45 miles west of Key West. Fisher's legacy lives on through the Mel Fisher Maritime Heritage Society Museum, where visitors can marvel at and even touch some of the riches salvaged from the Atocha and the Santa Margarita.

Every evening, the docks at Mallory Square come alive with a vibrant celebration of another tropical day's end. Musicians, jugglers, mimes, and the occasional fire-eater entertain the gathering crowd while local food vendors ensure no one goes hungry. This daily ritual has become one of Key West's most cherished traditions. As night descends, Key West offers a plethora of eclectic, upscale, and tropical dining establishments and bars with live music, spanning from New Orleans-style jazz to local trop-rock. The island's dining options are as diverse as its mesmerizing sunsets. For theater enthusiasts, Key West boasts several intimate theaters showcasing performances by local acting troupes. Additionally, classical symphony performances are not uncommon. Art enthusiasts will find an abundance of galleries to explore, while literary buffs can delve into the works of local authors. Those interested in hands-on experiences can participate in creative workshops to craft their own original creations.

Florida Keys boast some of the world's finest beaches, exceptional diving sites, and top-notch fishing spots. However, there's more to explore beyond these natural wonders. Here's list of the top 10 things to experience in this picturesque slice of Florida. Situated 70 miles west of the idyllic Key West, Dry Tortugas National Park comprises a cluster of small islands, coral reefs, and an impressive fortress. While it's not advisable to embark on a spontaneous trip to Dry Tortugas, with a bit of planning, you and your family can embark on a journey to one of America's most exceptional and storied national parks.

As the nation's inaugural underwater park, John Pennekamp State Park invites visitors to immerse themselves in a Jacques Cousteau-like underwater world within easy reach of downtown Miami. This park is primarily submerged within the boundaries of the Florida Keys National Marine Sanctuary.

Spanning 1.5 million acres of swampland, sawgrass prairies, and subtropical jungles, Everglades National Park stands as one of the most extraordinary public parks in the United States. Situated at the southern tip of Florida, this park shelters 14 rare and endangered species, including the American Crocodile, the Florida Panther, and the West Indian Manatee. A significant portion of the park remains uncharted, reserved for adventurers and researchers, but visitors have ample opportunities to hike, camp, and canoe.

Your journey to the Florida Keys begins as you leave Homestead and Florida City, venturing down an 18-mile stretch of US 1 that passes through the Everglades, known locally as "The Stretch." In most parts, it's just a two-lane highway, which may occasionally be impeded by leisurely-moving boat trailers. Exercise patience, as there are passing zones that expand to four lanes every few miles. The drive is serene and tranquil, setting the stage for a vacation state of mind. Continue your voyage to Key Largo, Islamorada, cross the Seven-Mile Bridge, and traverse a tropical haven on your way to Key West.

No visit to the Florida Keys is complete without a jaunt down Key West's renowned Duval Street. This lively thoroughfare is a hotbed of revelry, granting access to renowned drinking establishments like Sloppy Joe's at the corner of Greene and Duval. Nestled at mile marker 84.5, Theater of the Sea offers a marine mammal adventure where you can swim alongside dolphins, sea lions, and stingrays. They also host marine performances, glass-bottom boat tours, and a pristine beach for relaxation.

If you're seeking a more secluded state park experience in the Florida Keys, consider a visit to Bahia Honda State Park. This tranquil island forms part of the Lower Florida Keys and is situated not far from the Seven Mile Bridge. At Bahia Honda, you'll discover serene beaches with clear, warm waters, offering ample opportunities for snorkeling, hiking, and camping.

Near the southern tip of Key West, you'll find Fort Taylor, a waterfront fortress that remained in active service until 1947 and still houses the largest American collection of sea-coast cannons. The fort is also home to a beach cherished by locals for picnicking and swimming. Guided tours of the fort are available daily at 11 a.m.

Key West boasts a unique historical gem known as the "Little White House." While not a true White House replica, this captivating structure served as the naval headquarters during the Spanish-American War and later functioned as President Harry S. Truman's Winter White House during visits by military and political dignitaries. Today, the house operates as a museum, showcasing Cold War artifacts and more.

For an exceptionally distinctive lodging experience in the Florida Keys, don't miss the Jules Undersea Lodge in Key Largo. This unassuming hotel is the sole underwater hotel in the United States, offering accommodations submerged 30 feet below the ocean's surface. Access to your room resembles a quaint retro submarine, and scuba diving is required to reach it.

FOREST CAPITAL MUSEUM STATE PARK

REGION: NORTHEAST DISTRICT   **COUNTY:** TAYLOR   **CITY:** PERRY

DATE VISITED: **WHO I WENT WITH:**

RATING: ☆ ☆ ☆ ☆ ☆   **WILL I RETURN?**   YES / NO

The importance of forestry in Florida dates back to the early 19th century. The museum honors this heritage. The heart of the museum is dedicated to longleaf pines and the 5000 products made from them. The museum offers a fundamental understanding of the evolution, ecology and productivity of forests. The more than 50-year-old longleaf pines growing on the museum grounds form a majestic canopy and create a pleasant walking trail for visitors.

The museum contains displays that recount the history of the forest industry as well as the wildlife of the forest. The beauty of Florida's native wood is displayed in a map of Florida with each of the 67 counties carved from a species of wood native to its area. The Forest Capital Museum is an octagonal structure made from cypress and pine wood with high beamed ceilings, topped with a glass dome. The whole family will enjoy the exhibits featuring live animals found in the area. Adjacent to the museum is the Cracker Homestead built in 1864 which depicts life on a Florida homestead with a house, barn, well, arbor, and garden. The term "cracker" was used to describe the cracking sound of long whips used to herd their cattle. Rangers lead interpretive tours during special events and upon request.

It is possible to rent three covered pavilions accommodating up to 60 people each. Pavilions can be reserved for family reunions, birthday parties, corporate events, and more. Well-behaved dogs are welcome at Forest Capital Museum State Park. They must be kept on a 6-foot handheld leash at all times and cannot be left unattended. Pets are not permitted in buildings.

FORT CLINCH STATE PARK

REGION: NORTHEAST DISTRICT **COUNTY:** NASSAU **CITY:** FERNANDINA BEACH

DATE VISITED: **WHO I WENT WITH:**

RATING: ☆ ☆ ☆ ☆ ☆ **WILL I RETURN?** YES / NO

At Fort Clinch State Park, history meets nature. A row of cannons pointing across the St. Mary's River into Georgia are silent testimony to the strategic importance of Fort Clinch during the Civil War. The historic fort is only one aspect of this diverse park. Maritime hammocks with massive arching live oaks provide a striking backdrop for hiking and biking on the park's many trails. The park is known for its gopher tortoises, painted buntings, and other species of wildlife. Among the wildlife of the park are the rare purple sandpiper, alligators, and white-tailed deer. Visitors can also see dolphins and manatees. Camping, fishing, and shark-tooth hunting are popular activities. In addition to exploring Fort Clinch, activities include sunbathing, surfcasting, birding, and shelling. Visitors can also enjoy picnicking, swimming, beachcombing, and wildlife viewing. The park drive provides 3.3 miles of paved road for those wishing to ride a touring bicycle through the oak-shaded canopy drive that ends at the visitor center for historic Fort Clinch. A 6-mile off-road multi-use trail is located adjacent to the park drive and provides a more adventurous ride through the maritime forest as dune elevation changes provide rolling hills and turns. The trail is considered intermediate and caution should be exercised on this trail. There are several miles of beach with hard-packed sand that can be ridden with large tire bicycles during low tides. Helmets are recommended for all cyclists, and Florida law requires helmets for cyclists 16 years of age and younger. Hiking along the beaches of the Cumberland Sound, visitors can stand on the northernmost reaches of Florida and look over to Cumberland Island National Seashore where wild horses sometimes roam the beaches.

The park offers outstanding birding opportunities and is one of the first stops on the Great Florida Birding and Wildlife Trail. The park offers a variety of habitats for more than 100 species of birds that inhabit the park permanently or stop here during the migratory season. Favorite viewing areas include the Egans Creek Overlook and directly south of the jetty. The Great Florida Birding Trail Exhibit is located at the beach parking area.

Nestled at Florida's most northeasterly tip, Fort Clinch State Park offers 69 campsites in two separate and unique campgrounds. Each campsite is equipped with a fire pit, picnic table, drinking water, and 30- and 50-amp electrical outlets. A dump station is free for registered campers, and a fee is available for day visitors. Well-behaved pets are welcome at both campgrounds. Surrounded by wilderness and shaded by magnificent live oaks, the primitive group camp facility offers a great wilderness retreat and excellent hiking opportunities. Considered one of the best group camping facilities in the state park system, three spacious sites in the group campground accommodate up to 75 campers. Each site, located adjacent to Egans Creek Marsh, has a fire pit, access to potable water, and restrooms within 100 feet of the camping area. Modern, accessible restrooms are equipped with hot and cold water.

Fishing in the park is quite popular, and anglers have many opportunities to spend the day fishing. Popular locations include surf fishing along the Atlantic shoreline and St. Marys Inlet as well as adjacent to the jetties near Fort Clinch, which is accessible by the east and west inlet parking areas. Depending on the season, the most popular fish caught within the park are redfish, black drum, whiting, flounder, mullet, sheepshead, sea trout, and an occasional grouper. The park does not sell fishing licenses. All fishing within the park must comply with regulations regarding size, number, method of fishing, and season. Visitors who want to launch a canoe or kayak from the park can use the East or West Inlet parking areas accessed through the Fort Clinch visitor center parking lot. The visitor center picnic area is located in a maritime hammock area surrounded by relic dunes and oak trees. Visitors will find freestanding grills, picnic tables, and a playground for children.

FORT COOPER STATE PARK

REGION: CENTRAL WEST DISTRICT **COUNTY:** CITRUS **CITY:** INVERNESS

DATE VISITED: **WHO I WENT WITH:**

RATING: ☆ ☆ ☆ ☆ ☆ **WILL I RETURN?** YES / NO

The park offers a place to relax, hike, study nature and learn about Florida's rich history. Lake Holathlikaha is popular for fishing and boating. As part of the Great Florida Birding Trail, the park offers nearly 5 miles of self-guided trails with excellent bird and wildlife viewing. Along the trails, you will find benches plus interpretive signs that provide insight into the surrounding areas. The park's diverse natural areas provide refuge for many plants and animals, including threatened and endangered species. Among the wildlife of the park are white-tailed deer, wild turkey, opossum, bobcat, sheep, herons, and cardinals.

A paved pathway connects the park to the multi-use paved Withlacoochee State Trail. The Seminole Heritage Trail kiosks are a series of four interpretive panels that provide insight into the lives of the Seminole Indians who lived in this area and the reason for Fort Cooper's construction. Park visitors can enjoy the picnic facilities and playground under a hardwood hammock near the lake. Private boats are prohibited.

A primitive group camp is available for organized groups. Three sites are available that can accommodate up to 25 people and one smaller site for eight or fewer. The camp is nestled in an oak hammock with a fair amount of shade. There are no showers or electricity. However, restrooms and drinking water are available. Each site has a picnic table, grill, and fire pit.

FORT FOSTER STATE HISTORIC SITE

REGION: CENTRAL WEST DISTRICT   **COUNTY:** HILLSBOROUGH   **CITY:** ZEPHYRHILLS

DATE VISITED: **WHO I WENT WITH:**

RATING: ☆ ☆ ☆ ☆ ☆   **WILL I RETURN?** YES / NO

Fort Foster is a reproduction of the fort originally built on the site in December 1836 by Colonel William S. Foster and his 430 men. Fort Foster is the only standing replica of a Second Seminole War fort in the United States. Fort Foster State Historic Site is part of Hillsborough River State Park, located on the east side of U.S. 301 from the park. During the Second Seminole War, Fort Foster's purpose was to defend a bridge crossing over the Hillsborough River and act as a supply point for soldiers in the field. The fort was garrisoned intermittently from December 1836 to April 1838.

Today, park staff and re-enactors provide living, historical displays of life at Fort Foster. Each year, the site offers two living history events: Fort Foster Rendezvous in January and the Candlelight Experience at Fort Foster in December. The fort was designed for war and was not built to modern safety standards. Uneven terrain, uneven floors and stairs in a blockhouse can be dangerous. The interpretive center contains more than 100 artifacts found at the historic Fort Foster site. The exhibits provide an understanding of both sides of the conflict between the Seminole Nation and the U.S. Army.

FORT GEORGE ISLAND CULTURAL STATE PARK

REGION: NORTHEAST DISTRICT   **COUNTY:** DUVAL   **CITY:** JACKSONVILLE

DATE VISITED: **WHO I WENT WITH:**

RATING: ☆ ☆ ☆ ☆ ☆   **WILL I RETURN?** YES / NO

A site of human occupation for over 5,000 years, Fort George Island was named for a 1736 fort built to defend the southern flank of Georgia when it was a colony. Today's visitors come for boating, fishing, off-road bicycling, and hiking. A key attraction is the restored 1920s clubhouse. Once an exclusive resort, it is now a visitor center with a meeting space available for special functions. Behind the club, small boats, canoes, and kayaks can be launched on the tidal waters.

Fort George Island Cultural State Park offers a loop bicycle ride through history. Pick up a copy of the Fairway Loop Trail guide at the Little Talbot Island Ranger Station or in the brochure rack in front of the Ribault Club on Fort George Island. The loop is 4.4 miles and consists of paved road and hard-packed gravel. For off-road bicyclists, there is a 3-mile biking/hiking trail that traverses the interior of the former Fort George Island golf course. The trail is suitable for large-tire bikes. Helmets are recommended for all cyclists, and Florida law requires helmets to be worn by cyclists 16 years of age and younger. Park at the Ribault Club's Visitor Center and hike north to discover one of the tallest dunes on the eastern seaboard, Mount Cornelia, a true Florida hill.

Bring binoculars to catch a close-up of least terns, royal terns, and black skimmers. Wading birds like wood storks, great blue herons, and snowy egrets fish along the salt marsh of the Fort George River. Pileated woodpeckers, great horned owls, and bald eagles can be spotted among the live oaks. Fishing the Fort George River from shore is a popular activity. All fishing within the park must comply with regulations regarding size, number, method of fishing, and time of year. A fishing license may be required. Well-behaved dogs are welcome at Fort George Island Cultural State Park on our hiking trails, pavilions, paved park roads, parking lots, and multi-use trails.

FORT LAUDERDALE

REGION: SOUTHEAST DISTRICT   **COUNTY:** BROWARD   **CITY:** FORT LAUDERDALE

DATE VISITED: **WHO I WENT WITH:**

RATING: ☆ ☆ ☆ ☆ ☆   **WILL I RETURN?**   YES / NO

Fort Lauderdale is a coastal city, situated 30 miles (48 km) north of Miami along the Atlantic Ocean. It serves as the county seat and is the largest city in Broward County, with a population of 182,760 according to the 2020 census, making it the tenth largest city in Florida. After Miami and Hialeah, Fort Lauderdale is the third largest principal city (as defined by the U.S. Census Bureau) in the Miami metropolitan area, which had a population of 6,166,488 in 2019.

Established in 1838 and first incorporated in 1911, Fort Lauderdale derives its name from a series of forts built by the United States during the Second Seminole War. These forts were named after Major William Lauderdale (1782–1838), the younger brother of Lieutenant Colonel James Lauderdale. The city's development did not begin until 50 years after the forts were abandoned at the end of the conflict. Three forts named "Fort Lauderdale" were constructed, including the first one at the fork of the New River, the second one at Tarpon Bend on the New River between the present-day Colee Hammock and Rio Vista neighborhoods, and the third one near the site of the Bahia Mar Marina.

Over 300 miles of navigable inland waterways weave through Greater Fort Lauderdale, passing by grand estates, citrus groves, and the unique Everglades, attracting boats of all sizes and shapes. The famous Intracoastal Waterway stretches south to Miami, with waterfront homes adorning its shores, earning the area the nickname "Venice of America." In addition to being a popular tourist destination, Fort Lauderdale has a diverse economy encompassing marine industries, manufacturing, finance, insurance, real estate, high technology, avionics/aerospace, film, and television production. The city's favorable climate with an average year-round temperature of 75.5 °F (24.2 °C) and 3,000 hours of sunshine per year attracts numerous visitors. The city's Port Everglades serves as the embarkation point for nearly 4 million cruise passengers annually, making it the third largest cruise port in the world. With over 50,000 registered yachts and 100 marinas, Fort Lauderdale is also renowned as the yachting capital of the world.

The region where Fort Lauderdale would later be established had been inhabited by the Tequesta Indians for over two thousand years. However, when Spanish explorers made contact with them in the 16th century, it had devastating consequences. The Tequesta had no immunity to the diseases brought by the Europeans, such as smallpox, leading to a significant decline in their population over the next two centuries. Conflicts with neighboring Calusa tribes also contributed to their downfall. By 1763, only a few Tequesta remained in Florida, and most of them were relocated to Cuba when Spain ceded Florida to the British under the Treaty of Paris (1763) after the Seven Years' War. The area underwent various changes in control, passing between Spain, the United

Kingdom, the United States, and the Confederate States of America, but it remained largely undeveloped until the 20th century.

Before the 20th century, the Fort Lauderdale area was referred to as the "New River Settlement," and around the 1830s, approximately 70 settlers lived along the New River. One of the settlers, William Cooley, who traded with the Seminole Indians, faced a tragic event in 1836 when a group of Seminoles attacked his farm while he was trying to salvage a wrecked ship. The attack resulted in the death of his wife, children, and the children's tutor, prompting all the white residents in the area to abandon the settlement and seek refuge first at the Cape Florida Lighthouse on Key Biscayne and then in Key West.

The first U.S. stockade, named Fort Lauderdale, was constructed in 1838 and became a site of conflict during the Second Seminole War. After the war's end in 1842, the fort was abandoned, and the region remained sparsely populated until the 1890s. Development only began to take shape when Frank Stranahan arrived in 1893 and started operating a ferry across the New River. Additionally, the Florida East Coast Railroad completed a route through the area in 1896, further spurring organized development. Fort Lauderdale was eventually incorporated as a city in 1911 and designated as the county seat of the newly formed Broward County in 1915.

Fort Lauderdale experienced its first significant development during the 1920s, a period known as the Florida land boom. However, this growth was followed by economic challenges due to the devastating impact of the 1926 Miami Hurricane and the Great Depression in the 1930s.

In July 1935, a tragic event occurred when an African-American man named Rubin Stacy was accused of robbing a white woman. During his transportation to a Miami jail, the police were intercepted and attacked by a mob. The mob, comprised of about 100 white men, proceeded to hang Stacy from a tree near the location of the alleged robbery. His body was brutally shot with approximately 20 bullets. This heinous crime was later exploited by the press in Nazi Germany to undermine U.S. criticism of Germany's persecution of Jews, Communists, and Catholics.

With the outbreak of World War II, Fort Lauderdale played a significant role as a major U.S. base. It housed a Naval Air Station that trained pilots, radar operators, and fire control operators, and a Coast Guard base was established at Port Everglades.

Before July 1961, only white individuals were permitted on Fort Lauderdale's beaches, and there were no designated beaches for African-Americans in Broward County until 1954. In 1965, a road was finally constructed leading to the "Colored Beach," now known as Dr. Von D. Mizell-Eula Johnson State Park, located in Dania Beach. African Americans started a series of wade-in protests on July 4, 1961, at beaches where they were denied access, demanding a road to the Negro beach. On July 11, 1962, a court ruling by Ted

Cabot challenged the city's policy of racial segregation at public beaches, leading to the desegregation of Broward County beaches in 1962.

Today, Fort Lauderdale has become a prominent yachting hub and is one of the nation's largest tourist destinations. It serves as the focal point of a metropolitan area with a population of 1.8 million people.

The northwestern part of Fort Lauderdale is physically disconnected from the rest of the city and is linked only by the Cypress Creek Canal, passing under I-95. This particular area of Fort Lauderdale shares its southern border with the cities of Tamarac and Oakland Park. Additionally, the northeastern portion of Oakland Park also borders Fort Lauderdale on its western side. Moving to the southern part of Fort Lauderdale, it is bordered on its northern side by Wilton Manors.

Off the coast of Fort Lauderdale lies the Osborne Reef, an artificial reef created using discarded tires with the initial purpose of providing fish habitat while disposing of land-based trash. However, this endeavor turned into an ecological disaster. The tire dumping began in the 1960s, but the tires faced harsh and corrosive conditions in the ocean environment, causing the nylon straps used to secure them to wear out, cables to rust, and tires to break free. Once free, the tires posed a significant threat as they drifted towards the shore, colliding with a living reef tract, causing destruction in their path. Over the years, thousands of tires have washed up on nearby beaches, particularly during hurricanes, further exacerbating the environmental impact.

In response to this ecological problem, local authorities are now collaborating with the U.S. Army, Navy, and Coast Guard to remove the approximately 700,000 tires and mitigate the damage caused by the Osborne Reef.

Fort Lauderdale experiences significant seasonal fluctuations in its population due to the influx of "snowbirds" from the northern United States, Canada, and Europe who come to Florida during the winter and spring months. The city is renowned for its beautiful beaches, vibrant bars, lively nightclubs, and its history as a popular spring break destination, particularly in the 1960s and 1970s, when tens of thousands of college students flocked to the area.

However, in the mid-1980s, the city began taking measures to discourage college students from visiting Fort Lauderdale during spring break, implementing strict laws to prevent the mayhem that occurred in previous decades. Consequently, the number of college visitors declined significantly, dropping from an estimated 350,000 in 1985 to about 20,000 by 1989. Since the 1990s, Fort Lauderdale has shifted its focus to cater to those seeking a resort lifestyle, either seasonally or year-round, and has become a host city for various professional events, concerts, and art shows.

The arts and entertainment district of Fort Lauderdale, known as the Riverwalk Arts &

Entertainment District, stretches along Las Olas Boulevard from the beach to downtown. It features the Broward Center for the Performing Arts as its western anchor and extends to the intersection of Las Olas and A1A, which is considered the epicenter of Fort Lauderdale Beach. This location gained fame from the Elbo Room bar, featured in the 1960 film "Where the Boys Are," contributing to the city's reputation as a spring break mecca. The city and its suburbs boast over 4,100 restaurants and more than 120 nightclubs, many of which are located within the arts and entertainment district.

Fort Lauderdale also serves as the setting for the 1986 movie "Flight of the Navigator" and hosts Langerado, an annual music festival. Lastly, the Fort Lauderdale International Film Festival has been a yearly event since 1986, showcasing a variety of films and promoting the city's cultural scene.

Hugh Taylor Birch State Park is a sprawling 180-acre park located along the beach. It offers various recreational activities such as nature trails, camping, picnicking areas, and canoeing. The park also houses the Terramar Visitor Center, which features exhibits about the park's ecosystem. The park's history dates back to 1893 when Hugh Taylor Birch purchased ocean-front property for a meager price and eventually owned a 3.5-mile stretch of beachfront. The Bonnet House, another historical landmark in Fort Lauderdale, was gifted by Birch to his daughter and son-in-law as a wedding present in 1919. The site has since been listed on the National Register of Historic Places and declared a historic landmark by the City of Fort Lauderdale.

The Henry E. Kinney Tunnel on U.S. Route 1 is a unique feature as it is the only tunnel on a state road in Florida. Constructed in 1960, the tunnel spans 864 feet and goes beneath the New River and Las Olas Boulevard.

Just a short distance from the beach, the Riverwalk Arts and Entertainment District in downtown Fort Lauderdale offers a vibrant mix of cultural attractions, shops, parks, and restaurants. Along the Riverwalk, visitors can enjoy various attractions, including the Broward Center for the Performing Arts, the Museum of Discovery and Science with its AutoNation 3D IMAX Theater, Florida Grand Opera, Fort Lauderdale Historical Center, Stranahan House, and the Museum of Art.

Las Olas Boulevard, a popular street in downtown Fort Lauderdale, stretches from the Central Business District to A1A and Fort Lauderdale Beach. It serves as a prominent destination for both locals and tourists due to its convenient location near the beach, Fort Lauderdale-Hollywood International Airport, and Port Everglades. The boulevard is known for its unique and eclectic shopping and dining options, making it a favorite among South Florida residents.

Apart from its museums, beaches, and vibrant nightlife, Fort Lauderdale also hosts the Fort Lauderdale Swap Shop, a large indoor/outdoor flea market, and the world's largest drive-in movie theater with 13 screens. Additionally, the city is home to North

Woodlawn Cemetery, an African-American cemetery listed on the National Register of Historic Places, Calvary Chapel Fort Lauderdale, a prominent evangelical megachurch, and the annual Fort Lauderdale International Boat Show, a renowned event showcasing nearly 500 boats, yachts, and mega-yachts.

Fort Lauderdale is a popular destination for sun-seekers from around the world who come to play, relax, and sometimes even work. While it was once perceived as a playground exclusively for the wealthy and famous with luxurious lifestyles, loyal visitors know that the region offers a diverse range of accommodations and experiences.

The city boasts various attractions, such as Butterfly World in Coconut Creek, a vast 10-acre park with aviaries, botanical gardens, and butterflies, making it the largest butterfly park globally and the first in the Western Hemisphere. Another popular activity is the Jungle Queen Dinner Cruise, which takes tourists on a historical tour along the New River, passing Millionaire's Row, and making a stop to observe rare birds, monkeys, and an alligator exhibition during the three-hour journey.

For those interested in gaming, Fort Lauderdale provides several options. The Coconut Creek Seminole Casino offers slot machines and poker, along with casual dining selections in a buffet or table service setting. Gulfstream Park Racing & Casino in Hallandale Beach is Florida's premier Thoroughbred horse racing track, hosting prestigious Triple Crown races like the Florida Derby. Adjacent to the track, visitors can also enjoy two floors of casino action. Dania Jai Alai features the world's fastest game, Jai Alai, as well as poker and simulcasting of dog and horse racing. Isle Casino Racing at Pompano Park in Pompano Beach offers live harness racing, slots, poker, and simulcasting of Jai Alai, harness, and Thoroughbred racing. The Big Easy Casino in Hallandale Beach provides live Greyhound racing, slots, poker, simulcasting, and various dining options. For those seeking luxurious accommodation and entertainment, the Seminole Hard Rock Hotel & Casino offers spacious rooms and top-notch amenities.

FORT LAUDERDALE SWAP SHOP

REGION: SOUTHEAST DISTRICT   **COUNTY:** BROWARD   **CITY:** FORT LAUDERDALE

DATE VISITED: **WHO I WENT WITH:**

RATING: ☆ ☆ ☆ ☆ ☆   **WILL I RETURN?**   YES / NO

The Fort Lauderdale Swap Shop, situated in Fort Lauderdale, Florida, is a unique establishment that serves as both a 14-screen drive-in theater and the world's largest daily flea market. Locally promoted as Florida's second-most prominent tourist attraction and the biggest draw in the South Florida metropolitan area, the Swap Shop offers a one-of-a-kind entertainment and shopping experience. From 1989 to 2006, the Hanneford Family Circus was a regular feature in the Swap Shop's food court, entertaining the approximately 12 million annual visitors.

The Swap Shop offers a vibrant atmosphere where you can spend hours perusing both enticing and amusing knock-offs and used items, capturing the essence of its unique charm—never knowing when you might stumble upon a fantastic deal.

Featuring an array of offerings, including food, arcade games, clothing and accessories for both men and women, furniture, toys, and more, the Swap Shop has garnered a reputation as the go-to place for finding almost anything you might need at the right price. Beyond its flea market, the Swap Shop also draws automobile enthusiasts eager to explore the car museum. The drive-in movie theater, a cherished relic from the 1960s and 70s, remains popular, with upcoming movie listings available on their website.

To top it all off, the Swap Shop hosts one of the city's finest farmers' markets, offering a diverse selection of high-quality produce at budget-friendly prices, and it's open seven days a week.

The Thunderbird Drive-in Theater was initially opened by Betty and Preston Henn on November 22, 1963. It started with a single screen, which is still operational today as Screen 9. Initially, the drive-in garnered attention for showing adult films, which raised concerns among passing motorists. In the early days, the parking lot was even divided by a fence, segregating white and African American customers.

Following a trip to the American West Coast in 1966, Preston Henn decided to introduce a flea market to the venue, providing the local community with a massive collective rummage sale and promoting the growth of numerous small businesses in southeastern Florida. This addition marked the beginning of a period of expansion, with the drive-in eventually featuring 11 screens by 1980 and gaining widespread popularity.

In 1979, an outdoor food court was added to the Swap Shop. A decade later, a stage was incorporated, and the food court was enclosed and equipped with air conditioning. Initially, the circus shared the stage with music acts from the 1960s and 1970s, including notable artists like K.C. and the Sunshine Band, Willie Nelson, Loretta Lynn, and Three Dog Night.

In 1989 the Henns introduced regular concerts, hosted a circus with daily performances, incorporated a carnival, a video game arcade, and a range of other attractions.

It's worth noting that as of this year, the Swap Shop has ceased animal performances and enclosures in support of those who oppose circuses with animal acts, aligning with a more animal-friendly stance.

The Swap Shop continued to expand into the 1990s, with the introduction of Screens 12 and 13. The growth persisted into 2005 when the former Thunderbird Drive-in began projecting onto its fourteenth screen. However, on October 24, 2005, Hurricane Wilma caused damage to several of the screens, and at present, only 13 out of the 14 screens are operational.

In addition to the Fort Lauderdale Swap Shop, the Henns also own and operate two other similar venues: the Margate Swap Shop (which closed in 2007), the Lake Worth Swap Shop and Drive-in, and the Tampa Fun-Lan Swap Shop and Drive-in.

The Swap Shop is conveniently situated at 3291 West Sunrise Blvd., positioned between I-95 and the Florida Turnpike in Fort Lauderdale. Its operating hours are from Monday to Friday, from 8:00 a.m. to 5:00 p.m., while on Saturdays and Sundays, the shops remain open slightly later, until 6:30 p.m. Additionally, some hotels offer transportation services to the Swap Shop for their guests. Visitors also have the option of taking the Tri-Rail to reach the Swap Shop on Saturdays from various points across Broward, Palm Beach, and Miami-Dade counties.

FORT MATANZAS NATIONAL MONUMENT

REGION: NORTHEAST DISTRICT   **COUNTY:** ST. JOHNS   **CITY:** ST. AUGUSTINE

DATE VISITED: **WHO I WENT WITH:**

RATING: ☆ ☆ ☆ ☆ ☆   **WILL I RETURN?**   YES / NO

The Fort Matanzas National Monument serves as a historical site dedicated to preserving the fortified coquina watchtower, which was finalized in 1742. This watchtower played a crucial role in safeguarding the southern entryway to the Spanish military settlement of St. Augustine. Additionally, the monument encompasses roughly 300 acres of the Florida coastal ecosystem, comprising dunes, wetlands, maritime forest, and the diverse plant and animal life that inhabit this environment. This area also serves as a refuge for several threatened and endangered species.

Under the orders of Governor Manuel de Montiano, construction of the fort commenced in 1740 and was successfully completed in 1742. The fort's design was the work of engineer Pedro Ruiz de Olano, who had previously contributed to the Castillo de San Marcos. The construction labor force comprised convicts, slaves, and troops from Cuba. The fort, known as Torre de Matanzas (Matanzas Tower) to the Spanish, was constructed using coquina, a prevalent shellstone building material in the region. Pine pilings were employed to stabilize the marshy terrain, creating a foundation for the fort. The fort featured a square layout with sides measuring 50 feet and a prominent 30-foot tower. Its standard garrison consisted of one commanding officer, four infantrymen, and two gunners, although additional troops could be stationed if required. The fort was equipped with five cannons, including four six-pounders and one eighteen-pounder, all capable of covering the inlet, which was located less than half a mile away.

In 1742, as the construction of Fort Matanzas was nearing completion, a British fleet led by Oglethorpe approached the inlet with twelve ships. Upon encountering cannon fire from the fort, the British scouting boats were driven off, and the warships ultimately departed without engaging the fort in a full-scale battle. This brief encounter marked the sole instance in which Fort Matanzas fired upon an enemy force.

In 1763, Spain ceded control of Florida following the Treaty of Paris, only to regain it through the Treaty of Paris in 1783. However, with the decline of the Spanish Empire, minimal efforts were made to maintain the fort. By the time the United States assumed control of Florida in 1821, Fort Matanzas had deteriorated to the extent that it was uninhabitable for soldiers. Consequently, the United States never utilized the fort, allowing it to fall into a state of disrepair and ultimately become a ruin.

The fort derived its name from Matanzas Inlet, which earned its appellation due to the "matanzas" (Spanish for "slaughters") that occurred on its northern shore in 1565. These "matanzas" refer to the executions carried out by the Spanish against Jean Ribault and his group of Huguenot Frenchmen, who were the last remnants of the Fort Caroline colony.

In 1916, the U.S. Department of War initiated a significant restoration effort to address the extensive decay of the fort's structure. By 1924, substantial progress had been made, with the repair of three vertical fissures in the fort's walls and the stabilization of the entire structure. During the same year, Fort Matanzas was officially designated as a National Monument. On August 10, 1933, the fort was transferred from the War Department to the National Park Service.

Under the management of the National Park Service as a historic site, Fort Matanzas National Monument was added to the National Register of Historic Places on October 15, 1966.

Additionally, the Fort Matanzas National Monument Headquarters and Visitor Center, located at 8635 A1A approximately 15 miles south of St. Augustine, Florida, was constructed in 1936. Situated on Anastasia Island, this facility serves as the gateway to the Fort Matanzas National Monument, which is accessible via a short five-minute boat ride. The Visitor Center, designed in the National Park Service Rustic architectural style by the National Park Service's Eastern Division of Plans & Design, includes a museum. This center was officially listed on the National Register of Historic Places in 2008, encompassing two contributing buildings and one contributing site across 17.3 acres of land.

The main building at the Fort Matanzas National Monument Headquarters and Visitor Center is a two-story structure that incorporates an arched breezeway, serving as both the visitor center and housing for park rangers. The first-floor walls are constructed from coquina block masonry, while the second floor is composed of wood framing with wood siding. This building features a hipped roof.

Adjacent to this structure is another one-story building situated approximately 50 feet to the north. It also boasts a hip-roof design and is constructed with coquina walls. This building primarily functions as a utility building and currently serves as a ranger office.

Visitors gather at the visitor center before embarking on a brief five-minute boat journey to reach the historic Fort Matanzas, which is located on Rattlesnake Island across Matanzas Inlet.

The architectural planning and design of these buildings, along with the surrounding landscaping, were undertaken by architects from the Eastern Division Branch of Plans and Design within the National Park Service.

In addition to the buildings, the designed features of the site encompass flagstone walkways and sidewalks, an exterior staircase, a retaining wall, parking areas, and roads with curbs.

The Fort Matanzas National Monument offers a serene and shaded picnic area, conveniently located near the main visitor center entrance and parking. This picnic spot is nestled beneath the comforting shade of ancient oak trees, forming a natural canopy. Within this area, visitors can also access a public restroom facility, the trailhead for a nature trail, and a sidewalk leading to the visitor center. This gated section of the park is open for visitors from 9:00 AM to 5:30 PM daily.

Starting from the primary parking lot at the Visitor Center, visitors can access a scenic boardwalk that winds through the oldest and highest part of the barrier island. This area is known as a "hammock," characterized by a lush forest. The shaded trail spans less than a mile in length, providing enchanting views of the diverse tree canopy and opportunities to observe various forms of wildlife in a maritime forest setting.

Throughout the day, park rangers and volunteers are readily available to answer questions and offer interpretive programs related to the park's natural and cultural aspects. The specific topics, locations, and schedules for these programs may vary depending on the season, weather conditions, and visitor attendance. Upon arrival at the Visitor Center, guests can inquire with the staff to learn about the upcoming opportunities.

The Fort Matanzas National Monument also presents ample opportunities for saltwater fishing, catering to a wide variety of fish species. Visitors can enjoy the outdoors with their families while angling in both the river and ocean areas. To engage in fishing activities within the park, individuals must possess a saltwater fishing license. Fishing is permitted along the park's shoreline, with the exception of the designated area next to the ferryboat docks. During low tide, access to fishing spots becomes more convenient.

FORT MOSE HISTORIC STATE PARK

REGION: NORTHEAST DISTRICT   **COUNTY:** ST. JOHNS   **CITY:** ST. AUGUSTINE

DATE VISITED: **WHO I WENT WITH:**

RATING: ☆ ☆ ☆ ☆ ☆   **WILL I RETURN?** YES / NO

Fort Mose Historic State Park is a waterfront historic site. The park offers picnic areas, an observation and birding boardwalk, a kayak launch boardwalk, a visitor center, and a museum. There are many educational opportunities available, especially for those interested in history or wildlife viewing. Those with a penchant for history will enjoy the interactive museum that tells the full story of the first legally sanctioned free African settlement in what was to become the United States. The museum features interactive audio, video and tactile stations, as well as paintings, historical maps, archaeological artifacts, and hands-on activities. Although there are no remains of earth and wood structures, visitors can see the area where the settlement once stood.

The park is conveniently located near all St. Augustine activities including attractions, historical sites, churches, lodging, and restaurants. Fort Mose's open spaces and two wheelchair-accessible boardwalks provide ideal opportunities for viewing coastal shorebirds and birds of prey. Visitors interested in birds will have many opportunities to view species such as the great blue heron, bald eagle, and white ibis. The floating boardwalk platform on the water directly to the east of the museum provides a useful area to launch canoes and kayaks or tie up for the day's activities. There are two picnic areas at Fort Mose. One is a covered picnic pavilion near the main boardwalk, equipped with a large picnic table, grill, and handicap accessible trash cans. The second location is directly behind the visitor center and can accommodate more people with 10 tables, two of which are handicapped accessible. This picnic area is not covered but has a shady oak canopy. There is one manual wheelchair available in the park during visitor center hours on a first-come, first-served basis. Fort Mose is an ideal location for your special event. The park has parking on the main boardwalk.

FORT PIERCE INLET STATE PARK

REGION: CENTRAL EAST DISTRICT **COUNTY:** ST. LUCIE **CITY:** FORT PIERCE

DATE VISITED: **WHO I WENT WITH:**

RATING: ☆ ☆ ☆ ☆ ☆ **WILL I RETURN?** YES / NO

The shores and coastal waters of this park provide plenty of recreational opportunities. The beautiful half-mile beach invites visitors to swim, snorkel, surf, and scuba dive. Beach walks, picnicking, or simply relaxing on the sand are also popular. Dynamite Point was once a World War II naval diver training site but is now a birdwatcher's paradise. Jack Island Preserve, located 1 mile north of the park, has trails for hiking, biking, and nature study. The Coastal Hammock Trail takes hikers through one of the few remaining oak hammocks on a barrier island in South Florida. It is a pleasant, peaceful walk that takes only 30 minutes. Many native trees can be seen here, including gumbo limbo, redbay, and a variety of oaks.

The park has a paved bike path that starts outside the park, winds through the park, and leads to a playground, picnic area, or the beach. All cyclists are advised to wear helmets, and Florida law requires helmets to be worn by cyclists 16 years of age and younger. At the west end of the Marsh Rabbit Run Trail, visitors can climb an observation tower for a bird's-eye-view of the Indian River and the island.

Kayaking on the Indian River Lagoon is a great way to spend the day. The park offers several kayak launch sites, most of which are only 30-40 yards from shore. Along the south end of the park is Fort Pierce Inlet, a popular fishing spot for anglers. A variety of fish can be caught, including bluefish, snook, red drum, flounder, and trout. All fishing within the park must comply with regulations regarding size, number, method of fishing, and season. A fishing license may be required.

FORT WALTON BEACH

REGION: NORTHWEST DISTRICT   **COUNTY:** OKALOOSA   **CITY:** CRESTVIEW

DATE VISITED: **WHO I WENT WITH:**

RATING: ☆ ☆ ☆ ☆ ☆   **WILL I RETURN?**   YES / NO

The City of Fort Walton Beach is a comprehensive government organization with a workforce of approximately 300 employees, dedicated to delivering services to a population of over 21,000 residents. These services encompass a wide range of essential functions, including police and fire protection, cultural and recreational activities such as parks, libraries, museums, and two golf courses. Additionally, the city oversees planning and zoning efforts, public works responsibilities related to streets, sidewalks, and rights-of-way, as well as utility services covering water, sewer, stormwater management, garbage collection, and recycling programs.

Historically, Fort Walton Beach is situated along the Florida Panhandle's Gulf Coast, featuring the Santa Rosa Sound to the south and the northern boundaries formed by Choctawhatchee Bay and Cinco Bayou. The city's establishment dates back to 1937, and despite its growth and development, it has retained a "small-town" ambiance while offering the advantages of an urban community.

Within Fort Walton Beach, there are eleven distinct neighborhoods, with seven of them positioned along the shoreline. Each of these neighborhoods possesses its own unique character and appeal, contributing to the city's diverse identity.

Fort Walton Beach is also steeped in Native American heritage, with a history tracing back 14,000 years. Its earliest permanent settlers arrived shortly after Florida's territorial status commenced in 1821. In the early 1860s, the Walton Guards established a camp in the region, initially named Camp Walton in honor of Colonel George Walton, who served as Florida's acting governor. In 1868, John T. Brooks acquired 111 acres in what is now downtown Fort Walton Beach, leading to the establishment of Brooks Landing. However, the most pivotal factor in the city's growth was the inception and subsequent expansion of Eglin Air Force Base in 1937.

The city takes pride in its nationally recognized public and charter schools, characterized by a favorable teacher-to-student ratio. These schools are thoughtfully integrated into neighborhoods, connected by fitness trails, sidewalks, and public parks. Fort Walton Beach is home to numerous locally-owned and operated businesses, which thrive due to the city's affordability and the amenities it provides. This combination reflects the city's dedication to fostering a positive business environment conducive to the growth of companies.

There is a wide range of activities and attractions to enjoy in and around Fort Walton Beach, ensuring that there's always something to do and explore. The City of Fort Walton

Beach Heritage Park & Cultural Center is an integral part of the city, comprising several museums and a National Historic Landmark. These museums include the Indian Temple Mound Museum, Camp Walton Schoolhouse Museum, Garnier Post Office Museum, Fort Walton Temple Mound, and the Civil War Exhibit building. Collectively, they serve as a cultural hub, showcasing the rich history of the Fort Walton Beach area. This history encompasses a timeline extending from prehistoric times, approximately 12,000 years ago, through the Civil War era in the context of the region, the establishment of the first school in 1912, and the closure of the post office in the 1950s. The Emerald Coast Science Center, situated just west of downtown Fort Walton Beach, offers an array of exhibits and interactive demonstrations. These include new Robotics exhibits, a Hurricane Simulator, SMALLab Learning (sponsored by IMPACT100 of Northwest Florida), a live animal kingdom exhibit, and much more. The science center is a dynamic destination for exploring various aspects of science. For enthusiasts of aviation warfare and armament history, the Air Force Armament Museum is a must-visit attraction in the Fort Walton Beach area. The museum boasts a remarkable collection of over 15,000 artifacts, spanning from the early days of aviation warfare during World War I to the modern era of high-tech bombs and aircraft. Those seeking extreme sports and entertainment can explore the Emerald Coast Dirt & Vert facility, the sole complete extreme sports facility along the coast in Northwest Florida. This facility encompasses a 9,000 square foot skatepark/street course, a BMX Racing track, and Burly BMX/Freestyle Dirt Jumps, all in one location.

The Uptown Shopping District offers a diverse shopping and dining experience with over 60 national and local retail stores and restaurants. It is a prime destination to find a wide range of items. Moreover, the district hosts several major events throughout the year, attracting a large number of visitors.

The Downtown Arts & Entertainment District is a vibrant area featuring unique shops, restaurants, the Heritage Park & Cultural Center, the Emerald Coast Science Center, and much more. Within the downtown vicinity, you'll discover an antique district housing numerous antique and collectibles shops. For a fun-filled family activity, Goofy Golf is a longstanding favorite, offering two 18-hole miniature golf courses that have entertained people of all ages for over half a century. And, of course, no trip to the Fort Walton Beach area would be complete without experiencing the beauty of America's Most Beautiful Beaches, which are a hallmark of this picturesque region.

FORT ZACHARY TAYLOR HISTORIC STATE PARK

REGION: SOUTHEAST DISTRICT | **COUNTY:** MONROE | **CITY:** KEY WEST

DATE VISITED: | **WHO I WENT WITH:**

RATING: ☆ ☆ ☆ ☆ ☆ | **WILL I RETURN?** YES / NO

A visit to Fort Taylor is a one-of-a-kind experience that allows you to not only birdwatch and swim, but also immerse yourself in history. Fort Taylor is a National Historic Monument housing the largest cache of Civil War armament in the world. Construction of the fort began in 1845 as part of a mid-19th century plan to defend the southeast coast through a series of forts after the War of 1812. Tour guides and interpretive panels explain how the fort played important roles in the Civil War and Spanish-American War. On the third weekend of each month, local historical re-enactors conduct historical displays. Fort Taylor is also the site of many annual events, including Civil War reenactments. In addition to its historical significance, the park is the southernmost state park in the continental United States.

The fort is part of the Great Florida Birding Trail. Bird lists are available at the ranger's office. The park boasts Key West's favorite beach at the southern end of the park, offering opportunities for picnicking, swimming, snorkeling, paddle boarding, and fishing. Fishing is very popular in the Florida Keys, and Fort Zachary Taylor is no exception. Fish can be caught from the rock pier adjacent to the main shipping channel. Snapper, jacks, grouper, tarpon and other local favorites can challenge anglers of all ages. A fishing license is required. You can bring your own kayaks, canoes or paddleboards. Be sure to see the new coral reef that is being created here in Key West. Fort Zachary Taylor offers some of the best snorkeling from the beach in the Florida Keys. Good for beginners. The water is shallow, but deep enough for swimming and snorkeling. Water shoes are recommended. Picnic tables and charcoal grills are available in the park. A "pack in pack out" rule applies, so be sure to take your trash with you. Take the Tropical Hammock Trail to learn about native plants or walk the Fort View nature trail to admire the 19th century fortification from the outside. Bicycling is known as the best form of transportation in Key West. There are plenty of bike racks and trails at Fort Zachary Taylor.

GREEN CAY NATURE CENTER AND WETLANDS

REGION: SOUTHEAST DISTRICT   **COUNTY:** PALM BEACH   **CITY:** BOYNTON BEACH

DATE VISITED: **WHO I WENT WITH:**

RATING: ☆ ☆ ☆ ☆ ☆   **WILL I RETURN?**   YES / NO

Green Cay Nature Center offers stunning views of a 100-acre man-made wetland and serves as an educational hub for this distinctive ecosystem. The wetland boasts a 1.5-mile raised boardwalk equipped with informative signs detailing the various aspects of the habitat. The boardwalk highlights various features, including wildlife, the Cypress Swamp, Deep Zones, Hammock Islands, Emergent Marshes, and the Seminole Chickee Hut. Within the Nature Center, you'll discover a lecture hall, a gift shop, and a spacious exhibit room featuring live animals, all of which highlight the unique characteristics of wetlands.

The Wetland and Nature Center area was originally farmland, purchased by Palm Beach County from Ted and Trudy Winsberg in 1999 for $2.9 million, a fraction of its appraised value. The condition of the purchase was that it would be transformed into a wetland. A collaborative effort between the Palm Beach County Water Utilities Department and Palm Beach County Parks and Recreation Department commenced construction in July 2003. The site was converted into a nature center with 100 acres of wetland. Nutrient-rich water is pumped into the wetland from a nearby wastewater treatment plant. As the water flows through the wetland, natural processes involving plants and soil filter the water and reintegrate it into the water cycle.

A visit to Green Cay provides firsthand experience of the advantages of a wetland. Visitors can explore the habitat and observe various species of birds, mammals, reptiles, amphibians, insects, and fishes. Additionally, the Nature Center offers educational exhibits and programs that interpret this unique ecosystem, catering to a wide range of interests. Inside the Nature Center, interpretive exhibits shed light on different aspects of the wetland ecosystem, offering an engaging and close-up perspective. The exhibits cover topics such as the Turtle Pond, Wetland Diorama, Alligator Hole, Educational Murals, Frog Terrarium, History of Green Cay, and nature movies screened throughout the day. The boardwalk at Green Cay Nature Center and Wetlands is available for use from sunrise to sunset, allowing visitors to explore the area during daylight hours. Public restrooms are open from 6:45 a.m. until sunset, providing facilities for those enjoying the wetlands.

GULF ISLANDS NATIONAL SEASHORE

REGION: NORTHWEST DISTRICT   **COUNTY:** ESCAMBIA   **CITY:** PENSACOLA

DATE VISITED: **WHO I WENT WITH:**

RATING: ☆ ☆ ☆ ☆ ☆   **WILL I RETURN?** YES / NO

The Gulf Islands National Seashore, known as America's largest national seashore, stretches across 160 miles from east to west, encompassing both Florida and Mississippi. It consists of thirteen distinct areas to explore, with six of them located in Coastal Mississippi, offering numerous opportunities to immerse oneself in the natural beauty of the seashore. As of 2022, it ranked as the eighth-most visited unit within the National Park Service.

Among the six barrier islands in Coastal Mississippi, Cat Island, Horn Island, Petit Bois Island, and Ship Island are part of the Gulf Islands National Seashore, each offering unique attractions for visitors. Cat Island features bayous and marshes that serve as habitats for various bird species and alligators. It's noteworthy that most of the island is privately owned, except for its western half and southern tip. Petit Bois Island, whose name translates to "little woods," boasts a nearly 6-mile length, making it an ideal spot for swimming and fishing. Horn Island, a popular destination, offers expansive beaches and opportunities for swimming, boating, and sunbathing, as well as diverse flora and fauna to observe.

Ship Island, accessible via ferry service provided by Ship Island Excursions, is home to Fort Massachusetts, a well-preserved brick fortification dating back to the mid-19th century. With historical ties to the War of 1812, Ship Island offers informative fort tours for history enthusiasts. In addition to swimming, sunbathing, bird-watching, hiking, and fishing options, Ship Island features a boardwalk that makes traversing the island easy. Visitors can also find restrooms, drinking water, and covered picnic areas, making it an ideal destination for a full day of activities.

The area is characterized by exceptionally white sand. Within the Florida District of the seashore, you'll find offshore barrier islands boasting pristine quartz sand beaches that stretch along miles of undeveloped coastline. Additionally, the area features historical fortifications, nature trails, and the Perdido Key Historic District, which preserves shore batteries that were active during World War I and World War II. Near Pensacola, Florida, on the mainland, you can explore attractions like the Naval Live Oaks Reservation, beaches, and military forts, all of which are accessible by automobile.

The Mississippi District of Gulf Islands National Seashore encompasses a variety of natural features and attractions, including unspoiled beaches, historical sites, wildlife sanctuaries, islands that are accessible only by boat, bayous, nature trails, picnic areas, and campgrounds. Among these, the Davis Bayou Area stands out as the sole part of the National Seashore in Mississippi that can be reached by automobile. Other islands like

Petit Bois, Horn, East Ship, West Ship, and Cat can only be accessed via boat. Additionally, the Gulf Islands Wilderness, spanning 4,080 acres (16.5 km2), provides special protection to portions of Petit Bois Island and Horn Island in Mississippi.

During the 2004 and 2005 Atlantic hurricane seasons, significant damage occurred to public infrastructure in this area due to storms. Subsequently, extensive efforts were made to fully restore this infrastructure. Today, all roadways, parking areas, campgrounds, and visitor centers have been repaired and are operating normally. Some trails, boardwalks, and dune crossovers were still undergoing repairs as of late 2010, particularly in the vicinity of the Fort Pickens campground.

In September 2020, Hurricane Sally struck the Gulf Islands Seashores, resulting in extensive damage. The impact of the hurricane was particularly severe on Perdido Key, where flooding waters caused the flattening of some dunes. Johnson Beach National Seashore, a part of the Gulf Islands National Seashore located at the eastern end of the island, bore the brunt of the storm. Many dunes were flattened, and the tip of the island was eroded, leading to the formation of three small isolated islands off the coastline. Restoration efforts were initiated to replenish the sand and vegetation to rectify the storm damage. However, this restoration process can be protracted, especially in the face of subsequent storms and strong winds.

The establishment of the Gulf Islands National Seashore was authorized on January 8, 1971, and it is overseen by the National Park Service. The designation of the wilderness area within the seashore was made on November 10, 1978. Prior to this, Santa Rosa Island had been under protection as a national monument from 1939 to 1946.

A significant environmental event occurred with the Deepwater Horizon oil spill, which commenced on April 20, 2010. This catastrophic event led to the release of extensive quantities of oil and tar. These pollutants began washing ashore, in varying degrees, along the Gulf Islands National Seashore on June 1, 2010. By June 23, 2010, successive waves of oil pools and globs had begun to cover the beaches on Santa Rosa Island. Consequently, a ban was imposed on fishing and swimming in the affected areas. The oil-spill disaster had a profound impact on all the major islands within the Gulf Islands National Seashore.

Gulf Islands National Seashore offers four visitor centers, each of which is staffed by National Park personnel. Two of these visitor centers are situated in Florida, while one is located in Mississippi.

Within the National Seashore, there are two developed campgrounds, with the option for primitive camping in designated areas. In Florida, the Pickens Campground is a developed facility that provides water and electrical hookups for both recreational vehicles and tents. The campground features paved roads, including access to individual campsites. The natural environment here is characterized by sand scrub oaks, small brackish ponds, and a remaining pine forest on a barrier island nestled between Pensacola Bay and the Gulf of Mexico. Central restrooms and showers are available for campers' use. Additionally, a campground store, which had been closed due to storm damage from Hurricanes Ivan and Dennis in 2004 and 2005, reopened in late 2010. While there are no sewer hookups at the campsites, a dump station is provided. This campground is located approximately 1.5 miles (2 km) from Fort Pickens.

In Mississippi, the Davis Bayou Campground is another developed site offering water and electrical hookups for RVs and tents. Paved roads run throughout the campground and connect to individual campsites. The natural setting consists of an oak and pine forest adjacent to a brackish bayou that leads to the Mississippi Sound. Central restrooms and showers are accessible for campers. As in Florida, there are no sewer hookups at the campsites, but a dump station is available. This campground is located at the end of a road that leads through the Davis Bayou Area.

Primitive camping is permitted on various barrier islands, accessible either by boating or hiking. It is allowed on Perdido Key, Florida (east of Johnson Beach), as well as on government-owned properties on Petit Bois, Horn, East Ship, and Cat islands in Mississippi.

GUMBO LIMBO NATURE CENTER

REGION: SOUTHEAST DISTRICT   **COUNTY:** PALM BEACH   **CITY:** BOCA RATON

DATE VISITED: **WHO I WENT WITH:**

RATING: ☆ ☆ ☆ ☆ ☆   **WILL I RETURN?**   YES / NO

The Gumbo Limbo Environmental Complex, also known as the Gumbo Limbo Nature Center, is a nature center that operates in partnership with the city of Boca Raton, Florida, the Gumbo Limbo Coastal Stewards (Gumbo Limbo Nature Center, Inc.), and the Greater Boca Raton Beach and Park District. It is situated at 1801 N. Ocean Blvd. in Boca Raton and spans twenty acres of protected barrier island, located between the Intracoastal Waterway and the Atlantic Ocean. While Gumbo Limbo does not have direct beachfront access, it is part of the beachfront-to-intracoastal Red Reef Park. The name "Gumbo Limbo" is derived from the common name of the Bursera simaruba tree species, which is abundant in the park.

The nature center comprises an indoor museum featuring exhibits, small aquariums, and a gift shop. Additionally, it boasts significant outdoor facilities, including large aquariums that showcase various ecosystems inhabited by fish, turtles, and other marine life. There is also a boardwalk trail that traverses the adjacent woods, as well as a butterfly garden designed for observing butterflies. The center organizes events such as sea turtle nesting season observations, with valuable assistance from local community volunteers in running the center and its activities.

Gumbo Limbo Nature Center is widely recognized for its dedicated efforts to protect the area's sea turtles. The beaches in South Florida play a crucial role as nesting grounds for three species of sea turtles: loggerhead, green, and leatherback. Unfortunately, all of these sea turtle species are currently classified as either threatened or endangered. Gumbo Limbo collaborates closely with the Florida Fish and Wildlife Conservation Commission to safeguard the local sea turtle populations.

Since the 1980s, the Boca Raton Sea Turtle Conservation and Research Program, based at Gumbo Limbo Nature Center, has employed Marine Conservationists and Marine Turtle Specialists. They are responsible for monitoring, documenting, and studying sea turtle activities along the five-mile stretch of Boca Raton's city beach. This team also handles reports of deceased or injured turtles from the Boynton Beach Inlet to the Boca Raton/Deerfield Beach border.

For more than thirty years, Gumbo Limbo's sea turtle conservation team has been providing assistance to sick and injured sea turtles in the Boca Raton area. In 2010, with the collaborative efforts of the City and the Friends of Gumbo Limbo, a rehabilitation facility was established on the center's premises to care for injured turtles. The primary objective of the rehabilitation program is to nurse these turtles back to health until they are fit for release into their natural habitat.

Gumbo Limbo's rehabilitation center is one of just six such facilities in Florida that accept turtles afflicted with Fibropapillomatosis (FP). FP is a condition associated with certain strains of the herpes virus. Warm and polluted waters have been linked to increased cases of FP. Many of the turtles at Gumbo Limbo afflicted with FP come from lagoons and bays near densely populated areas where runoff introduces pollutants such as fertilizers, pesticides, and pet waste into the water, resulting in poor water quality. FP often manifests as benign tumors that resemble cauliflower. Tumors on the flippers can hinder a turtle's ability to swim, while those on the eyes and mouth can affect their ability to locate and consume food. The center performs surgical removal of these tumors to help affected turtles recover.

The Gumbo Limbo Environmental Complex serves as a research facility for the Department of Biological Sciences at Florida Atlantic University. Ongoing research at this facility includes the study of sea turtle behavior, sensory perception in sharks, and the examination of salt levels affecting seagrasses. Visitors have the opportunity to observe the research facility and engage in discussions with the researchers conducting these studies.

HENDERSON BEACH STATE PARK

REGION: NORTHWEST DISTRICT   **COUNTY:** OKALOOSA   **CITY:** DESTIN

DATE VISITED: **WHO I WENT WITH:**

RATING: ☆ ☆ ☆ ☆ ☆   **WILL I RETURN?**   YES / NO

This protected strip of the Emerald Coast is for more than just relaxation. Fishing, a nature trail, and campsites are connected to the beach by a boardwalk are just some of the featured areas of this park. This special place was created to preserve and protect the natural features of this area, the last remaining coastal scrub area in Destin. The park has such activities as bicycling, birding, hiking, picnicking, swimming, wildlife viewing, and full camping facilities. There are no trails or bike paths in the park, but many campers ride their bikes on the mile-long paved road. You can also bike into the park and take a ride to the beach. Bicyclists should ride with helmets, and Florida law requires helmets for bicyclists 16 and younger.

The park has 60 campsites that can accommodate either tents or RVs, with a mixture of back-in and pull-through sites. The sites have water, electricity (all sites have both 30 and 50-amp service except campsites #28 and #29); picnic tables, and ground grills. Pets are welcome at campsites. A nearby 0.75-mile nature trail leads through ancient but still growing and changing dunes with vegetation known as coastal scrub. The trail offers views of the park and, in some places, the Gulf of Mexico. The trail features a high dune formed around the remains of a bunker that was built decades ago when the area was used by the military. Guided tours are available upon request. Destin is known as the luckiest fishing village in the world. Visitors may catch popular species such as pompano, redfish, flounder, catfish, whiting, and sometimes cobia. Fishing is prohibited between piers and fish cleaning stations are not available. All fishing within the park must comply with regulations regarding size, number, method of fishing, and time of year. A fishing license may be required. In spring and fall, birdwatchers can enjoy wading and shorebirds, as well as migratory birds.

Dolphins, sea turtles, and fish can be spotted on the beach, and small species of reptiles are often seen on the nature trail. The park is also home to rabbits, rats, and gopher tortoises, which can be seen from time to time when the park is quiet. There are six pavilions with grills, picnic tables, and three restrooms in the area for day use. There is a modern playground for children overlooking the Gulf of Mexico. The playground is located in the day use portion of the park, at the beginning of the nature trail. There are outdoor cold showers in the day use areas. These are located next to the day use bathhouses.

HOLLYWOOD

REGION: SOUTHEAST DISTRICT   **COUNTY:** BROWARD   **CITY:** HOLLYWOOD

DATE VISITED:	WHO I WENT WITH:

RATING: ☆ ☆ ☆ ☆ ☆   **WILL I RETURN?** YES / NO

Hollywood, located between Miami and Ft. Lauderdale, is renowned for its picturesque beach, making it an ideal destination for a beach vacation. The area boasts a variety of oceanfront hotels and resorts, catering to those seeking a weekend getaway or a relaxing staycation. Visitors can explore unique shopping options, enjoy beachfront dining experiences, and relax at bars along Hollywood's Broadwalk. Additionally, the city offers year-round activities, opportunities for water sports, and live music entertainment.

The distinctive Hollywood Beach Broadwalk is an iconic promenade extending nearly 2.5 miles along the Atlantic Ocean. Recognized as one of America's Best Beach Boardwalks by Travel + Leisure magazine, this brick-paved pathway welcomes pedestrians, joggers, cyclists, rollerbladers, and attracts millions of visitors annually. Along the promenade, you'll find the Hollywood Beach Theatre, a water playground for children at Charnow Park, captivating public art installations, and various other attractions. Hollywood Beach is also home to numerous luxury hotels and condominiums, including renowned establishments like the Diplomat Resort & Spa Hollywood, Trump Hollywood, and Margaritaville Hollywood Beach Resort.

Accessible Beach Access Points can be found at the following streets and along the Broadwalk: Carolina Street, Connecticut Street, Johnson Street, New York Street, Tyler Street, Harrison Street, Oregon Street, between Iris Terrace and Magnolia Terrace.

The city of Hollywood is a coastal community situated in southeastern Broward County, positioned midway between Miami and Fort Lauderdale. Established by Joseph Young in 1925, Hollywood covers an area of approximately 30 square miles and ranks as Broward's third-largest municipality, boasting a population of approximately 143,000 residents. Hollywood enjoys a pleasant climate with an average annual high temperature of 83 degrees and a low temperature of 68 degrees. The city takes pride in its abundant green spaces, including over 60 parks, five golf courses, and seven miles of unspoiled beaches.

Hollywood has evolved into a vibrant business center, boasting over 10,000 companies within its boundaries. Remarkably, approximately 80 percent of Port Everglades, the world's second-busiest cruise port, is situated within Hollywood. The port is home to Royal Caribbean's Allure of the Seas and Oasis of the Seas, which are the largest cruise ships globally. Additionally, Hollywood provides convenient access to both the Fort Lauderdale/Hollywood International Airport and the Miami International Airport, serving as significant gateways to Latin America. Notably, Hollywood is home to the Memorial Healthcare System, one of the nation's largest healthcare networks, including its flagship hospital, Memorial Regional, and the Joe DiMaggio Children's Hospital, Broward County's largest standalone children's healthcare facility.

The historic Downtown Hollywood district is a bustling commercial, entertainment, and cultural arts hub. Featuring attractions such as the Artspark at Young Circle and a plethora of bars and restaurants, Downtown Hollywood hosts a multitude of events, including concerts, music festivals, dance exhibitions, art shows, and more. Visitors can enjoy an eclectic range of music genres, including live jazz, blues, rock, Latin, and R&B, all within a few steps of each other.

Surfing is allowed in extended areas, from Douglas Street north to the Dania Beach/Hollywood border. It's also permitted from Madison Street south to Eucalyptus Terrace. Under certain conditions and when the bather load is low, surfing may be allowed in other beach areas marked with a black flag. Consult the nearest lifeguard. For safety reasons, it is strongly advised to wear a leash while surfing.

Kite boarding is allowed at the Meade Street launching area. Kite boarding is permitted from Monday through Friday, with holidays being the exception.

Surf fishing is allowed after 6:00 p.m. and before 9:00 a.m. Certain areas of the beach may be opened for fishing when conditions are suitable. Please check with the nearest lifeguard for guidance.

Paddlecraft, including stand-up paddleboards, kayaks, and canoes, can utilize the entire length of the municipal beach before 10:00 a.m. and after 5:00 p.m. Paddlecraft are allowed at all hours between Madison Street and Liberty Street. In the area south of Liberty Street and north of Madison Street, paddlecraft must remain 100 yards from the shore between 10:00 a.m. and 5:00 p.m. Whenever going offshore, please ensure you carry a personal flotation device and a signaling device for safety.

Overall, Hollywood offers a warm, welcoming atmosphere with a world-class beach, making it a cherished destination in the heart of South Florida.

To fully embrace the beauty and pleasures of Hollywood, take some time to explore Hollywood North Beach Park, one of the city's most exquisite beaches. Covering 52 acres on the barrier island between the Atlantic Ocean coast and the Intracoastal Waterway, this park offers various family-friendly amenities, such as picnic shelters, fishing piers, and public beach access, making it ideal for families with children.

Throughout the beach area, numerous other activities and experiences await. Hollywood Beach is a haven for water sports enthusiasts, offering jet ski rentals for an exhilarating ride on the water. Surfers can grab their boards and ride the waves. If you prefer a more laid-back experience, relax under an umbrella, lay your towel on the sandy shore, and soak up the South Florida sun. Or, take a leisurely stroll along the shoreline with the warm sand beneath your feet.

If you've had your fill of sun and sand during your visit, venture west across the Stranahan River to explore two of Hollywood's top outdoor adventure destinations: Anne Kolb Nature Center and West Lake Park.

Most visitors arrive at Fort Lauderdale-Hollywood International Airport (FLL), which is approximately 5 miles north of Hollywood. The drive from the airport via Dania Beach to Hollywood Beach takes approximately 15 minutes by car or taxi.

47 **HONEYMOON ISLAND STATE PARK**

REGION: CENTRAL WEST DISTRICT   **COUNTY:** PINELLAS   **CITY:** DUNEDIN

DATE VISITED: **WHO I WENT WITH:**

RATING: ☆ ☆ ☆ ☆ ☆   **WILL I RETURN?** YES / NO

A short drive from Tampa, Honeymoon Island offers visitors an escape from the bustle of city life. Honeymoon Island has over 4 miles of beach to explore along with a 3-mile trail through one of the last virgin pine forests. Looking to the sky, eagles, ospreys and great horned owls can be seen, while ground animals include gopher tortoises, raccoons, and armadillos. Rattlesnakes are common on Honeymoon Island, so be careful. A trip to the Rotary Centennial Nature Center helps visitors learn about the park's history and natural resources. Swimming, fishing, shelling, hiking, and biking are popular activities. Surf and pass fishing can yield catches of flounder, snook, trout, redfish, snapper, whiting, sheepshead, pompano, Spanish mackerel, cobia, ladyfish, and tarpon. All fishing within the park must comply with regulations regarding size, number, method of fishing, and season. A fishing license may be required. Kayaks can be rented through the concession or, if you have your own, explore Pelican Cove, which lies between the sand spit and nature trail. Surfing is allowed in the park.

A picnic area is located at the north end of the island. There are picnic tables, two covered pavilions, restrooms, and grills. Beach lovers will find plenty of activities: the main beach has areas for swimming, there is a pet beach at the south end, and there is shell collecting and walking at the north end, which turns into a sandy spit. Showers are located along the boardwalks leading to the main beach areas. Parking is available for the beach, at the picnic area and at the Rotary Centennial Nature Center. There is a playground located in the picnic area on the north end of the island. The park is also the ferry terminal for access to another unspoiled state park, Caladesi Island.

48

ISLAMORADA

REGION: SOUTHEAST DISTRICT	**COUNTY:** MONROE	**CITY:** MIAMI

DATE VISITED: **WHO I WENT WITH:**

RATING: ☆ ☆ ☆ ☆ ☆   **WILL I RETURN?**   YES / NO

Islamorada, also occasionally referred to as Islas Morada, is a legally recognized village located in Monroe County, Florida, within the United States. It is situated directly between Miami and Key West, spanning across five islands: Tea Table Key, Lower Matecumbe Key, Upper Matecumbe Key, Windley Key, and Plantation Key, all part of the Florida Keys. As of the 2020 census, the village had a population of 7,107 residents, marking an increase from 6,119 residents in 2010.

The name "Islamorada" translates to "purple island" and originates from early Spanish explorers who visited the area.

Historically, Islamorada served as one of the stations for the Overseas Railroad.

In 1935, Islamorada suffered a nearly direct hit from the devastating Labor Day Hurricane, which tragically led to the loss of 423 lives. Today, a memorial stands at Overseas Highway mile marker 82, containing the ashes of more than 300 hurricane victims.

Renowned baseball player Ted Williams started visiting Islamorada in 1943 and remained its most prominent resident for 45 years. Following his retirement from baseball, he became the national spokesperson for Sears sporting goods and gained fame for his exceptional fishing skills. Over the years, he welcomed numerous celebrities to his home in Islamorada and took them on local fishing excursions.

The village officially became incorporated on December 31, 1997, prior to which the term "Islamorada" referred to the developing community on Upper Matecumbe Key.

Islamorada's geographical coordinates are 24°56′9″N latitude and 80°36′49″W longitude. According to the United States Census Bureau, the village covers a total area of 6.7 square miles (17 km2), with 6.4 square miles (17 km2) of land and 0.3 square miles (0.78 km2), or 3.73%, consisting of water.

The village is traversed by U.S. Route 1, known as the Overseas Highway, which extends north for 74 miles (119 km) to Miami and southwest for 80 miles (130 km) to Key West.

Situated approximately 19 nautical miles (35 km; 22 mi) to the southwest of John Pennekamp Coral Reef State Park, Islamorada's strategic location between the Atlantic Ocean and the Gulf of Mexico places it along the migratory routes of many large fish species. As a result, Islamorada is informally recognized as the "Sportfishing Capital of the World."

Visitors can engage in a wide range of activities related to the water, whether they're on it, below it, above it, or near it, with options available around the clock.

And if you're looking for more to do, there are several noteworthy attractions to explore in the area:

Theater of the Sea provides opportunities for close encounters with dolphins. The History of Diving Museum features fascinating exhibits, including a treasure chest dating back to the 16th century. At Windley Key Fossil Reef Geological State Park, visitors can explore an ancient quarry originally excavated by the laborers of Henry Flagler's railroad. Lignumvitae Key Botanical State Park is home to a lush tropical forest waiting to be discovered. Indian Key Historic State Park is a small island that houses the remains of structures dating back to the 1800s, providing a glimpse into the area's historical past. Hikers have the opportunity to wander along scenic, tropical nature trails within Long Key State Park. For those seeking high-quality music and theater performances, the Coral Shores Performing Arts Center is the place to be. Music enthusiasts can revel in the pleasant, tropical evenings and full-day music festivals at the outdoor ICE Amphitheater, situated by the waterfront within Islamorada Founders Park. This expansive 40-acre park offers various attractions, including an Olympic-sized pool, a shallow-water beach, and options for water sports rentals.

The exhibits at the Keys History & Discovery Center showcase a wide range of topics, including the early inhabitants of the Florida Keys, the pioneering families that settled there, legendary figures in sportfishing, the significance of Henry Flagler's Florida Keys Over-Sea Railroad, and reflections on the Keys' nature, art, and history.

Travelers embarking on group tours throughout the Florida Keys, whether they're multi-generation families or special interest groups, can discover unique experiences that cater to almost every interest and preference.

The region offers a blend of activities, enjoyment, and relaxation suitable for the entire family. This includes the exciting experience of hand-feeding tarpon at the docks of Robbie's Marina and the opportunity to visit one of Florida's original marine mammal parks, known as the Theater of the Sea.

Diving enthusiasts are drawn to the area for the chance to explore the exceptional reef systems and vibrant patch reefs, and many are equally captivated by the intriguing exhibits at the History of Diving Museum.

The culinary scene in Islamorada beckons diners with a diverse array of options, featuring seafood straight from the docks, along with crowd-pleasing land-based dishes and ethnic cuisines. These tantalizing offerings are found in charming settings like tiki-covered bars, waterside fish houses, upscale beachfront cafes, and intimate island bistros.

For those who love to shop, there's a selection of appealing boutiques and art galleries to explore. Art enthusiasts can indulge in the monthly Third Thursday Art Walk, hosted by the Morada Way Arts & Cultural District.

Islamorada's beachfront accommodations and top-notch hospitality create an attractive and relaxed setting, making it a highly sought-after destination for tropical weddings.

JOHN B. STETSON HOUSE

REGION: CENTRAL EAST DISTRICT   **COUNTY:** VOLUSIA   **CITY:** DELAND

DATE VISITED: **WHO I WENT WITH:**

RATING: ☆ ☆ ☆ ☆ ☆   **WILL I RETURN?** YES / NO

The Stetson Mansion holds a unique place in Florida's architectural history as the state's premier luxury residence and the grandest dwelling constructed during the 19th century. Built in 1886 by the renowned hat maker and philanthropist, John B. Stetson, this mansion served as his winter retreat and stands as the sole exquisitely detailed "Gilded Age" estate ever built in Florida. After meticulous restoration and timeless updates, it has been preserved to reflect its former glory.

This remarkable mansion was a hub for lavish parties and gatherings, hosting both local residents and some of the nation's most prominent and influential figures during the "most prosperous era" in American history. The dedication to preserving its grandeur extended to extraordinary measures, such as Henry Flagler's construction of a private railway spur to deliver the finest architectural materials and Thomas Edison's installation of electric lighting.

The mansion's architectural design is a captivating blend of eclectic and unconventional elements, featuring intricate interior carvings, 16 patterns of exceedingly rare and detailed parquet wood flooring, and an astonishing 10,000 panes of original leaded glass windows. What sets it apart from other historic sites is its fully modernized infrastructure and furnishings, harmoniously combining the past and present to celebrate classic elegance with contemporary design. Unlike typical Victorian or Stetson museums filled with relics and antiques, this mansion retains every original architectural detail and exudes a warm and inviting atmosphere.

During a tour, visitors are immersed in the rich history of the mansion and its inspiring restoration story, with access to every part of the home, including "behind the scenes" areas. The mansion boasts five new kitchen areas and thirteen distinct bathrooms, all tastefully designed to complement the home's timeless style.

For the first time in over a century, this private estate is open to the public for tours, corporate events, lectures, weddings, receptions, and exclusive parties. The extensive restoration, carried out with the same care and attention as if it were still owned by a wealthy family, allows guests to experience this "National Historic Place" property and create cherished memories. The mansion is a national treasure that the current custodians are proud to share with the community, considering themselves stewards rather than mere owners.

The Stetson Mansion is an opportunity to discover the beauty of the mansion itself and the remarkable story of John B. Stetson, a forward-thinking and generous American whose cowboy hats have become iconic symbols of Americana, even though the man behind them remains relatively unknown. Reportedly, the expansive three-story home is only about half the size of what Mr. Stetson originally envisioned constructing on his vast 300-acre orange grove. During the construction phase, Mr. Stetson's younger and beautiful wife, Elizabeth, who was not particularly enthusiastic about the Florida project, visited DeLand and managed to persuade John B. Stetson to significantly scale down the mansion's construction from its grandiose original plans. Consequently, the home now spans just under 10,000 square feet and is situated on over 2 acres of land adorned with various features, including gardens, gazebos, fountains, patios, and a pool. Over the years, rumors have circulated about the existence of a concealed tunnel or wine vault on the property, though the current owners have yet to discover it - emphasizing the word "yet."

Adjacent to the main house is an 800-square-foot structure designed in a Polynesian style, featuring a stunning ceiling that soars to an impressive height of over 15 feet. Initially intended to serve as the mansion's kitchen, it later found use as a private schoolhouse for the Stetson children during their winter stays at the mansion. Mr. and Mrs. Stetson would even allow some of the workers' children to occasionally join in on these lessons. Each year, the Stetsons traveled to Florida with not only their servants and a governess but also a headmaster or headmistress for their children, who resided in the rear quarters of the schoolhouse. The schoolhouse's high planked arched ceiling not only captivates with its visual appeal but also transports one's imagination to the exotic waters of the South Pacific.

Today, the schoolhouse has been transformed into a lovely one-bedroom zen guesthouse/retreat, complete with a spa bath and gourmet kitchen, while still preserving many of its charming architectural elements that render it so distinctive. In addition, a serene meditation garden known as "Sophie's Garden" has been thoughtfully created next to the schoolhouse, offering visitors a space to dream, reflect on their life's journey, or simply unwind and appreciate the beauty of nature.

The sole recent addition to the estate is a new three-car garage and carriage house, which was completed in 2009. A significant amount of time was dedicated to searching for a design that seamlessly integrates with the original architectural style of the mansion and complements the inner courtyard of the estate.

The original carriage house, located across the street from the mansion, had once been combined with another structure to create the current residence that is no longer associated with the estate.

Behind the pool area, there was a brick building partially submerged in the ground, initially constructed to house the original steam heating furnace. Originally, it featured a glass hip roof. However, this building had been without a roof for many decades and had been repurposed as a compost bin. In recent times, the walls have been reinforced, the furnace removed, and a new roof installed. Today, this building serves as storage for some of the mansion's original details and as a repository for various Christmas decorations.

Between 1887 and 1906, it is documented that the Stetsons played host to a remarkable array of distinguished individuals. Their guest list included prominent figures such as the Astors (notably, John Jacob Astor, who tragically perished aboard the Titanic), the Mellons, the Vanderbilts, the Carnegies, Henry Flagler, Baron Frederick DeBary (renowned for DeBary Hall), President Grover Cleveland, and King Edward VII (who was the Prince of Wales at the time). Among the noteworthy friends of John B. Stetson was the world-renowned inventor, Thomas Edison, who oversaw the installation of electrical systems in the mansion. As a matter of fact, the Stetson Mansion holds the distinction of being one of the world's earliest residences designed and constructed with Edison electricity.

The Stetson Mansion's inclusion among America's top 300 historic homes is a source of pride for its current owners. J.T. Thompson elaborates on this recognition, stating, "The house attains this status due to its exceptional architecture and historical significance. Architecturally, it stands out for its incorporation of various styles and innovative features into a single residence, resulting in the creation of this magnificent structure. Historically, its significance lies in the notable guests who frequented the Stetson Mansion and the pivotal decisions made within its walls that have had a lasting impact on the history of Florida."

Another remarkable aspect of the mansion's history is that it represents Florida's inaugural luxury residence. It stands as one of the few enduring relics of the Gilded Age in the Sunshine State, and its lavishness becomes immediately evident upon entering the front door. This undoubtedly did not go unnoticed by Mr. Stetson's esteemed guests from the A-list.

Although Elizabeth did not harbor great enthusiasm for her winter visits to Florida, she did bring some elements of culture and art from the Philadelphia area during her annual trips. The absence of cultural and societal amenities at the time was a source of discontent for Elizabeth. Thanks to visionaries like the Stetsons, DeLand would later earn the moniker "The Athens of the South" due to their foresight and contributions in cultivating culture and ingenuity.

The mansion was renowned for hosting extravagant parties and receptions for some of the most elite members of society. One can only imagine the opulence and privilege experienced by those fortunate few during that era. Now, the opportunity to step back in time and become guests in this American masterpiece is within reach, as the mansion has been revitalized to offer everyone the chance to partake in its rich history while reaffirming the idea that anything is achievable.

John B. Stetson, one of the twelve children born to Stephen and Susan Batterson Stetson, came into the world in 1830 in Orange, New Jersey. His father was engaged in the hat-making trade, and John decided to leave school at a young age to apprentice as a hatter. However, his health took a toll, prompting him to travel to Colorado in search of gold and a recovery in his well-being. It was during his time in the West that he encountered the distinctive 10-gallon sombreros worn by Mexican Vaqueros and was inspired to create his own waterproof version. In the years that followed, his signature hat, known as "The Boss of the Plains," became synonymous with his name. This hat not only provided protection from the elements for cowboys but also allowed them to offer water to their horses from it.

In 1865, a rejuvenated John returned to the East, settling in Philadelphia. He initially opened a hat repair business in a one-room shop located at the northeast corner of 7th and Callowhill Streets. However, his talent for hat trimming quickly propelled him into hat manufacturing. Guided by the principle of producing only hats of the highest quality, his business flourished so rapidly that he required larger premises within just over a year. He relocated his business to 4th Street above Chestnut, and before long, his hats were being sold in the majority of retail establishments throughout Philadelphia.

In 1869, John B. Stetson introduced an innovative concept by employing traveling salesmen, which increased the demand for hat production and necessitated more manufacturing space. Another groundbreaking idea of his was to relocate his factory to the tranquil northeast area of the city, providing the necessary room for expansion. Over time, this 12-acre site accommodated multiple five and six-story hat factory buildings, along with the establishment of the Stetson Hospital.

John B. Stetson's commitment to "delivering quality work at fair prices" and his exceptional care for his employees, their families, and even the surrounding neighborhood set him apart from the typical manufacturers of his era. His factory buildings were initially constructed using brick and incorporated advanced safety features such as automatic sprinkler systems, fire extinguishers on each floor, and various other safety devices. Additionally, the manufacturing equipment he utilized was of unparalleled quality, making his facility the premier hat manufacturing facility globally.

Furthermore, John B. Stetson initiated one of the most progressive apprenticeship programs of his time. He paid wages above the standard scale and offered bonuses linked to specific achievement levels. He designated several rooms within his factory for his employees to use for religious, social, and other communal activities. Driven by his patriotic spirit, he organized a military unit composed of young male workers, providing them with uniforms, training, and even establishing an armory for their use.

John B. Stetson's genuine concern for the well-being of his employees was evident in his various initiatives. He initially established a dispensary, which later expanded its services to cater to the local community. Equipped with state-of-the-art medical equipment and staffed by highly skilled professionals, it offered services and treatment for a minimal charge of $1.00 for three months, with free assistance provided to those unable to pay. As the demand for healthcare services grew, Mr. Stetson took the step of constructing a free hospital on adjacent land near his factory.

Additionally, he established the John B. Stetson Building Association, offering his workers access to below-market rate loans, which was a significant assistance.

In 1885, at the behest of his friend Henry Deland, John Stetson visited Persimmon Hollow, now known as Deland, where he spent the subsequent 20 winters. During his time there, he became actively involved in local business and community leadership.

Beyond his business endeavors, John B. Stetson was a notable contributor to the YMCA and various other charitable organizations in Philadelphia. In 1888, he endowed an academy in DeLand, Florida, which later became Stetson University. The institution initially offered programs in liberal arts, music, and business and currently includes a college of law in St. Petersburg, Florida. John B. Stetson passed away in 1906 in his DeLand mansion home and was laid to rest in the family Mausoleum in the Ashland section of West Laurel Hill Cemetery in Bala Cynwyd, PA.

Following his death, his son, G. Henry Stetson, assumed control of the company until changing fashion trends led to a decline in hat sales, ultimately resulting in the closure of the plant in 1971. Subsequently, in 1977, the buildings were gifted to the City of Philadelphia. During the Great Depression, John B. Stetson's Elkins Park Estate was sold, and the mansion on the property was demolished. A road in the area still bears the Stetson name in his honor.

JOHN PENNEKAMP CORAL REEF STATE PARK

REGION: SOUTHEAST DISTRICT **COUNTY:** MONROE **CITY:** KEY LARGO

DATE VISITED: **WHO I WENT WITH:**

RATING: ☆ ☆ ☆ ☆ ☆ **WILL I RETURN?** YES / NO

Known for being the first undersea park in the country, John Pennekamp Coral Reef State Park covers an impressive 70 nautical miles. The park has four different types of boat tours. While many visitors view the park's colorful coral reefs and vibrant marine life on a glass-bottom boat cruise, you can get an even closer look by snorkeling or scuba diving. Kayaking and canoeing on the park's waters are popular activities. The park has several miles of paddling trails through the mangroves and in Largo Sound. There are three areas where saltwater fishing is allowed from shore. Fishing from a boat is allowed in park waters, but there may be designated protected areas, including those within the Florida Keys National Marine Sanctuary. Directions can be obtained at ranger stations. All fishing within park boundaries must comply with regulations regarding size, number, method of catch and season. A saltwater fishing license is required.

Visitors can also enjoy walking on short trails through tropical hammocks, picnicking, or swimming at the beach. The visitor center features several large saltwater aquariums filled with sea creatures, and nature videos are shown in its theater.

Full-facility and youth/group campsites are available. The campground has 42 reservable campsites, each with 30-amp, 50-amp and 110 electrical outlets. Each site also has water and sewer hookup, a picnic table and a grill. There is a primitive group campsite at the end of the road to the campground. It has a large grill, fire circle and picnic table, as well as a water tap. There is no electricity at this site, but there is a restroom near the pond. The park has a boat ramp. For overnight stays on a personally owned boat, there are dock slips in the marina and mooring buoys in Largo Sound. The park has picnic tables and grills throughout the park. Additionally, pavilions are available on a first-come, first-served basis.

JUNGLE ISLAND

REGION: SOUTHEAST DISTRICT   **COUNTY:** MIAMI-DADE   **CITY:** MIAMI

DATE VISITED: **WHO I WENT WITH:**

RATING: ☆ ☆ ☆ ☆ ☆   **WILL I RETURN?** YES / NO

Jungle Island, a beloved landmark in South Florida, is a cozy zoological park situated in the heart of Miami, nestled between downtown Miami and South Beach. Building on a storied legacy that dates back to 1936, Jungle Island serves as a haven for some of the world's rarest and most exotic animals. Visitors to the park can partake in captivating animal shows and informative exhibits as they wander amid streams and waterfalls beneath a lush canopy of tropical trees. For those seeking a more hands-on experience, there are opportunities for interactive encounters with intriguing animals and guided behind-the-scenes VIP tours. Jungle Island provides visitors with immersive real-life jungle adventures, emphasizing elements of adventure, animals, discovery, and play. Additionally, the park offers event facilities, including the newly renovated Treetop Ballroom and scenic outdoor spaces, including a private beach, making it Miami's go-to destination for extraordinary events.

Jungle Island, the premier entertainment hub in Miami, seamlessly combines the allure of Miami's tropical landscape with a jungle inhabited by extraordinary animals from around the world. Building on its remarkable 80-year history, today's Jungle Island is a modern theme park, featuring remarkable attractions like incredibly rare twin orangutans and an impressive array of over 300 vibrant birds, including the world's only trained Cassowary.

The story of Jungle Island traces back to 1936 when it was originally known as Parrot Jungle. Founded by Franz Scherr with the vision of a place where birds could soar freely, Parrot Jungle was initially situated in southern Miami. It gained fame for its diverse collection of exotic birds, including the famed high-wire bicycling cockatoo, Pinky, and the world-renowned pink flamingos that graced the opening credits of the television series Miami Vice.

Throughout the years, the park underwent transformations under the guidance of its current owners, who acquired it in 1988. After enduring the ravages of Hurricane Andrew, the owners embarked on the mission to relocate the park to Watson Island. In 2003, after extensive construction efforts, the Watson Island site officially opened its doors as Parrot Jungle Island.

The evolution of the park led to its rebranding as Jungle Island, a name better suited to encompass the diverse range of animals, plants, and experiences it offers.

True to its name, Jungle Island features an array of extraordinary flora, from the remarkable African sausage tree to a collection of rare cycads. Visitors can explore the park by wandering along 1.35 miles of winding, covered trails while enjoying numerous special exhibits, attractions, and tours. As Miami's most vibrant and distinctive destination, Jungle Island continues to enchant the multitude of visitors who flock to Miami each year.

JUNGLE QUEEN RIVERBOAT

REGION: SOUTHEAST DISTRICT   **COUNTY:** BROWARD   **CITY:** FORT LAUDERDALE

DATE VISITED: **WHO I WENT WITH:**

RATING: ☆ ☆ ☆ ☆ ☆   **WILL I RETURN?**   YES / NO

The Jungle Queen Riverboat has been plying the waters of Fort Lauderdale since 1935, amassing over 80 years of maritime expertise. Their wealth of experience truly shines through in their exceptional guest treatment, adept navigation of sometimes narrow river passages, and their ability to create an entertaining atmosphere. On top of their history, they boast one of the most visually appealing tour boats on the water.

The focal point of the tour, along the New River, showcases some of the most stunning and opulent residences in Florida. These homes are the exclusive domain of the ultra-wealthy, earning the nickname "billionaire's row" rightfully. From television producer Michael Mann, the creative force behind the iconic show Miami Vice, to the heir of Kohl's department stores, this stretch is home to some of the world's wealthiest individuals. Not to be outdone, the yachts of luminaries like Steven Spielberg also make appearances.

While you may not recognize the names of some of these affluent and influential figures, such as Wayne Huizenga, who co-founded companies like Blockbuster, Auto Nation, and Waste Management, their sprawling multimillion-dollar compounds are deserving of admiration and plenty of photos during your Jungle Queen Riverboat Cruise.

With decades of experience traversing the Intercoastal Waterway, their seasoned guides ensure that your trip is both informative and memorable. These guides are not only knowledgeable but also quick-witted, providing insights into the surrounding residences, vessels, and other noteworthy landmarks while injecting a dose of humor along the way.

Their fully equipped riverboat features an onboard bar where you can enjoy beer, wine, or even a mixed drink in the comfort of the boat.

During the Island Dinner and Show Cruise, you'll embark on a narrated sightseeing voyage down Fort Lauderdale's New River, often referred to as the "Venice of America." This informative cruise will provide you with insights into the who, what, when, and how much as you glide along Millionaire's Row, showcasing the lavish homes of the Rich and Famous, awe-inspiring Mega Yachts, and other remarkable sights. Your journey will lead you to a secluded private tropical island, where you'll be treated to an All-You-Can-Eat BBQ Dinner, featuring delectable offerings such as baby back ribs, chicken, and all the accompanying fixings. While indulging in this feast, you'll be entertained by live performances. Following dinner, prepare to be amused by a Variety Show brimming with laughter, live comedy, magic tricks, music, and more. Don't forget to allocate some time for a brief exploration of the beautiful tropical island, adorned with lush foliage, alligators, and tropical birds, enhancing your overall experience.

JUPITER

REGION: SOUTHEAST DISTRICT   **COUNTY:** PALM BEACH   **CITY:** JUPITER

DATE VISITED: **WHO I WENT WITH:**

RATING: ☆ ☆ ☆ ☆ ☆   **WILL I RETURN?** YES / NO

Jupiter, located in Palm Beach County, holds the distinction of being the northernmost town in the county. Positioned at a distance of 84 miles to the north of Miami and 15 miles to the north of West Palm Beach, Jupiter stands as the northernmost community within the Miami metropolitan area.

Jupiter has garnered recognition for its exceptional qualities as a beach town. It was notably designated as the 9th Best Southern Beach Town to reside in by the Stacker Newsletter in 2022. Additionally, in 2018, WalletHub ranked it as the 12th Best Beach Town in the United States. Furthermore, in 2012, Coastal Living magazine honored Jupiter by naming it the 9th Happiest Seaside Town in the United States, celebrating its coastal charm and quality of life.

Jupiter offers stunning beaches, world-class championship golf courses, a plethora of scuba diving sites, and the rich historical heritage.

Jupiter is widely recognized as one of Florida's most golf-centric regions, boasting miles of splendid fairways. Golf enthusiasts can indulge in their passion at over 50 courses in and around Jupiter, including notable options such as Jupiter Dunes, Cypress Links, Jonathon's Landing, Emerald Dunes Golf Club, and the PGA National Resort.

For those who cherish the beach, popular destinations for sun and recreation include Jupiter Beach Park, Juno Beach Park, and the unique Blowing Rocks Beach on Jupiter Island. Diving enthusiasts are in for a treat with access to more than 30 artificial reefs, such as the King Neptune reef featuring a nine-foot statue of King Neptune and his turtles, and the expansive Breakers Reef, spanning two miles with a ledge teeming with fish.

Sightseeing opportunities abound in the area, with highlights including the Jupiter Inlet Lighthouse and Museum, offering insights into the region's maritime history, and the Dubois Home, a historic pioneer residence dating back to 1898, which is listed on the National Register of Historic Places and was constructed on an ancient Indian Shell Mound, adding to its historical significance.

Jupiter boasts approximately 3.4 miles of stunning coastline featuring beautiful beaches. These beaches are renowned for their warm, crystal-clear waters and are naturally adorned with features like dunes, mangroves, and sea grape trees that enhance the area's natural charm. To ensure the cleanliness and protection of these beloved natural resources, both the County and Town are involved in their maintenance, with support from the Friends of Jupiter Beach, a local nonprofit organization dedicated to preserving these assets for the enjoyment of residents and visitors alike.

Each section of Jupiter's beachfront offers a unique experience, catering to various preferences, whether you're in the mood for a picnic, surfing, shell hunting, or bringing your furry companion along. Here's some useful information to help residents and tourists plan their beach visit while ensuring a pleasant experience for everyone:

Palm Beach County's Ocean Rescue oversees the guarded areas of Jupiter's beaches, which include portions of DuBois Park, Jupiter Beach Park, Carlin Park, Ocean Cay Park, and Juno Beach Park.

Pavilions at beaches and beach parks are maintained by Palm Beach County, and pavilion rentals can be arranged through their website.

Free parking lots can be found at DuBois Park, Jupiter Beach Park, Carlin Park, Ocean Cay Park, Juno Beach Park, and a lot situated between crossover #27 & #28. Street parking is also available along the A1A corridor.

Sea turtle nesting season along Jupiter's beaches runs from March 1 to October 31. During this season, it's crucial to avoid disturbing nesting turtles, refrain from interfering with nests or hatchlings, fill in any holes, and knock down sandcastles before leaving the beach to support the conservation efforts.

JUPITER INLET LIGHTHOUSE AND MUSEUM

REGION: SOUTHEAST DISTRICT	**COUNTY:** PALM BEACH	**CITY:** JUPITER

DATE VISITED: **WHO I WENT WITH:**

RATING: ☆ ☆ ☆ ☆ ☆   **WILL I RETURN?** YES / NO

In 1853, the construction of a lighthouse near Jupiter Inlet received congressional approval. In the subsequent year, the federal government officially designated a lighthouse reservation spanning 61.5 acres for this purpose. However, a survey conducted in the 1920s revealed that the reservation's actual size was 122 acres, twice the originally designated area.

The responsibility for overseeing the construction of the Jupiter Inlet Lighthouse was assigned to Lieutenant George Gordon Meade of the U.S. Army Corps of Topographic Engineers. Notably, Meade would go on to achieve fame as a Major General in the Union Army, where he famously defeated Robert E. Lee at the Battle of Gettysburg a decade later. Lieutenant Meade was responsible for selecting the construction site and creating the initial design for the lighthouse. Subsequently, Lieutenant William F. Raynolds, who succeeded Meade, further enhanced the design by increasing the tower's height and incorporating a double wall. The actual construction of the light station in 1859 and 1860 was supervised by Edward A. Yorke, a civilian.

Shortly after receiving authorization for the lighthouse, engineers encountered a significant challenge. A storm had blocked the inlet, causing the waters inside to become stagnant and fostering the spread of malaria. As a result, all construction materials had to be transported down the Indian River in small, shallow-draft barges from the nearest inlet near Fort Pierce.

The initial work crew was dispatched in late 1855, but they were forced to return home due to the outbreak of the Third Seminole War. Construction finally commenced in January 1859, but the challenging climate and logistical obstacles made progress slow. Construction was temporarily halted that summer, leaving the lighthouse far from completion.

Work resumed in January 1860, and the majority of the construction on the 108-foot lighthouse, the adjacent oil house, and the keepers' house was completed in just five months. The tower was officially illuminated on July 10, 1860.

With the onset of the American Civil War, Assistant Keeper Augustus Lang and other local Confederate sympathizers disabled the light, keeping it dark throughout the war. The inlet naturally reopened in 1862, allowing it to be used by Confederate blockade runners operating between Florida and the Bahamas. Union gunboats patrolled offshore and dispatched rowed cutters into the Indian River.

The Jupiter Inlet Lighthouse was relit on June 28, 1866, resuming its role as an active aid to navigation. James Armour, who had assisted the Union Navy in recovering parts and supplies removed from the lighthouse during the war, became one of the new keepers. In 1869, he was promoted to Head Keeper, and remarkably, he served as the lighthouse keeper for 40 years until his retirement in 1906. In honor of his service, Captain Armour's Way was named after him.

From 1860 to 1939, a total of more than 70 different lighthouse keepers took on varying lengths of service at the Jupiter Inlet Lighthouse. At any given time, three keepers were responsible for the operation and maintenance of the lighthouse and its premises. Their primary duties included fueling the lighthouse lamp with oil, winding the mechanism that rotated the lens, and maintaining watch through the night.

In 1939, the civilian Lighthouse Service merged with the US Coast Guard. Keeper Charles Seabrook and his assistants chose to enlist in the Coast Guard. Military personnel continued to serve as keepers of the lighthouse until it became fully automated in 1987.

In 2008, the Jupiter Lighthouse Reservation was designated as the Jupiter Inlet Lighthouse Outstanding Natural Area by Congress. The ownership of the lighthouse and the former Coast Guard station was transferred to the Bureau of Land Management in 2019. The historic Fresnel lens is still the property of the Coast Guard. The lighthouse remains an active public Aid to Navigation, boasting one of only 13 active First-Order Fresnel lenses in the entire United States. The Loxahatchee River Historical Society (LRHS), a non-profit organization, first established a lighthouse museum on the site in 1973. Since 1994, LRHS has acted as the modern custodians of the Jupiter Light through a formal agreement to restore and preserve the lighthouse, provide visitor access, and offer historical interpretation.

The Jupiter Inlet Lighthouse Outstanding Natural Area (JILONA) received federal designation from Congress in May 2008 with the purpose of safeguarding and enhancing the unique and nationally significant historic, natural, cultural, scientific, educational, scenic, and recreational values of the federal land surrounding the Lighthouse. This designation aims to benefit both current and future generations of people in the United States. Within JILONA, you can encounter 25 special status species, discover cultural evidence of 5,000 years of human presence, and explore a north-side hiking trail leading to a lagoon overlook that traverses three distinct Florida habitats. Another noteworthy aspect is that JILONA was included as a unit of the Bureau of Land Management's (BLM) National Conservation Lands, making it one of only three Outstanding Natural Areas in the country. These extraordinary lands are spread across the Western United States, Alaska, and Florida. They represent our nation's most recent system of protected public lands and hold the same significance as our National Parks, National Forests, and National Wildlife Refuges.

JILONA provides visitors with picturesque hiking trails situated on both the north and south sides of Beach Road. The North Trail winds its way through Florida Scrub and tropical hammock areas, leading to a sheltered observation platform overlooking a tranquil mangrove lagoon. An optional loop within this trail passes through a rare sand pine forest. On the other hand, the South Trail loop grants access to the Indian River, offers views of the lighthouse, and allows for encounters with a diverse array of flora and fauna.

Furthermore, there is a shoreline observation pier that is now open to the public and can be visited as part of daily admission to the Jupiter Inlet Lighthouse & Museum or through various programs organized by the Bureau of Land Management.

For families with children, there is a small playground located in Lighthouse Park. Additionally, leisurely waterfront activities such as fishing, paddleboarding, and birdwatching are popular recreational options in the vicinity of the museum. Visitors are encouraged to bring their cameras and binoculars for the opportunity to spot exceptional plant and animal life. Lighthouse Park also offers recreational facilities such as soccer fields, tennis courts, and pickleball courts.

KENNEDY SPACE CENTER

REGION: CENTRAL EAST DISTRICT   **COUNTY:** BREVARD   **CITY:** CAPE CANAVERAL

DATE VISITED: **WHO I WENT WITH:**

RATING: ☆ ☆ ☆ ☆ ☆   **WILL I RETURN?** YES / NO

The Kennedy Space Center was initially known as NASA's Launch Operations Center when it was established on July 1, 1962. However, it was later renamed in honor of President John F. Kennedy after his tragic death. President Kennedy's vision to land astronauts on the moon within a decade served as an inspiration and challenge to the agency.

Throughout its history, the Kennedy Space Center has played a pivotal role in leading the United States on groundbreaking journeys into space. From this Florida location, NASA has launched rockets, courageous astronauts, and advanced spacecraft on missions to Earth's orbit, the moon, and beyond, venturing into the vast universe.

Despite facing both triumphs and tragedies, the Kennedy Space Center remains dedicated to exploring the wonders of the universe.

At the Kennedy Space Center Visitor Complex, the attractions and tours are organized into Mission Zones based on different chronological eras of space exploration. These Mission Zones cover the entire journey of space exploration, starting from its early days to current and ongoing missions. Visitors have the opportunity to experience and interact with the captivating story of human endeavors in space up close and firsthand. It's a place where you can ignite your passion for inspiration and immerse yourself in the wonders of space exploration.

One day is an absolute minimum for visiting the Kennedy Space Center, as it takes at least 6 to 8 hours to explore it thoroughly. If you want to see all the exhibits and exhibition halls on the grounds of the Kennedy Space Center, even 8 hours might not be enough. If you plan to have a meal at the space center, it may take even longer. So, it's worth planning your trip to the Kennedy Space Center wisely.

If you have booked a hotel in another part of Florida, such as Orlando or Miami, you need to consider the travel time to Cape Canaveral. Therefore, it's essential to plan your day at the Kennedy Space Center wisely to make the most of your visit and see as much as possible in one day.

Additionally, you need to take into account the current weather conditions during your visit to Florida. If your visit to the Kennedy Space Center and Cape Canaveral falls during the summer months, July and August, be prepared for high temperatures and very high humidity. Many attractions at KSC (Kennedy Space Center) are outdoors, so you need to adapt to the Florida weather conditions.

The place attracts thousands of tourists daily. You will likely arrive here by rental car or your own means of transportation. There are clear signs on the roads leading to the Visitor Center of the Kennedy Space Center.

After entering the Kennedy Space Center Visitor Complex, there are parking fees to be paid. You will receive a ticket and receipt confirming the parking fee at the Kennedy Space Center, which you need to display on your car's front windshield.

Next, you will be directed to the appropriate part of the parking lot, which has numbered sections from 1 to 6. The parking area is huge, so there is plenty of space. Then, you need to walk a few hundred meters to the Kennedy Space Center, where ticket counters and ticket vending machines are located. You can purchase tickets using a credit card without having to wait in line at the ticket counter.

Inside this massive complex, there are restaurants, places to buy cold drinks, and restrooms. Facilities like mother-and-child rooms and all amenities imaginable facilitate exploring this facility.

The entire Kennedy Space Center Visitor Complex is located within the Merritt Island National Park, surrounded by splendid, wild nature. Along the way, you can see birds typical of Florida (see Florida animals) and alligators floating in the lakes scattered around the complex. Bus drivers sometimes draw visitors' attention to the local fauna and flora.

After entering, head to the information desk, where you will be informed where to start the tour and receive an additional map. There's an option to rent an Audio Tour – headphones, where the guide's voice explains the various attractions within the Kennedy Space Center complex. Also, if you want to bring souvenirs from this fantastic trip, there are several souvenir shops on the premises, well-stocked with fantastic gadgets related to the Kennedy Space Center and space exploration.

To access certain parts of the Kennedy Space Center, you can take special shuttle buses, and the stops are clearly marked within the complex. The shuttle buses within the Kennedy Space Center Visitor Complex are free. Usually, the waiting time for the next bus does not exceed 15 minutes.

The bus stops at two major attractions within the center: the Observation Tower, where you can go up and have a top view of the Kennedy Space Center and the vastness of the place. From a distance, you can see all the individual sections of the center. The hangar where space shuttles are stored and serviced, once the largest building in the world, the roads where the crawler-transporters move, transporting space shuttles, and the rocket launch pads.

Along the way, the guide on the bus also points out the launch pad, which is the exact spot from where space shuttles take off. It's worth listening attentively and absorbing the information provided by the well-informed bus guides/drivers.

The next bus stop is the Apollo/Saturn V Center. Here, after watching a film about the Apollo mission, you can see and experience the Apollo launch in a special room simulating the space flight control center in Houston, and relive the rocket launch. According to the guide, it's the original mission control center from those times. The deafening roar of the rocket engines, vibrating windows, and the experience is almost as if you were there, witnessing the rocket launch into space.

Exhibitions at Kennedy Space Center:

Mission Status Update at Astronaut Encounter Theater
Here, you will learn about NASA's current space flights, the current NASA space program, and upcoming plans related to space exploration.

Exploration Space: Explorers Wanted
Introduction to the space exploration center. Do you dream of traveling in space? Would you like to fly to space? Maybe this place is just for you.

Space Shuttle Atlantis and Shuttle Launch Experience
Here, you will experience the NASA program and get to know the space shuttle Atlantis. After watching a film and audio-video presentation, the exhibited Atlantis shuttle leaves a strong impression on visitors. It's a great opportunity to take pictures of an American space shuttle and learn about the history of space shuttles. There are plenty of artifacts and items related to space shuttle missions. An incredibly interesting exhibition and a wonderful experience.

Eye on Universe: The Hubble Space Telescope
Get to know better this famous, cosmic Hubble telescope, observing and exploring deep space. Learn about the discoveries made by scientists as they peer into the universe through the lenses of the Hubble telescope.

Astronaut Encounter
Inquire at the information desk about the schedule for live lectures. In this air-conditioned hall, real astronauts who have been in space speak and share their experiences. It's a fantastic experience, and it's worth listening to what the pioneers of space have lived through and seen.

Angry Birds Space Encounters
Angry Birds fans will fall in love with this place. Inter-galactic chasing of eggs, while the most peculiar flock of birds competes with Space Pigs. You have to experience it, even if you're not a fan of the Angry Birds Universe.

Rocket Garden

This is the best place to start your tour of the Kennedy Space Center, as it is right in front of the entrance. Each rocket is thoroughly described here, and you will immediately recognize them from TV photos, realizing that these American rockets are not as large as they appear on television. You will also see how small and cramped the space capsules returning to Earth with astronauts are. Some of them you can even enter inside.

Early Space Exploration

Here, you will get to know the Mercury Mission Control, featuring various consoles and other artifacts related to the early American space missions during the exploration of the cosmos.

Astronaut Memorial

This place commemorates the victims of space exploration. It honors the well-known astronauts who lost their lives and dedicated themselves to humanity.

Space Walk of Honor

Learn about the pioneers in space exploration and the sponsors of NASA's space programs.

Children's Play Dome

A playground for children. It's a shaded area where kids can play to their heart's content, and parents can take a little break. Children should not be left unattended in this area.

KEY WEST

REGION: SOUTHEAST DISTRICT   **COUNTY:** MONROE   **CITY:** KEY WEST

DATE VISITED: **WHO I WENT WITH:**

RATING: ☆ ☆ ☆ ☆ ☆   **WILL I RETURN?**   YES / NO

Key West, also known as Cayo Hueso in Spanish, is an island located in the Straits of Florida. It is part of the City of Key West, along with other separate islands like Dredgers Key, Fleming Key, Sunset Key, and the northern part of Stock Island.

The island of Key West is approximately 4 miles long and 1 mile wide, covering a total land area of 4.2 square miles. It is situated at the southernmost tip of U.S. Route 1, the longest north-south road in the United States. Key West is about 95 miles north of Cuba at their closest points and around 130 miles southwest of Miami by air, 165 miles by road, and 106 miles north-northeast of Havana.

The city of Key West serves as the county seat of Monroe County, which includes a majority of the Florida Keys and part of the Everglades. The city's total land area is 5.6 square miles. Its official city motto is "One Human Family."

Key West holds the distinction of being the southernmost city in the contiguous United States and is the westernmost island connected by a highway in the Florida Keys. The main street in Key West is Duval Street, spanning 1.1 miles and crossing from the Gulf of Mexico to the Straits of Florida and the Atlantic Ocean. It also serves as the southern terminus of U.S. Route 1, State Road A1A, and the East Coast Greenway. Key West is a popular port of call for passenger cruise ships, and it has the Key West International Airport providing airline service.

Naval Air Station Key West is an important year-round training site for naval aviation due to the favorable tropical weather. The island was also chosen as the site for President Harry S. Truman's Winter White House. The central business district is situated along Duval Street and covers much of the northwestern corner of the island.

The Overseas Highway, also known as "The Highway That Goes to Sea," is a modern marvel that stretches from Miami to Key West, following the path originally blazed by Henry Flagler's Florida East Coast Railroad in 1912. Today, the highway offers a scenic route that can be completed in less than four hours from Miami, but travelers are encouraged to take their time and appreciate the ever-changing beauty of the surrounding seas and wilderness, as well as the breathtaking sunrises and sunsets.

Before its transformation into the Overseas Highway, the route was initially a railroad line, but after a devastating hurricane in 1935, the railway was severely damaged, leading to its discontinuation. The construction of the highway started shortly after, utilizing some of the original railway spans and specially designed columns on individual keys.

The completion of the Overseas Highway in 1938 marked a significant milestone, enabling motorists to embark on an incredible 113-mile journey through 42 bridges from Miami to Key West. Over the years, some bridges have been replaced and expanded, such as the renowned Seven Mile Bridge in Marathon.

Driving the Overseas Highway offers spectacular views, but it also means there are stretches without stops, except for pulling off into the water. However, with adequate preparation, the experience of driving this highway is unforgettable.

Key Largo is the first major key you'll encounter, and you can take a break at the Florida Keys Overseas Heritage Trail for some refreshing outdoor activities. As you continue, Islamorada offers the History of Diving Museum, showcasing diving artifacts and the quest for underwater exploration. In Marathon, you'll find the Dolphin Research Center, where you can learn about and interact with dolphins.

Eventually, you'll reach Key West, the final destination of the Overseas Highway adventure. Key West offers a vibrant nightlife with local bars and a famous daily Sunset Celebration at Mallory Square. Must-see attractions include the Ernest Hemingway Home and the southernmost point of the continental U.S. marked by a concrete buoy.

Key West is a seafood lover's paradise, and visitors can indulge in fresh and perfectly cooked seafood. The city also boasts numerous breweries and bars, including the classic Sloppy Joe's. When it comes to accommodation, Key West offers a range of options, from newly renovated hotels to charming bed and breakfasts.

Getting to Key West can be done by driving along the single road on and off the island or flying into Key West International Airport. While cars are convenient for exploring the island, most areas are easily walkable, and visitors can also dock their boats at various locations.

With just four miles in length and one mile in width, Key West boasts some of the most picturesque beaches in the county. Whether you seek relaxation, family fun, or adventurous activities, Key West's beautiful beaches have something to offer for everyone.

One of the famous beaches in Key West is South Beach, located at the southernmost tip of the island. It's essential to note that this is not the same South Beach known for its party scene in Miami. Instead, Key West's South Beach is a beloved spot among families due to its tranquil and shallow waters. The beach offers a laid-back atmosphere, and its shoreline is technically part of the Southernmost Beach Cafe. Visitors can enjoy the beautiful crystal-clear water and find a few makeshift food stalls. However, it's worth noting that there are no public restrooms available at this beach.

Smathers Beach is the most popular beach on the island and stretches about two miles down Roosevelt Boulevard. It provides ample opportunities for all-day entertainment and beach activities. Visitors can enjoy food vendors, water sports rentals, and beach volleyball. The beach is easily accessible with free parking along the boulevard, and amenities like restrooms and lounge chair rentals are available without an entry fee.

For a less crowded option, Higgs Beach is a great choice. Located within walking distance of Smathers Beach, Higgs Beach tends to attract fewer crowds due to the way tides flow in the area, leading to some ocean debris and seaweed. However, the city diligently maintains the beach, cleaning up driftwood regularly. The water is clear, making it suitable for snorkeling, and visitors might even spot stingrays near the pier.

Rest Beach may be small, only stretching about 300 yards, but it offers breathtaking views of the Atlantic Ocean and boasts the most beautiful sunrises and sunsets on the island. If you prefer to sleep in, head to Mallory Square for the famous nightly sunset celebrations. Rest Beach also features a yoga deck, where classes are frequently offered.

Dog Beach is the sole beach on the island that permits dogs to roam freely, making it an ideal spot for exercising your four-legged friend. The area is relatively small, around 20 feet across, and has a rocky terrain that dogs seem to enjoy. To find Dog Beach, look for Louie's Backyard, as the eatery is adjacent to the beach, and there is a small sign indicating its location.

The best time to visit Key West is during the months of March to May. This period falls between the peak tourist season and hurricane season, ensuring pleasant temperatures ranging from the low 70s to 80s Fahrenheit, fewer rainy days, smaller crowds, and more affordable flight and hotel prices. On the other hand, winter (November to February) is the busiest season with lively activities, but it comes with expensive flight and car rental costs, and hotels and vacation rentals are often fully booked. Alternatively, the months from June to October offer incredible deals, but it is also the time of the Atlantic hurricane season, posing potential risks.

Key West, like other parts of Florida, is susceptible to hurricanes. The hurricane season runs from June 1 to November 30 each year, with the most powerful storms usually forming in August, September, and October. Due to the island's complete surround by water, hurricanes often lead to mandatory evacuations.

During the colder months up north, many travelers head south to Key West for its warm weather and blue skies. From November to February, it is the peak travel season in Key West, especially starting with Thanksgiving week, when the Florida Keys' tourist season officially begins. During this time, restaurants and hotels are fully booked, flight prices are higher, and traffic in and out of Key West becomes heavy. If you plan to visit at this time, it's essential to book flights, hotels, and rental cars early to secure availability and save money, as it is generally more expensive.

One of Key West's most famous events is Fantasy Fest, a 10-day festival featuring costumes and masks held at the end of every October. This festival includes unique costumes, X-rated parties, and a nighttime costume parade down Duval Street. If you attend, be prepared to witness wild costumes and join the enthusiastic crowd of locals and visitors, as Fantasy Fest has been a tradition for over 40 years.

Key West has a pleasant climate throughout the year, with average high temperatures of 82 degrees Fahrenheit and average lows of 73 degrees Fahrenheit. This makes it an ideal year-round destination, whether you're looking to escape the winter cold or enjoy a tropical paradise in the summer. The winter weather attracts visitors with temperatures in the mid-70s during December, January, and February, while the summer months of June, July, and August offer warm water temperatures in the Gulf of Mexico and Atlantic Ocean, perfect for a relaxing beach vacation.

No matter when you plan to visit Key West, it's essential to be aware of the weather conditions to pack accordingly and plan your activities accordingly.

Fishing in Key West offers a diverse range of options to suit different preferences and experiences. You can try deep sea fishing, light tackle offshore fishing, flats fishing, and backcountry fishing, depending on your interests and desired location. Additionally, there are plenty of areas where you can fish from shore or the Overseas Highway bridges, making it suitable for beginners who want to give fishing a try.

The waters surrounding the Southernmost Point of the United States are home to some of the most sought-after gamefish, including bonefish, tarpon, permit, redfish, and snook. Just a little further out in the Atlantic, you can find a plethora of sport fishing favorites like blue and white marlin, swordfish, and sailfish. Whether you're a beginner, seasoned angler, or just want to give fishing a shot, Key West offers some of the finest fishing experiences in the world.

The best season for fishing in Key West depends on various factors, including water temperature. During the winter months from December to February, the catch may be more challenging to come by due to windier waters, making backcountry fishing a recommended option. The "backcountry" refers to the Florida Bay, the inner curve of the Keys. Springtime, from March to May, is considered the prime season for fishing all types of fish in the local waters. The waters start to warm up, and tarpon become more abundant. From June to August, the weather is the hottest, making it great for fishing, but it can be uncomfortable for inexperienced anglers due to the heat. The fall months of September and October are the second-best time for fishing in Key West, as the summer crowds have thinned out, and the water remains warm and teeming with fish. Spring in Key West, from March to May, offers pleasant weather and fewer crowds compared to other parts of the United States. The average air temperature during this season is around 77 degrees Fahrenheit (25 degrees Celsius), with ocean and gulf temperatures above 70 degrees Fahrenheit (21 degrees Celsius). It's a good time to take advantage of vacation packages from resorts in the area. When packing for spring, a sweater may not be necessary, but it's still advisable to bring a long-sleeved shirt for cooler evenings. While March and April are relatively dry, May and June can bring rain, so packing an umbrella and raincoat is a good idea. Summer in Key West, from June to August, is the hottest time of the year, but it's also the rainiest due to the Atlantic Hurricane Season. Tourist crowds are high during this season, and the weather can be sweltering with high humidity. Expect about 17 days of rain per month on average. For summer packing, leave the long sleeves at home as temperatures stay in the upper 70s for highs and lows. Lightweight and breathable clothing, like linens, are ideal for the beach, but you might also need some business casual wear for upscale establishments with strict dress codes. Fall in Key West, from September to November, sees the end of the hurricane season and various festive events taking place, such as the city-wide Fantasy Festival and the Key West Holiday Fest during Thanksgiving. Fall packing should include a mix of clothing, as the nighttime temperatures drop and hurricanes or tropical storms are still possible. Bring both long and short-sleeved shirts, a light jacket, a raincoat, an umbrella, and suitable beach attire to be prepared for any weather. Winter in Key West, from late December to mid-March, is the best time to visit due to low rainfall and high temperatures. The Master Chef's Classic is an outdoor event during this season, allowing visitors to enjoy delicious cuisines by the sea. For winter packing, bring a light jacket or sweater for the cooler nighttime temperatures, which can go down to 64 degrees Fahrenheit (18 degrees Celsius) in January and February. During the day, shorts, light T-shirts, sandals, sunscreen, and a beach blanket are suitable for enjoying the winter sun.

To save money, visitors can take advantage of free parks and museums, walk instead of using rideshare services, and enjoy free rum tastings at the First Legal Rum Distillery. Additionally, places like the Children's Animal Park and the Florida Keys Eco-Discovery Center offer free and educational experiences for all ages.

KEY WEST BUTTERFLY AND NATURE CONSERVATORY

REGION: SOUTHEAST DISTRICT   **COUNTY:** MONROE   **CITY:** KEY WEST

DATE VISITED: **WHO I WENT WITH:**

RATING: ☆ ☆ ☆ ☆ ☆   **WILL I RETURN?** YES / NO

The Key West Butterfly and Nature Conservatory, situated at 1316 Duval Street in Key West, is a butterfly park. It provides a home for approximately 50 to 60 diverse butterfly species from all over the world, all within a controlled environment enclosed by glass walls.

Within the conservatory, you'll find lush flowering plants, beautiful waterfalls, and tall trees. Additionally, it's home to various species of birds that can fly freely and coexist with the butterflies. These birds include American flamingoes, red-factor canaries, zebra finches, cordon-bleu finches, and "button" or Chinese painted quail.

For visitors interested in learning more, there's a dedicated learning center. Here, guests can observe live caterpillars up close as they feed and go through the process of becoming butterflies on their respective host plants.

LAKE KISSIMMEE STATE PARK

REGION: CENTRAL WEST DISTRICT   **COUNTY:** POLK   **CITY:** LAKE WALES

DATE VISITED: **WHO I WENT WITH:**

RATING: ☆ ☆ ☆ ☆ ☆   **WILL I RETURN?** YES / NO

The park is located off State Road 60, 15 miles east of Lake Wales. White-tailed deer, bald eagles, sandhill cranes, turkeys, and bobcats have been seen in the park, located on the shores of lakes Kissimmee, Tiger, and Rosalie. The park's abundance of water, wetlands and numerous different habitats offer observers views of a variety of waterfowl and birds of prey. The park offers some of the best fishing opportunities in the state. A variety of fish that can be caught include largemouth bass, crappie, catfish, chain pickerel, and bluegill. All fishing within the park must comply with regulations regarding size, number, method of fishing, and season. A fishing license may be required. Visitors can launch boats from the park, and explore the 35,000 acres of Lake Kissimmee and the neighboring lakes and creeks on the Kissimmee Chain of Lakes. The scenic 10-mile Buster Island Paddling Trail is Florida's 53rd state designated paddling trail. It is suitable for experienced paddlers and offers excellent fishing and wildlife viewing opportunities as it encircles Buster Island. The park has an on-site boat ramp and marina. Daily access and use of the boat ramp and marina may be impacted by wind-blown debris that can potentially block the canal and marina. The marina includes accessible parking spaces, restrooms, and a fishing area.

Nature lovers can hike more than 13 miles of trails to observe and study abundant plant and animal life. Six miles of trails are available for horseback riding. A large picnic area is located near the day use area of the park. There are numerous picnic tables and four pavilions, two of which are handicapped accessible.

The park has full-facility campsites as well as a primitive camping facility. The youth camping area can accommodate up to 50 people. Sixty campsites are available with electric and water hookups. A dump station is located nearby. Well-behaved pets are welcome at the campground. Primitive equestrian camping is available at Lake Kissimmee State Park. You should be prepared: water, electricity, and restrooms are not available. Park amenities include a playground and an observation tower providing a view of Lake Kissimmee. Dark skies make stargazing a popular nighttime activity for visitors.

59

LAKE OKEECHOBEE

REGION: CENTRAL EAST D., SOUTHWEST D., SOUTHEAST D. **COUNTY:** GLADES, OKEECHOBEE, MARTIN, PALM BEACH, HENDRY **CITY:** CLEWISTON, PAHOKEE, OKEECHOBEE, BELLE GLADE

DATE VISITED: **WHO I WENT WITH:**

RATING: ☆ ☆ ☆ ☆ ☆   **WILL I RETURN?** YES / NO

Lake Okeechobee, also referred to as Florida's Inland Sea, stands as the largest freshwater lake in the state of Florida. Among all 50 states in the United States, it ranks as the tenth largest natural freshwater lake, and it's the second largest one entirely contained within the contiguous 48 states, following Lake Michigan.

Lake Okeechobee spans an impressive 730 square miles (1,900 km2) but is quite shallow given its size, with an average depth of only 9 feet (2.7 meters). What sets it apart is not only its title as Florida's largest lake or the largest in the southeastern United States, but also its vastness, making it impossible to see across, giving it a resemblance to an ocean.

The primary source of Lake Okeechobee is the Kissimmee River, which flows directly north of the lake. The lake's borders are shared among Glades, Okeechobee, Martin, Palm Beach, and Hendry counties, with all five counties converging at a single point near the lake's center.

The earliest known inhabitants around Lake Okeechobee were the Calusa people, who referred to the lake as Mayaimi, meaning "big water." This name was documented in the 16th century by Hernando de Escalante Fontaneda. The term "Okeechobee" itself originates from the Hitchiti words "oki" (water) and "chubi" (big). In the later part of the 16th century, René Goulaine de Laudonnière mentioned a large freshwater lake in southern Florida known as Serrope. By the 18th century, this mostly legendary lake was recognized by British mapmakers and historians under the Spanish name Laguna de Espiritu Santo. In the early 19th century, it was identified as Mayacco Lake or Lake Mayaca, named after the Mayaca people who had settled near the lake in the early 18th century, originally hailing from the upper St. Johns River region. The present-day Port Mayaca on the lake's eastern side still holds that name.

Along the southern shore of Lake Okeechobee, three islands – Kreamer, Ritta, and Torey – were once inhabited by early settlers. These settlements featured essential amenities like general stores, post offices, schools, and even local elections, with agriculture being the primary occupation. However, farming in the fertile but muddy muck of the area presented significant challenges. Over the first half of the 20th century, farmers adopted agricultural machinery, including tractors, to work in the mucky soil. By the 1960s, all these settlements had been abandoned.

Initially, the entire Lake Okeechobee area fell within the boundaries of Palm Beach County when the county was established in 1909. In 1963, the lake was divided among the five counties that surround it.

The predominant fish species found in Lake Okeechobee include largemouth bass, crappie, and bluegill. Pickerel, while present, are not as frequently caught in the lake.

Okeechobee, encompassing the lake, waterways, and the neighboring countryside, offers a diverse representation of Florida's natural beauty. Here, you'll find a captivating landscape characterized by the graceful canopy of moss-covered live oak trees that conceal clusters of sabal palms. The transition from wetlands to the lake's shore is marked by a complex interweaving of aquatic plants, creating a distinctive boundary.

Occasionally, you might spot a solitary alligator basking in the sun along a riverbank, appearing tranquil at first glance. However, this calm exterior can be deceiving. The area also boasts a vibrant avian population, with wild birds suddenly taking flight in a burst of dynamic motion.

From the soft, pastel hues of dawn to the breathtaking spectacle of a vibrant sunset, Okeechobee caters to the desires of all outdoor enthusiasts who appreciate the wonders of nature.

Lake Okeechobee plays a central role in a region of Florida that has a historical association with agriculture. However, in recent years, it has gained recognition for its exceptional fishing, boating, and trail opportunities.

This lake is encircled by the Herbert Hoover Dike, which was constructed in 1928. Surrounding the dike, the fertile soil supports a thriving sugarcane industry, and the flatland areas are crisscrossed with roads that allow you to explore the lush sugarcane fields and the towns that thrive on this industry. On both sides of the lake, waterways flow into Lake Okeechobee, making it an integral part of a 152-mile boating route known as the Okeechobee Waterway, which cuts through the heart of Florida.

Clewiston, situated along the southern shoreline of the vast 750-square-mile Lake Okeechobee, offers a plethora of attractions for vacationers, particularly those keen on pursuing the renowned largemouth bass and speckled perch found in the lake. To assist in this pursuit, fishing guides and resorts in the area are readily available. Additionally, local anglers can try their luck with catches like bluegills, Okeechobee catfish, and black crappies.

Clewiston is not only famous for its fishing but also goes by the moniker "America's Sweetest Town." Therefore, it's highly recommended to embark on the Sugarland tour of a local farm and mill, where you even have the opportunity to sample sugarcane. A three-hour boat cruise is also available, providing insights into the lake's rich historical and natural heritage. For further exploration, the Clewiston Museum, housed in the former police station and jail, offers a wealth of information.

Clewiston holds an annual Sugar Festival every April and extends its hospitality to visitors at the historic Clewiston Inn, built circa 1938. This inn is an excellent spot to savor a homemade Southern-style meal. While there, don't forget to drop by the Everglades Lounge to enjoy a cold drink and admire its renowned wildlife mural.

Clewiston's diverse Hispanic population ensures a variety of excellent taquerias where you can indulge in authentic Mexican specialties.

Starting from Clewiston, you have the opportunity to access the Lake Okeechobee Scenic Trail (LOST), a 110-mile path that encircles the vast Lake Okeechobee atop a 35-foot dike. This elevated trail offers stunning panoramic views of the lake and its vibrant birdlife. LOST is part of the broader Florida National Scenic Trail, designed for both cyclists and hikers. Along the trail, you'll find campgrounds and resorts in towns like Pahokee, Belle Glade, Moore Haven, and others on the outskirts, catering to those adventurous individuals who aim to complete the entire loop. An annual Big O Hike event takes place in November, during which participants frequently report sightings of various wildlife, including manatees, alligators, wild turkeys, bobcats, deer, wild hogs, egrets, osprey, kites, and numerous bird species. A National Audubon Society Wildlife Sanctuary safeguards this ecosystem, which is intricately connected to the broader Everglades wetland system. Specially marked roads also allow motorists to drive to the top of the dike for their own scenic views.

To the west of Clewiston, along the Caloosahatchee River, which forms the western portion of the Okeechobee Waterway, you'll find LaBelle, a charming rural town with a historical town hall and a bookstore. The town is surrounded by acres of citrus fields, adding to its picturesque setting. LaBelle's Old Florida charm comes to life every February when it hosts the Swamp Cabbage Festival along the river. Swamp cabbage, a traditional pioneer food, is derived from the bud of Florida's state tree, the cabbage palm. Nearby, the Ortona Lock & Dam offers recreational opportunities such as picnicking, camping, fishing, and boat launching.

The town of Okeechobee offers a relaxed, small-town atmosphere and provides options for overnight stays at campgrounds along the Kissimmee River, which flows into Lake Okeechobee. Additionally, you can embark on a pontoon or airboat ride from the local marina. Okeechobee celebrates its rich fishing and farming heritage with annual events such as the Speckled Perch Festival and the Okeechobee Cattlemen's Rodeo in March.

Originally, the Seminole Indians referred to this lake as "Big Water" in their native language, and they heavily relied on it for sustenance in the past. Today, the Big Cypress Seminole Reservation is situated nearby their ancestral "Big Water." Visitors can delve deeper into Native American culture by exploring the informative Ah-Tah-Thi-Ki Museum. Additionally, they can savor a meal at the Swamp Water Café and embark on an airboat excursion to an Indian camp through the Billie Swamp Safari.

60

LINCOLN ROAD

REGION: SOUTHEAST DISTRICT   **COUNTY:** MIAMI-DADE   **CITY:** MIAMI

DATE VISITED: **WHO I WENT WITH:**

RATING: ☆ ☆ ☆ ☆ ☆   **WILL I RETURN?**   YES / NO

In 1912, developer Carl Fisher embarked on a remarkable endeavor by transforming a mangrove forest into what we now know as Lincoln Road. This development took place 47 years after the conclusion of the Civil War. In a somewhat unconventional move, Fisher chose to name this iconic street after the assassinated Abraham Lincoln, who played a pivotal role in preserving the Union. This decision marked a form of creative disruption in the distinctly 'southern' region of South Florida. It's noteworthy that just one year later, in 1913, the City of Miami dedicated a memorial to the Confederacy.

Carl Fisher's impact extended beyond Lincoln Road; he was responsible for several significant projects. He established the "Brick Yard," which became the venue for the Indianapolis 500. He also played a pivotal role in the creation of two major transcontinental highways: the Lincoln Highway (east/west) and the Dixie Highway (north/south). Fisher's vision extended to the development of the Sunset Islands and, according to many accounts, the naming of Miami Beach itself. His grand vision for Lincoln Road was to transform it into "the Fifth Avenue of the South," and he succeeded in achieving this ambition. By the 1940s, Lincoln Road was home to prestigious establishments such as Bonwit Teller, Burdines, Saks Fifth Avenue, Cadillac, and Lincoln.

However, by the late 1950s, Lincoln Road was in need of revitalization. The City of Miami Beach enlisted the talents of Morris Lapidus to rejuvenate the city's central district. Lapidus created what is now recognized as the second open-air mall in the United States.

In contrast to the famed Bauhaus architect Mies Van de Rohe's adage, "Less is more," Morris Lapidus adhered to the belief that "Too much is never enough." His whimsical and exuberant Mid-Century Modern approach to the area truly embodies this philosophy. His design elements, including fountains, lush plantings, and architectural embellishments, celebrate the uniqueness of our subtropical South Florida region while making the foreign seem familiar. Lincoln Road's architectural vernacular is so distinctive that it has earned a place on the National Register of Historic Places, making it a one-of-a-kind destination known worldwide.

In the 1980s, Lincoln Road underwent yet another revitalization. During the early '80s, something unusual was observed – there were more cattle egrets, typically associated with rural areas, than pigeons on Lincoln Road. Like in many other cities, the abundance of vacant storefronts presented significant opportunities for artists. In 1984, the Art Center South Florida was established, and it played a pivotal role in rekindling public interest in Lincoln Road. By the late 1990s, Lincoln Road had successfully reclaimed its status as one of the foremost streets in the United States.

Along the pedestrian walkway of Lincoln Road, you can witness a captivating array of architectural styles that span from 1912 to the present day. These styles include Mediterranean Revival, Depression Moderne, Art Deco, Mid Century Modern, and contemporary designs that have earned accolades. Notable contemporary additions include the Frank Gehry-designed New World Symphony building located at the eastern end of the road and the Herzog & De Meuron-designed parking garage at 1111 Lincoln on its western edge. These architectural gems collectively contribute to the road's unique and diverse architectural heritage.

Lincoln Road also boasts an impressive collection of tropical plants from around the globe, meticulously curated and maintained by Fairchild Tropical Botanic Garden, featuring over 1,250 orchids. Among the noteworthy plantings are magnificent examples of flowering trees such as the royal poinciana, sausage tree, and tabebuia, as well as various palm species like the Saba palms, date palms, and Caribbean thatch palms. The landscaping also incorporates ecologically significant plants that support interactions with rare birds and insects. One notable example is the native coontie cycad (Zamia integrifolia), found on multiple blocks, which sustains one of the largest colonies of the endangered Atala butterfly.

The Lincoln Road District is anchored on its eastern edge by the New World Symphony, known as America's Orchestral Academy, and Florida International University's Miami Beach Urban Studio. On the western side, it is anchored by the Colony Theater, which houses Miami New Drama. Between these cutting-edge institutions, Lincoln Road is also home to Oolite Arts, whose evolution from Art Center South Florida played a crucial role in the revitalization of the road during the 1980s. Additionally, Rankontur Films, situated in the area, has produced content that has helped introduce South Florida to a broader global audience.

LION COUNTRY SAFARI

REGION: SOUTHEAST DISTRICT **COUNTY:** PALM BEACH **CITY:** LOXAHATCHEE

DATE VISITED: **WHO I WENT WITH:**

RATING: ☆ ☆ ☆ ☆ ☆ **WILL I RETURN?** YES / NO

Lion Country Safari made its debut in the summer of 1967 in the rural western part of Palm Beach County. It featured numerous free-roaming lions and a few other animal species. This drive-through safari park is widely regarded as the first cageless zoo in the United States, revolutionizing the field of zoology. It brought the experience of an African game park, traditionally an expensive and time-consuming journey, within reach of families who might not otherwise have the opportunity to enjoy an African safari. The choice of South Florida's Western Palm Beach County as the park's location proved ideal due to its year-round tropical climate, ample land, a growing local population, and a constant influx of tourists from around the world.

Lion Country Safari, situated in West Palm Beach, has become a prominent figure in Palm Beach County's tourism industry. It provides a unique and affordable opportunity for visitors to explore the largest drive-through safari in Florida. The park holds accreditation from the Association of Zoos and Aquariums and has earned recognition as one of the top three zoos in America by USA Travel Guide, one of the ten best safari parks by USA Today, and Palm Beach County's premier local attraction. Covering 320 acres, the park offers a combination of a drive-through safari, a walk-through adventure park, and an award-winning KOA campground.

At Lion Country Safari, large herds of animals representing six continents roam freely while human visitors remain enclosed in their vehicles. The park is home to hundreds of WILD animals, including lions, wildebeest, giraffes, the largest recorded herd of zebras in North America, ostriches, chimpanzees, and rhinoceroses. These animals inhabit wide-open, naturalistic habitats that aim to replicate their native environments.

Lion Country Safari actively participates in various sustainable initiatives to reduce waste and incorporate more eco-friendly products. The park is also engaged in numerous conservation and breeding programs, known as Species Survival Plans, which focus on threatened species like rhinoceroses, zebras, oryxes, siamangs, and more. These programs play a crucial role in ensuring the survival of healthy, sustainable populations of these endangered species in human care. They serve as a vital lifeline, or figurative arks, as wild populations continue to decline and face the risk of extinction.

LUMMUS PARK

REGION: SOUTHEAST DISTRICT   **COUNTY:** MIAMI-DADE   **CITY:** MIAMI

DATE VISITED: **WHO I WENT WITH:**

RATING: ☆ ☆ ☆ ☆ ☆   **WILL I RETURN?** YES / NO

Nestled between the Atlantic Ocean and Ocean Drive, occupying the space between 5th Street and 14th Place, Lummus Park has played a significant role as a backdrop in numerous television and film scenes. This beachfront park offers a range of amenities, including a playground, public restrooms, paved paths for walking or biking, and the 9th Street fitness area known as Muscle Beach South Beach. Lummus Park hosts a diverse range of events throughout the year, catering to both free and paid experiences. These events encompass concerts, marathons, festivals, beach parties, and more. For instance, in April, you can enjoy the vibrant Miami Beach Pride Parade, while February brings the renowned South Beach Wine & Food Festival. During July, the South Beach Mango Festival spans three days, celebrating South Florida's beloved sweet and juicy tropical fruit. Notably, the South Beach Triathlon, which supports Save the Children, commences with an ocean swim near Lummus Park.

Muscle Beach South Beach, a prominent attraction for fitness enthusiasts, provides an outdoor space for exercise, weightlifting, and gymnastics. It features two nature-inspired installations: MyEquilibria's Leopard Tree and MyBeast. Together, these functional structures offer more than 30 workout components. This installation, the first of its kind in a public park in the United States, brings together art and functionality on the beach, and it is accessible to both visitors and residents. A free mobile phone application is available to assist individuals of all fitness levels with workouts through a series of training sessions and tutorials.

In addition to these amenities, Lummus Park has seen several enhancements, including the installation of 114 new dimmable LED lights. These lights not only improve visibility but also reduce the amount of light visible from the beach. This lighting retrofit represents a long-term strategy to protect the native sea turtle population by significantly decreasing light pollution in areas where sea turtle disorientation incidents are most frequent during the sea turtle season. As the city continues to plan, design, and execute projects along the beachfront, sea turtle-friendly fixtures will replace existing lights on public property.

Lummus Park is accessible from sunrise to sunset, ensuring that you can enjoy it whenever the sun is shining. It's advisable to check the weather in Miami if you plan to spend the day outdoors, as the city occasionally experiences torrential downpours, which are more common during the summer months. However, don't let a brief rain shower deter you, as these showers typically pass as swiftly as they arrive. If you have a place to take shelter from the rain or a spot to people-watch under a roof with a cocktail in hand, you should be perfectly fine.

The park offers an abundance of activities suitable for all ages and activity levels. Covering over 25 acres, it boasts open field spaces, and various amenities. For the little ones aged 2 through 5, there are Tot Lots playgrounds, while bigger kids aged 5 through 12 have their own designated playgrounds. Additionally, the park features 18 volleyball courts and walking trails.

Getting to Lummus Park is quite convenient. It's a short drive of under half an hour from Fort Lauderdale Airport and just 10 minutes from Miami International Airport by car. Alternatively, rideshares, taxis, and the Line 7 bus (which may take up to an hour and a half) are transportation options. If you're already on the beachside, walking, biking, or even using a scooter are viable choices.

To gain a deeper understanding of the city, embark on an enlightening Art Deco walking tour organized by the Miami Design Preservation League, renowned for its critical acclaim. Established in 1976, the Art Deco Museum is conveniently situated right on Ocean Drive, welcoming visitors from 10 a.m. to 5 p.m. every Tuesday through Sunday. A visit to this museum allows you to delve into the rich architectural heritage, historical significance, and community culture of Miami Beach. The walking tours typically commence from this location, providing an excellent opportunity to explore and appreciate the city's unique charm and history.

Immerse yourself in culture by paying a visit to the Jewish Museum of Florida-FIU. This museum, established in 1936, is a captivating attraction that encompasses two meticulously restored, historic synagogues. It offers a diverse range of exhibits, including both permanent collections and rotating art displays. One notable exhibit is "MOSAIC: Jewish Life in Florida," featuring a fascinating collection of photos and artifacts that trace the rich history of the Florida Jewish community all the way back to 1763. Notably, museum members and children under the age of 6 enjoy free admission. Additionally, on Saturdays, the museum generously opens its doors to all visitors for free.

Make sure to save some room for a delectable meal at the renowned Joe's Stone Crab, conveniently located on Washington Avenue. This iconic establishment has been delighting patrons for over a century, consistently serving the freshest shellfish and seafood dishes you can find anywhere in the country.

MANATEE SPRINGS STATE PARK

REGION: CENTRAL WEST DISTRICT   **COUNTY:** LEVY   **CITY:** CHIEFLAND

DATE VISITED: **WHO I WENT WITH:**

RATING: ☆ ☆ ☆ ☆ ☆   **WILL I RETURN?** YES / NO

The park's 800-foot boardwalk runs through a majestic cypress forest overlooking one of Florida's breathtaking first-magnitude springs. The magnitude spring releases an astounding 100 million gallons of water daily. This makes it a popular cooling-off spot and a great place to stroll on the park boardwalk and gaze into watery depths. People have enjoyed the cool waters of Manatee Springs for more than 10,000 years, from early Paleo Indians to modern-day visitors to the park. True to its namesake, manatees can be seen in the cooler months, and birds, mammals, and fish are spotted year-round. Swimming activities can be enjoyed in the natural feature of this beautiful first-magnitude spring. Use caution - the current is swift.

The park also offers 8.5 miles of nature trails and a connection to the 32-mile Nature Coast State Trail. Bicycles are welcome on all park roads. Mountain bikers can enjoy 8 miles of wooded off-road trails in the park. Bicycles are not allowed on the boardwalk or sidewalks. All bicyclists are advised to ride with helmets, and Florida law requires helmets for bicyclists 16 years of age and younger. Freshwater fishing from the park's boardwalk along the spring run and in the Suwannee River is always popular. Popular fish include largemouth bass, catfish, and mullet. All fishing within the park must comply with regulations regarding size, number, method of fishing, and season. A fishing license may be required. Canoeing and kayaking are available year-round down the famous Suwannee River. Other activities include camping, picnicking, and snorkeling. Motorboats can tie off at a floating dock on the river. Dives are available on a first-come, first-served basis only. Places cannot be reserved.

The park has 80 campsites in three loops, each with its own bathroom with a hot shower and located a short walk from the spring. There is electricity and water at each campsite. The Magnolia 2 and Hickory campsites do not have sewer hookups, but there is a dump station. Pets are allowed and must be kept on a six-foot leash at all times and under owner control. The park has two group camping areas for youth groups focused on outdoor recreation. The group camp can accommodate up to 35 people. No pets are allowed in the youth camp area. Drinking water, an outdoor shower, a portable toilet, and a campfire circle are available on site. Pavilions in the picnic area near the spring are available for rent. There are six picnic tables at each pavilion. Water and electricity are available at each pavilion. Picnic tables are available on a first-come, first-served basis. Rangers-led programs are offered throughout the year. Most ranger-led programs are free with paid park admission.

REGION: CENTRAL EAST DISTRICT	**COUNTY:** BREVARD	**CITY:** MERRITT ISLAND

DATE VISITED: **WHO I WENT WITH:**

RATING: ☆ ☆ ☆ ☆ ☆   **WILL I RETURN?** YES / NO

The origins of Merritt Island National Wildlife Refuge are closely tied to the development of the United States' Space Program. In 1962, NASA acquired the lands and waters surrounding Cape Canaveral to establish the John F. Kennedy Space Center. While NASA constructed a launch complex and other space-related facilities, much of the area remained undeveloped. On August 28, 1963, the U.S. Fish and Wildlife Service entered into an agreement, marking the establishment of Merritt Island National Wildlife Refuge as the 286th refuge in the National Wildlife Refuge System. In 1975, a second agreement led to the creation of Canaveral National Seashore. Today, the Department of the Interior oversees most of the undeveloped portions of the Kennedy Space Center, managing them as both a National Wildlife Refuge and a National Seashore.

The administrative designation of Merritt Island Refuge in 1963, in accordance with the Migratory Bird Conservation Act, outlined the primary purposes of these lands and waters. These purposes include serving as an inviolate sanctuary for migratory birds and other wildlife species, as well as conserving and protecting these species, particularly those listed as endangered or threatened. The overarching goal is to restore or develop suitable wildlife habitat, aligning with the provisions of the Migratory Bird Conservation Act, found in 16 USC §715i.

Approximately 12,000 years ago, the first humans arrived in Florida by crossing the Siberian land bridge and traversing North America. During this period, the Florida peninsula was significantly larger than it is today, with sea levels situated 20 to 30 feet lower than their present levels. Archaeological findings indicate that Paleo-Indians coexisted with an array of large animals in Florida, including mastodons, giant armadillos, camels, bison, and mammoths. Nevertheless, their primary sustenance likely comprised plants, nuts, mammals such as rabbits, raccoons, opossums, squirrels, and deer, in addition to fish and marine life. As a result, hunting and fishing became essential means of subsistence for Florida's earliest inhabitants. Subsequently, the history of the Space Coast, encompassing both its cultural and natural facets, became rich and diverse.

Around 7,000 years ago, as the last glaciers retreated and sea levels rose, the barrier islands and lagoons that currently constitute Merritt Island National Wildlife Refuge took shape. Just inland from the barrier island, these Paleo-Indians were the earliest inhabitants of the Indian River Lagoon region. Their descendants settled in the area, relying on the abundant resources of the Indian River Lagoon, the St. Johns River, and the surrounding uplands for their livelihoods. By 2000 BC, these early Americans were crafting pottery and fashioning tools from materials like stone, shell, and animal teeth. Despite these advancements, they continued to live as hunter-gatherers, although the rising sea levels had already reduced the size of the peninsula to approximately its current dimensions. Over time, distinct tribes known today as the Ais and Timucuans emerged, residing along the shores of the Indian River. These tribes left behind significant evidence, including extensive mounds filled with discarded shellfish, animal remains, and broken pottery. These mounds have provided valuable insights into the lives and cultures of these indigenous peoples.

The initial interactions between North American Indigenous peoples and European explorers likely commenced around 1513 when Juan Ponce de León encountered the Ais Indians in a village near Cape Canaveral. During this period, Spanish explorers often experienced shipwrecks along the Florida coast. These encounters had significant impacts on Ais culture, and by the time a permanent Spanish settlement was established in St. Augustine, Florida, in 1565, the Ais were perceived as formidable warriors. Over time, diseases, conflicts, and food shortages contributed to the decline of these early cultures.

Over the following 200 years, Florida's population grew slowly, and the ethnic composition of its inhabitants became more diverse. What we now recognize as Brevard County was initially part of Mosquito County until Florida officially achieved statehood in 1845. Initially named St. Lucie County, it extended southward to include Dade County. Several boundary adjustments occurred until 1959 when Brevard County reached its present-day boundaries.

One of the early settlers in the Titusville area before the Civil War was Douglas Dummitt. He relocated from Tomoka, where he had served as the postmaster and engaged in sugarcane farming during the 1820s and 1830s. In addition to his sugarcane cultivation, Douglas was among the few individuals who ventured into orange cultivation, selling his initial orange crop in 1828. While still residing in Tomoka, he initiated experiments with various citrus cultivation techniques. He achieved this by planting wild sour-orange trees, which were likely descendants of Spanish-origin trees that had adapted to Florida's soil and climate. Douglas grafted cuttings from sweet orange trees, supposedly sourced from groves planted by the Turnbull colonists in New Smyrna, onto the sour-orange rootstock. These experimental trees survived the well-known freeze of 1835 and were later transplanted to the Dummitt Grove, now part of the Merritt Island National Wildlife Refuge, following the conclusion of the Second Seminole War.

Over the years, Dummitt expanded the size of his grove, and by 1859, he was producing an estimated 60,000 oranges annually. He played a crucial role in the growth of the Indian River citrus region by providing budwood to other growers, allowing them to establish new groves in the area. In 1873, Douglas Dummitt passed away at his orange grove, leaving behind a legacy of significant contributions to the political and economic development of the Indian River region.

The year 1854 marked a significant event in the region when the strip of land between the Indian River and Mosquito Lagoon, which had long served as a "haul over" for travelers, was officially enhanced and opened. This development was one of the initial major man-made improvements to the inland waterway system that had been utilized by Florida travelers for centuries. During this period, the haul-over measured approximately one-third of a mile in length, 10-12 feet wide, and had a depth of 3 feet. It was primarily utilized by shallow-draft vessels. Subsequent enhancements to the canal commenced in 1885, with the U.S. Army Corps of Engineers completing the work in the 1930s. Today, Haulover Canal is an integral part of the Intercoastal Waterway, accommodating thousands of vessels annually as they navigate between Mosquito Lagoon and the Indian River during their journeys up and down the east coast. The canal is also heavily used by fishermen and paddlers.

Overall, there was relatively little notable development in the region from the late 1920s until after World War II. However, following the war's commencement, there was a period of rapid growth, driven in part by the establishment of the United States' space industry complex at Cape Canaveral. The pursuit of space exploration and use began in 1950 with the creation of a missile testing range at Cape Canaveral. At that time, the federal government already owned the land surrounding the Cape Canaveral lighthouse, and it acquired the additional acreage required for the facility from private landowners. In 1958, the National Aeronautics and Space Administration (NASA) initiated its operations at Cape Canaveral. NASA's primary mission was to launch communication, meteorological, and scientific satellites. The agency gained national prominence in 1961 when President John F. Kennedy announced plans to land a man on the moon before the decade's end.

In 1963, the federal government acquired over 140,000 acres of land situated to the north and west of the Cape Canaveral area on Merritt Island. This land was intended for the development of a significant support facility for the launch complex, which would later become the John F. Kennedy Space Center. President Kennedy's vision became a reality when, on July 20, 1969, humans first set foot on the moon. The inaugural Space Shuttle mission, known as STS-1 (Space Transportation System), took place on April 12, 1981. The spacecraft Columbia completed 36 orbits around Earth during this 54.5-hour mission. This marked the United States' first manned spaceflight since the Apollo-Soyuz Test Project in July 1975.

At the time of NASA's acquisition of the land that now comprises the Merritt Island National Wildlife Refuge, several families were residing there and engaged in farming activities. Traces of old foundations and canals from that era can still be seen at various locations, particularly in the vicinity of Haulover Canal.

On August 28, 1963, the U.S. Fish and Wildlife Service entered into an Interagency Agreement with NASA to manage all the lands within the Kennedy Space Center that were not actively utilized for NASA KSC operations. These lands, known today as the Merritt Island National Wildlife Refuge, serve as habitat for more than 1,500 species of plants and wildlife. Through a robust and longstanding collaborative relationship between NASA, the Fish and Wildlife Service, and the National Park Service, this unique area exemplifies how nature and technology can harmoniously coexist.

Merritt Island National Wildlife Refuge is situated along the coast of Florida, approximately 60 miles east of Orlando. It was established through an agreement that overlaid the National Aeronautics and Space Administration's (NASA) John F. Kennedy Space Center. This refuge is located within one of the most ecologically productive estuaries in the United States.

National wildlife refuges offer individuals the opportunity to disconnect from the stresses of everyday life and reestablish a connection with the natural world. Merritt Island National Wildlife Refuge provides a wide range of recreational and educational activities. Whether you're interested in birdwatching, nature exploration, fishing, or seasonal hunting, there's an activity to cater to your interests.

To access certain areas of the refuge, such as the Black Point Wildlife Drive and Bio Lab Road, as well as to launch a boat at Bairs Cove, Beacon 42, and Bio Lab boat ramps, a Refuge Pass is required. Various types of passes can be obtained in person at the Visitor Center. Alternatively, Merritt Island Annual, Daily, and Foot/Bicycle passes can be purchased online through Recreation.gov.

MIAMI BEACH

REGION: SOUTHEAST DISTRICT   **COUNTY:** MIAMI-DADE   **CITY:** MIAMI

DATE VISITED: **WHO I WENT WITH:**

RATING: ☆ ☆ ☆ ☆ ☆   **WILL I RETURN?**   YES / NO

Miami Beach is a coastal resort city located in Miami-Dade County, Florida, United States. It is a part of the Miami metropolitan area in South Florida. Situated on barrier islands, both natural and human-made, Miami Beach is positioned between the Atlantic Ocean and Biscayne Bay, with the latter separating it from the mainland city of Miami. The southernmost 2.5 square miles (6.5 km2) of Miami Beach, along with Downtown Miami and PortMiami, collectively form the commercial center of South Florida. According to the 2020 census, Miami Beach's population is 82,890, and it has been a prominent beach resort destination since the early 20th century.

Miami Beach is responsible for more than half of the tourism in Miami Dade County. Miami Beach attracts around 13.3 million visitors annually. Miami Beach was created on swamps, consistently drained over one and a half decades by one of the city's founders - Carl Fisher. Therefore, though hard to believe, the flawlessly golden sand was simply brought here. Swamps and alligators are still an attraction, but not here, rather an hour away at Everglades National Park.

The name "Miami" comes from the Miami Indian tribe, which once inhabited this area. Miami is a paradise for wreck diving enthusiasts - there are as many as 75 wrecks here. Miami is the only city in the USA surrounded by two national parks.

Attractions - what to see when visiting Florida's most popular city?

Bayside Marketplace is a two-story outdoor shopping center surrounded by Biscayne Bay. It is the most popular and frequently visited attraction in Miami. Besides shopping centers and shops, Bayside Marketplace also serves as a cultural and entertainment hub. Visitors can find bars, restaurants, and properties set in picturesque coastal surroundings. One of the additional highlights is the live music performances held daily.

Miami Art Deco is a historic district located in South Beach. It houses 960 Art Deco-style buildings, constructed during the Great Depression of the 1940s in the architectural movement known as Streamline Moderne. This architectural style emerged in 1925 after a devastating hurricane left nearly 25,000 people homeless, shaping the city's development. Notably, the famous Italian fashion designer Gianni Versace resided in this area, adding to its popularity. In 1979, Miami Beach's Art Deco was added to the National Register of Historic Places. The Art Deco District boasts the largest collection of Art Deco architecture in the world, featuring numerous hotels, apartments, and other structures built between 1923 and 1943.

South Beach, also known as SoBe, is a popular area in Miami Beach, stretching from Biscayne Street (South Pointe Drive) one block south of 1st Street to about 23rd Street. While topless sunbathing by women is not officially legalized, it is tolerated on South Beach and in some hotel pools on Miami Beach. Before gaining popularity due to the TV show Miami Vice, the area was once plagued by urban blight, vacant buildings, and high crime rates. Despite its transformation into one of the most affluent commercial areas on the beach, pockets of poverty and crime still persist nearby.

For those who prefer to have fun or do some shopping, there is Ocean Drive. On Ocean Drive, you can find Villa Casa Casuarina, a building constructed in an incredibly refined Mediterranean style. A three-story mansion among palm trees with arched vaulted gates. In 1992, the building was purchased for nearly 3 million dollars by designer Gianni Versace, and it was on the steps to this residence that he was shot five years later. Today, it serves as a hotel. Miami Beach's Ocean Drive, particularly in the Art Deco District, was featured prominently in the films Scarface (1983) and The Birdcage (1996).

Lincoln Road, a famous east-west street between 16th and 17th Streets, is renowned for its outdoor dining and shopping options. It features galleries showcasing works from well-known designers, artists, and photographers like Romero Britto, Peter Lik, and Jonathan Adler. In 2015, Miami Beach residents passed a law prohibiting bicycling, rollerblading, skateboarding, and other motorized vehicles on Lincoln Road during busy pedestrian hours from 9:00 am to 2:00 am.

Downtown Miami is the city's central business district and is a cultural, commercial, and financial hub in southern Florida. It boasts museums, parks, banks, government offices, and a variety of shops and theaters.

Museums in Miami:

Frost Museum of Science: Formerly known as the Museum of Science in Miami, this interactive museum features a planetarium, aquarium, and exhibits related to technology and meteorology.

History Miami Museum: Located in the city center, it is the largest history museum in Florida, established in 1940. It houses four permanent exhibitions, a research center, and an archive. The museum also hosts the International Map Fair annually.

Institute of Contemporary Art in Miami: A museum of contemporary art situated in the Miami Design District. The museum supports scholarship programs and art exchanges and provides a space for international, talented, and emerging artists, offering free admission throughout the year.

Pérez Art Museum Miami: Founded in 1984, this museum of contemporary art features over 2,000 works from the 20th and 21st centuries by artists from around the world. It has recorded a record attendance of 150,000 visitors.

Lowe Art Museum: The first art museum in southern Florida, managed by the University of Miami. The museum showcases collections of ancient Greek and Roman art, Renaissance, Baroque, 17th, and 19th-century European and American art. Works by artists like Lippo Vanni, El Greco, Francisco Goya, Paul Gauguin, Claude Monet, and Julian Stańczyk can be admired here.

Jewish Museum of Florida: The only museum dedicated to over 250 years of Jewish history, art, and culture in Florida. The museum's collection comprises over 100,000 artifacts. It is located in the South Beach area and housed in two restored historic buildings that were once the synagogues of Miami Beach's first Jewish congregation.

Beaches of Miami:
Miami beaches are a perfect destination for water sports enthusiasts, diving, and sunbathing. One can relax and take a stroll along the beautiful Atlantic Ocean coastline. The most popular beach is undoubtedly South Beach.

South Beach is one of the most famous beaches in southern Florida, located at Ocean Drive. It is well-known worldwide and often seen on television, attracting famous celebrities and stars. Lummus Park, featured in the popular TV show "Miami Vice," separates the beach from the restaurants. Visitors can ride bikes, rollerblades, and skateboards on the beachfront boardwalk. Besides daytime activities, South Beach offers a vibrant nightlife with numerous nightclubs, bars, and clubs.

Surfside Beach is a beautiful beach in one of Miami's coastal districts. It might be less popular than South Beach, but it offers stunning views, luxurious hotels, and charming restaurants.

What dishes to try while relaxing in Miami?
Miami's cuisine reflects the city's diverse population, with influences from Latin American, Caribbean, and American gastronomy. The combination of these styles has formed Floribbean cuisine, which has become extremely popular and widely available in South Florida.

While in Miami, it's a must to try fresh seafood such as shrimp, lobster, octopus, and various types of fish. The climate also favors the cultivation of oranges, grapefruits, lemons, limes, mangoes, coconuts, and pineapples, and the culinary influences from around the world allow for exceptional flavor combinations in dishes. Where to taste local and international delicacies?

Seaspice Brasserie & Lounge; 422 NW North River Dr, Miami, FL 33128: This international restaurant is located by the river, just a few minutes from downtown. It perfectly embodies the ambiance of a waterfront eatery, offering dishes cooked on a wood-fired grill, fresh seafood, and cuisine inspired by various parts of the world.

Mama's Tacos; 710 Washington Ave Suite, Miami Beach, FL 33139-6248: A Mexican restaurant where every tourist can savor Latin American cuisine. The restaurant focuses on traditional Mexican dishes and creates an atmosphere reminiscent of small Mexican towns.

Old's Havana Cuban Bar & Cocina; 1442 SW 8th Street, Miami, FL 33135: A Cuban restaurant serving traditional Cuban dishes and beverages. Visitors can enjoy the flavors, atmosphere, and music from the sunny, tropical, lively streets of Havana.

Aromas del Peru; 13823 SW 88 St, Miami, FL 33186: A Peruvian restaurant established to spread the flavors of Costa, Sierra, and Selva cuisine abroad. The menu offers traditional Creole dishes with classic aromas from the capital city of Peru.

Beautiful beaches, immense prestige, and luxury of the city, as well as interesting landmarks and attractions, attract a vast number of tourists to Miami. Hotels located close to sunny beaches and in the city center are highly popular. In Miami, it's warm all year round, but it's best to avoid the hurricane season, which typically lasts from early August until the end of October. Those seeking tranquility should stay in the northern part of Miami Beach, while party-goers will enjoy South Beach. So, which place should you choose for accommodation?

East Miami is a five-star hotel located in the city center. It offers 4 pools, a restaurant, and a 24-hour fitness center. Nearby, guests can enjoy exclusive shops, restaurants, bars, spas, and cinemas. The apartments and rooms provide high, modern, and luxurious standards. On the 40th floor of the hotel, you can admire a picturesque city panorama.

DoubleTree by Hilton Grand Hotel Biscayne Bay is a comfortable hotel located directly by Biscayne Bay. Due to its central location, you can quickly reach Miami's most popular attractions, museums, restaurants, and other entertainment venues. The hotel features a modern fitness center and a large Olympic pool.

Hyatt Centric Brickell Miami is a hotel located 3 km from downtown Miami. Guests can enjoy a fitness center, a business center, and easy access to Miami's major attractions. Each room offers free Wi-Fi, complimentary toiletries, and modern amenities.

Courtyard Miami Downtown Brickell Area is another hotel located in the city center, just 1.6 km from Bayside Market. Guests can use the outdoor pool, restaurant, and fitness center. All rooms are equipped with 32-inch televisions. The restaurant serves local dishes prepared with fresh, local ingredients. It is very easy to reach the Art Deco District from here.

Mandarin Oriental Miami is a luxurious hotel located on Brickell Key island. All rooms have balconies with views of the picturesque city and Biscayne Bay. The hotel features a luxury spa and an infinity-edge outdoor pool. The hotel's location allows for quick access to the city center (approximately 3 minutes) and South Beach (10 km).

Hampton Inn & Suites by Hilton Miami is a hotel located in the city center. Guests can enjoy an outdoor pool, a fitness center, and assistance with organizing tours and activities. Just 3.2 km away, you can visit the AmericanAirlines Arena and the Bayside Market shopping center.

MIAMI CHILDREN'S MUSEUM

REGION: SOUTHEAST DISTRICT   COUNTY: MIAMI-DADE   CITY: MIAMI

DATE VISITED: WHO I WENT WITH:

RATING: ☆ ☆ ☆ ☆ ☆   WILL I RETURN? YES / NO

Miami Children's Museum is a non-profit educational organization. Its primary mission is to cater to the educational needs of children from various cultural backgrounds. The museum provides a range of interactive exhibits, programs, and educational resources that focus on the arts, culture, and local community. Miami Children's Museum encourages individuals of all age groups to engage in play, learning, imagination, and collaborative creation.

The institution is committed to enhancing the well-being of all children by nurturing a passion for learning through playful activities and enabling them to achieve their fullest potential. The ultimate goal of the museum is to establish ourselves as a top-tier establishment dedicated to serving children and their families.

The Miami Children's Museum is situated on Watson Island and occupies an impressive 56,500 square feet of space. This building was skillfully designed by the renowned architectural and design firm, Arquitectonica International Inc., which is based in Miami and has received numerous awards for its work. The unique design of the museum is centered around the four natural elements: earth, wind, water, and fire, creating an environment that is specifically tailored for children.

Within the facility, you'll find 17 different galleries, each offering a distinct learning experience. The museum also has a preschool program catering to children aged 12 months to 5 years, as well as a charter school serving students from kindergarten to 5th grade. The KidSmart educational gift shop is a great place to find educational materials and gifts for children. For events and presentations, we have a 200-seat auditorium available. Additionally, there's a Subway restaurant on-site, ensuring that visitors have access to dining options during their visit.

Miami Children's Museum was originally established in 1983 under the name "Miami Youth Museum." It began as a modest 2,000 square foot facility situated in a shopping center in West Kendall. Over the course of the past four decades, the museum has undergone multiple relocations and expansions, driven by both public and private support and engagement.

In the fall of 2003, the museum moved to its current location, boasting a state-of-the-art facility spanning 56,500 square feet near Downtown Miami. This move marked a significant turning point in the museum's history, as it experienced remarkable growth and welcomed over 5 million visitors. In recent years, annual visitation has consistently reached 445,000 people.

Miami Children's Museum has emerged as one of the largest children's museums in the United States. It plays a vital role within the community by integrating arts, culture, and community engagement into interactive learning experiences. The museum's strategic location on Watson Island ensures accessibility for many underserved and low-income populations.

Partnerships with other children's museums, cultural institutions, and local and national organizations allow the museum to offer a wide array of programs covering topics such as literacy, science, culture, history, careers, the environment, and more through the lens of the arts.

MIAMI DESIGN DISTRICT

REGION: SOUTHEAST DISTRICT   **COUNTY:** MIAMI-DADE   **CITY:** MIAMI

DATE VISITED: **WHO I WENT WITH:**

RATING: ☆ ☆ ☆ ☆ ☆   **WILL I RETURN?**   YES / NO

Over two decades ago, Craig Robins, a Miami native, had a keen insight into the potential of the Miami Design District. He embarked on a journey to acquire property in this neighborhood with the vision of revitalizing an overlooked part of Miami. His goal was to transform it into a vibrant and creative community by emphasizing exceptional architecture, innovative design, and immersive experiences. Today, this ambitious vision has become a reality.

The Miami Design District has evolved into a thriving community where both residents and visitors can indulge in remarkable shopping, dine at award-winning restaurants, explore world-class museums, and enjoy ample outdoor spaces. This transformation was made possible through meticulous planning and the infusion of rich cultural programming.

The district began to attract prominent design brands, significant art collections, captivating design installations, and world-class dining establishments. As new buildings sprang up and historical structures were rejuvenated, design showrooms flocked to the area. The core identity of the Miami Design District has always revolved around art and design, which has led to the continual growth and enrichment of this remarkable cultural neighborhood.

In 2011, L Catterton, formerly known as L Real Estate, joined forces with Craig Robins, becoming a partner in his visionary project. Together, they encouraged the luxury brands to recognize the distinctive potential of the Miami Design District. Both Robins and Catterton shared the belief that establishing flagship stores within the district would provide the luxury brands with a unique opportunity to showcase their entire range of products in architecturally innovative and distinctive spaces.

Today, the Miami Design District has emerged as the epicenter of the city's cultural scene. It offers unparalleled access to luxury fashion, cutting-edge architecture, round-the-clock exposure to the arts, and a world-class dining experience.

Much like any vibrant neighborhood, the Miami Design District is continually evolving. It is set to welcome more exceptional shops, restaurants, and galleries, in addition to a boutique hotel and residential spaces, all contributing to its ongoing growth and transformation.

The Miami Design District is a creative neighborhood that offers visitors unparalleled access to world-class dining, shopping, art, events, and a constant source of inspiration.

Within the district, you'll find over 170 brands, making it the ultimate destination for fashion enthusiasts. However, it's not just about clothing here; everywhere you look, you'll be surrounded by award-winning architectural marvels, like our Museum Garage, which the IPMI recognized as the "Best Design of a Mixed or Multi-Use Parking & Transportation Facility."

Beyond the fashion and design showrooms like Poliform and Holly Hunt, the district is home to three prominent cultural institutions: ICA Miami, the de la Cruz Collection, and Locust Projects. If you prefer a more relaxed visit, take a leisurely stroll through the neighborhood and appreciate the seasonal public art installations integrated into the district's pedestrian-friendly pathways.

The Miami Design District is also a culinary haven, boasting world-renowned chefs and even a few Michelin stars. And when the Miami heat calls for ice cream, the district offers artisanal options to cool you down. With its combination of luxury fashion, cutting-edge architecture, 24/7 access to the arts, and world-class dining, the Miami Design District proudly stands as the city's cultural epicenter.

MIAMI SEAQUARIUM

REGION: SOUTHEAST DISTRICT   **COUNTY:** MIAMI-DADE   **CITY:** MIAMI

DATE VISITED: **WHO I WENT WITH:**

RATING: ☆ ☆ ☆ ☆ ☆   **WILL I RETURN?** YES / NO

Miami Seaquarium is a distinctive South Florida attraction situated on a 38-acre tropical paradise with breathtaking views of the skyline. It serves as a haven for endangered sea turtles and manatees, while also providing entertainment and joy to visitors of all ages through its dolphins. The Seaquarium offers one-of-a-kind, interactive experiences that are both educational and enjoyable, making it a sought-after destination for those seeking things to do in Miami and South Florida. Since its inception in 1955, Miami Seaquarium has been committed to conservation efforts that have safeguarded numerous animals.

The institution is dedicated to raising awareness about environmental stewardship and conservation through educational initiatives brought to life with captivating animal presentations. These presentations feature a diverse array of creatures, including sea lions, cetaceans, penguins, and more.

Miami Seaquarium's unwavering commitment to conservation and animal care is evident in the daily actions of its devoted staff. From rescuing and rehabilitating animals to educating the future generation of veterinarians, caregivers, and animal enthusiasts, the core mission of Miami Seaquarium is to preserve the wonders of the natural world and provide exceptional care to the animals that call the Seaquarium their home.

Education plays a pivotal role at Miami Seaquarium, and the facility offers unique programs tailored to various groups, including homeschoolers, field trip participants, Boy Scouts, Girl Scouts, and more. Whether it's a camping adventure or a leisurely afternoon at the park, children have the opportunity to gain a fresh perspective on marine life.

66 years ago, Miami Seaquarium opened its doors to the public and established itself as one of South Florida's most beloved tourist destinations.

When Miami Seaquarium made its debut back in 1955, it held the distinction of being the world's largest marine attraction. However, even before human visitors arrived, the Seaquarium's first guests were the marine animals it aimed to care for. Among them was Mamie, a three-year-old orphaned manatee rescued several months prior to the Seaquarium's opening. She marked the beginning of a long history of marine life rescue and care at Miami Seaquarium. Today, this oceanarium stands as one of just four manatee Critical Care Facilities in the state of Florida.

Miami Seaquarium offers a wide array of distinctive interactive and educational experiences, making it an ideal choice for families in search of enjoyable activities to do in Key Biscayne with children. Whether you're interested in discovering sea turtles, meeting the latest additions to the marine world, or learning about the Seaquarium's conservation initiatives, there's something here for everyone.

The park also provides a diverse range of dining options to cater to various dietary preferences and appetites.

MONKEY JUNGLE

REGION: SOUTHEAST DISTRICT   COUNTY: MIAMI-DADE   CITY: MIAMI

DATE VISITED: WHO I WENT WITH:

RATING: ☆ ☆ ☆ ☆ ☆   WILL I RETURN?   YES / NO

Monkey Jungle is a unique eco-show park and discovery center that was established in 1935. It's nestled within a natural subtropical forest located in the southern part of Miami-Dade County. This special place provides a habitat where wildlife from the jungle can thrive much like they would in their native environments. Skilled Jungle Guides lead visitors deep into the forest for regularly scheduled shows and performances featuring the jungle's remarkable wildlife. These shows are not only entertaining but also showcase natural behaviors in their authentic habitats.

Visitors to Monkey Jungle, including guests, students, and scientists, have the extraordinary opportunity to explore and experience close encounters with these incredible creatures within the park's 30-acre natural jungle setting. Additionally, Monkey Jungle is available to host environmental festivals, birthday parties, and other events.

The history of Monkey Jungle traces back to 1933 when Joseph DuMond, an inquisitive animal behaviorist, arrived in South Florida. He released six Java monkeys into the dense subtropical forest, marking the beginning of a thriving troop that now roams freely at Monkey Jungle. This troop forms the foundation for the Eco-Show theater and scientific programs at the park.

Monkey Jungle, conveniently located near U.S. 1 and the Florida Turnpike in southern Miami-Dade County, pioneered many innovative concepts in its field. Unlike traditional circus acts and zoos, the primary focus here is on showcasing natural behaviors and facilitating interaction with Jungle Guide show hosts. The park is home to over 300 primates, with most of them roaming freely within a 30-acre preserve. It's also one of the few protected habitats for endangered primates in the United States and uniquely open to the general public for exploration.

As part of Monkey Jungle's ongoing efforts to engage and educate visitors about primates, there's a special feature known as the CAMEROON GORILLA FOREST showcase. Here, audiences witness dynamic interactions between Jungle Guides and the incredible apes based on their natural behavior.

Upon entering Monkey Jungle, visitors are immediately greeted by the Java monkey troop, which now numbers over 90 individuals. This interaction with the monkeys remains a highlight for visitors. Java monkeys are known for their skills in diving, collecting crabs and shellfish along riverbanks and mangrove swamps in the wild. Visitors can observe these water skills and other natural behaviors as the monkeys interact with the Guides, often wading or leaping into their pond during the WILD MONKEY SWIMMING POOL activity.

Additionally, Monkey Jungle serves as a hub for science, conservation, and education through its affiliation with the DuMond Conservancy for Primates & Tropical Forests, a not-for-profit organization.

MORIKAMI MUSEUM AND JAPANESE GARDENS

REGION: SOUTHEAST DISTRICT   **COUNTY:** PALM BEACH   **CITY:** DELRAY BEACH

DATE VISITED: **WHO I WENT WITH:**

RATING: ☆ ☆ ☆ ☆ ☆   **WILL I RETURN?** YES / NO

Visitors to South Florida are often amazed when they stumble upon a remarkable connection that dates back a century between Japan and the region. In this area, a community of young Japanese farmers came together with the aim of bringing about a farming revolution in Florida.

The reason we encounter the name Yamato, which is an ancient term for Japan, in Palm Beach County is due to the historical presence of the Yamato Colony, once a small community of Japanese farmers situated in what is now northern Boca Raton. The tale of the Yamato Colony commences with the visit of Jo Sakai to Florida in 1903. Sakai, originally from Miyazu, Japan, had recently graduated from New York University. He entered into an agreement with the Florida East Coast Railway to establish a proposed colony of Japanese farmers in the Boca Raton region. Following this, he returned to Japan to recruit settlers and bring them to Florida.

Initially, the Yamato Colony attracted young, unmarried men who engaged in pineapple cultivation for shipment to northern markets. However, as competition from Cuban pineapples intensified, including those grown by Yamato colonists, many local growers, including those in Yamato, shifted their focus to winter vegetables. While most settlers didn't stay in Yamato for extended periods, those who did occasionally returned to Japan to marry and bring their wives back to the colony. Families gradually formed. Ironically, prosperity during World War I and the real estate "boom" of the 1920s led to the departure of many settlers. By the onset of World War II, only a few Japanese residents remained. In May 1942, the U.S. government confiscated the farmland in the Yamato area that was still owned by Japanese settlers for military use. Although the pioneering Japanese community is gone, the name Yamato endures to this day.

The mission of the Morikami Museum and Japanese Gardens is to engage a diverse audience by offering Japanese cultural experiences that both educate and inspire.

Since its opening in 1977, Morikami has served as a hub for Japanese arts and culture in South Florida. Through changing exhibitions, monthly tea ceremonies conducted in the Seishin-an tea house from October to May, and educational outreach programs with local schools and organizations, Morikami strives to promote an appreciation for the vibrant culture of Japan.

The original structure, known as the Yamato-kan, takes its architectural cues from a traditional Japanese villa. It comprises a series of exhibition rooms arranged around an open-air courtyard, complete with a dry garden featuring gravel, pebbles, and small boulders. Inside the Yamato-kan, visitors can explore exhibitions that delve into the history of the Yamato Colony and the design philosophy of garden designer Hoichi Kurisu.

Responding to the growing demand for programming and versatile facilities, as well as the needs of an expanding community, the main museum building was inaugurated in 1993. This building draws inspiration from traditional Japanese design principles. It boasts three exhibition galleries, a 225-seat theater, an authentic tea house with a viewing gallery, classrooms, a museum shop, the Cornell Cafe, and lakeside terraces offering panoramic views for diners.

The Morikami Collections are home to a diverse array of over 7,000 Japanese art objects and artifacts. This includes a collection of 500 items related to tea ceremonies, over 200 textile pieces, and various fine art acquisitions.

The 16-acre area that surrounds the two museum buildings at Morikami comprises extensive Japanese gardens featuring winding paths, places to rest, a world-class bonsai collection, and lakes teeming with koi fish and various other wildlife. The broader 200-acre park encompasses nature trails, pine forests, and picnic areas.

In the year 2001, Morikami underwent a significant expansion and renovation of its gardens. These newly designed gardens reflect key periods in the history of Japanese garden design, spanning from the eighth to the 20th century. They effectively serve as an outdoor extension of the museum. As per the garden designer, Hoichi Kurisu, each garden aims to convey the character and concepts of a distinct counterpart in Japan, without attempting to replicate those gardens. Instead, they seamlessly blend together into a unified garden experience.

Morikami Museum and Japanese Gardens stands out as one of Palm Beach County's most cherished cultural attractions, thanks to its exceptional gardens and collections. Nestled within a peaceful natural setting, Morikami invites visitors to explore its diverse facets and uncover the rich heritage of Florida and its ties to Japan.

MOTE MARINE LABORATORY & AQUARIUM

REGION: SOUTHWEST DISTRICT	COUNTY: SARASOTA	CITY: SARASOTA

DATE VISITED:	WHO I WENT WITH:

RATING: ☆ ☆ ☆ ☆ ☆   WILL I RETURN?   YES / NO

Mote Marine Laboratory is a nonprofit marine research organization situated on City Island in Sarasota, Florida, and it also has campuses in eastern Sarasota County, Boca Grande, Florida, and the Florida Keys. It was established in 1955 by Eugenie Clark in Placida, Florida, under the name Cape Haze Marine Laboratory until it was renamed in 1967 in recognition of its major benefactors: William R. Mote, his wife Lenore, and his sister, Betty Mote Rose. The laboratory's primary mission is to advance marine science and education, with a focus on supporting the conservation and sustainable use of marine resources. In addition to its research efforts, it operates a public aquarium and education program to communicate its findings to the general public.

The early research at the lab primarily centered around studying sharks and other fish species. Since 1960, the laboratory has been based in Sarasota, Florida, and has been situated on City Island since 1978.

In recognition of its 55th anniversary in 2010, the laboratory received acclaim for its contributions to marine science, including resolutions in the Florida House and Senate. Eugenie Clark, the founder, was also inducted into the Florida Women's Hall of Fame in March 2010. When the laboratory celebrated its 60th anniversary in 2015, it launched a comprehensive fundraising campaign called "Oceans of Opportunity: the Campaign for Mote Marine Laboratory." Eugenie Clark remained actively involved with the laboratory as a senior scientist, director emerita, and trustee until her passing in February 2015.

As of 2017, Mote Marine Laboratory had a workforce of over 200 employees, which included Ph.D. scientists involved in more than 20 different research programs. These programs covered a wide range of marine-related topics, such as coral health and disease, chemical and physical ecology, phytoplankton ecology, ocean acidification, marine and freshwater aquaculture, fisheries habitat ecology, stranding investigations, ecotoxicology, conservation research on sharks and rays, fisheries ecology and enhancement, coral reef monitoring and assessment, coral reef restoration, environmental health, ocean technology, marine immunology, benthic ecology, marine biomedical research, environmental forensics, sea turtle conservation, manatee research, and dolphin research. The laboratory also collaborates with the Chicago Zoological Society to conduct the world's longest-running study on a wild dolphin population.

Since 1978, the laboratory has undergone expansion and now includes a 10.5-acre campus in Sarasota, the Elizabeth Moore International Center for Coral Reef Research and Restoration on Summerland Key, a public exhibit in Key West, an outreach office in

Boca Grande, and the Mote Aquaculture Research Park in eastern Sarasota County. Apart from its staff members, the laboratory benefits from the support of approximately 1,000 volunteers.

The public outreach branch of Mote Marine Laboratory is its aquarium, where visitors can view more than 100 marine species, with a particular emphasis on the species and ecosystems that are the focus of the laboratory's scientific research. This aquarium holds accreditation from the Association of Zoos and Aquariums, an organization that recognizes qualified facilities based on rigorous evaluations of animal care, conservation efforts, scientific research, facility quality, and more.

Established in 1980 on City Island in Sarasota Bay, the aquarium's exhibits showcase a variety of marine life, including sharks, manatees, sea turtles, seahorses, rays, skates, and various invertebrates like cuttlefish, octopuses, sea jellies, anemones, and corals. The aquarium also hosts special exhibits such as "Otters and Their Waters" and "The Teeth Beneath: The Wild World of Gators, Crocs, and Caimans," which highlight animals found in watershed areas, including North American river otters, American alligators, and spectacled caimans. Another special exhibit, "Oh Baby! Life Cycles of the Seas," explores marine courtship and reproduction, featuring the offspring of various species and their challenges in early-life survival through interactive displays, a baby shark touch tank, and more. Furthermore, the aquarium offers windows into active research laboratories and interactive exhibits designed to make scientific concepts accessible to visitors of all ages.

The aquarium also presents educational shark feedings, during which large sharks are trained to target specific areas for a food reward. Similarly, resident animals like sea turtles and river otters undergo feeding and training sessions designed to enhance their well-being and provide mental stimulation. These narrated training and feeding sessions are carefully tailored to prioritize animal care and, in some cases, to support behavioral research aimed at informing the conservation of wild populations.

Notably, until 2011, the aquarium was home to Harley, the last known spinner dolphin in captivity in the United States.

MOUNT DORA

REGION: CENTRAL EAST DISTRICT   **COUNTY:** LAKE   **CITY:** MOUNT DORA

DATE VISITED: **WHO I WENT WITH:**

RATING: ☆ ☆ ☆ ☆ ☆   **WILL I RETURN?** YES / NO

Mount Dora is a city situated in Lake County, Florida. According to the 2010 census, its population was recorded at 12,370 residents, and by 2019, it was estimated to have grown to 14,516 residents. This city is a part of the Orlando-Kissimmee metropolitan statistical area in Florida. Founded in the year 1880, Mount Dora is renowned for its quaint, small-town southern charm. Its downtown area is famous for housing numerous antique shops, and it offers picturesque views of Lake Dora. Notably, Mount Dora is the location of one of only three freshwater lighthouses in the state of Florida. The city is also recognized for its numerous monthly festivals and has earned the nickname "Festival City."

Mount Dora, a serene and leisurely escape located just an hour away from Orlando, provides a taste of the delightful Old Florida countryside lifestyle.

Within the confines of Mount Dora, you'll find a picturesque landscape featuring lakes, tranquil country inns, quaint shops, a historic railroad station, and a diverse selection of delectable dining options, all conveniently situated within walking distance of each other.

Designated as a trail town, Mount Dora offers a mountain biking trail, various parks, and a range of lakeside amenities. These include the scenic Palm Island Boardwalk, opportunities for boat rentals, a boat launch area, and a well-known lighthouse that adds to the city's charm.

The small-town atmosphere of Mount Dora is particularly appealing to antique enthusiasts, drawing visitors from across the state, the country, and even worldwide. The local shops and those in the surrounding areas are replete with nostalgic items, valuable antiques, collectibles, and estate jewelry, making it a haven for collectors.

In addition to its antique treasures, Mount Dora boasts a thriving culinary scene with outdoor cafes, gourmet restaurants, galleries, wineries, and charming bed and breakfast inns gracing its downtown district, adding to the city's appeal as a delightful destination.

Local folklore suggests that the origin of the name of the large, picturesque lake around which the city of Mount Dora developed is attributed to Ms. Dora Ann Drawdy (1819-1885). According to the legend, Ms. Drawdy settled in the mid-1800s in the area and made a lasting impression on federal surveyors with her warm hospitality. In 1846, these surveyors bestowed the name "Lake Dora" in her honor. Subsequently, in 1883, when the small town in the vicinity of the lake began to grow, it was officially named Mount

Dora, after the lake itself. It's worth noting that Ms. Drawdy's final resting place is in Umatilla. Historical research has uncovered that the earliest survey maps, dating back to 1848, indeed referred to the body of water as "Lake Dora." Curiously, on the 1850 U.S. Census, the William and Dora Ann Drawdy family is listed as farmers in Georgia, not Florida. However, they are documented as residents of Mount Dora before the 1860 census. This leaves a mystery regarding the true identity of the initial "Dora" for whom the lake was named. Following Ms. Drawdy, more settlers migrated to the region, including notable figures like Mr. Ross C. Tremain and Capt. John Philip Donnelly, who played essential roles in the growth and development of the burgeoning settlement. Tremain assumed the role of the town's inaugural official postmaster in 1880 when the town was informally known as Royellou, unofficially named after Tremain's three children: Roy, Ella, and Louis. Three years later, the town's name was officially changed to Mount Dora to reflect the unique geographical feature upon which it sits—a plateau located 184 feet above sea level, an uncommon topographical characteristic in Florida. The Alexander House, originally opened in 1883, served as a popular winter destination for hunters, fishermen, and boaters. It was a two-story hotel featuring ten rooms. Later, in 1893, the Alexander House underwent a name change and became known as The Lake House. Subsequently, in 1903, it was once again renamed, this time to Lakeside Inn. Remarkably, Lakeside Inn is still operational today and has hosted distinguished guests, including Presidents Coolidge and Eisenhower, as well as notable figures such as Thomas Edison and Henry Ford. The year 1887 marked a pivotal moment in the local economy with the introduction of the railroad, which not only brought tourists but also facilitated the transportation of goods. In 1891, Tremain played a key role by opening the town's first orange-packing house. Unfortunately, the surrounding citrus groves suffered severe damage due to the devastating freezes of 1894 and 1895. Concurrently, the 1890s saw the establishment of fertilizer factories and a cannery in the area. By 1910, the town had achieved the status of an incorporated municipality, obtaining a charter with Capt. John Philip Donnelly as its inaugural mayor. Mount Dora, with a population of 371 residents, boasted two general stores, a hardware store, a drugstore, two churches, and a town hall. It also saw the inception of its first newspaper, The Mount Dora Voice. Notably, Capt. John Philip Donnelly's Queen Anne-style residence, constructed in 1893, has since been listed on the National Register of Historic Places, serving as a testament to the town's rich history and heritage. The early 1920s marked a significant period of growth in residential and business sectors, signaling the transformation of Mount Dora from a rural town into a burgeoning city. During this era, Mount Dora made substantial investments in its public infrastructure. The installation of streetlights, the establishment of a water system, the addition of curbs, and the paving of roads were notable improvements. Moreover, the town saw the creation of its first two public parks, Gilbert Park and Donnelly Park. These parks were made possible through the generous donations of land by Earl Gilbert and J. P. Donnelly, prominent landowners in the area. They contributed prime pieces of land in both the downtown area and along the shores of Lake Dora.

The construction of the Mount Dora Community Building is another significant achievement from this period. Despite facing economic challenges during the late 1920s, a determined group of residents rallied together to raise funds for the project. In 1929, the impressive Mediterranean-style building was completed, boasting seating capacity for approximately 800, which equaled the town's population at the time. Over the years, this building has served as the city's primary venue for performances and meetings.

In 2009, despite economic difficulties, the citizens once again united to restore and renovate the Mount Dora Community Building. This effort resulted in improved seating, structural enhancements, an expanded lobby, while preserving the building's unique architectural style and exterior.

Here's an interesting piece of trivia: In 1981, the film "Honky Tonk Freeway" was shot in Mount Dora, and as part of the movie's set design, numerous buildings in Mount Dora were temporarily painted pink.

Today, Mount Dora continues to experience growth and has developed a strong artistic presence. It has retained its status as a beloved tourist destination, drawing visitors from far and wide.

----

⑦³ MUSEUM OF CONTEMPORARY ART NORTH MIAMI

REGION: SOUTHEAST DISTRICT	COUNTY: MIAMI-DADE	CITY: MIAMI

DATE VISITED:	WHO I WENT WITH:

RATING: ☆ ☆ ☆ ☆ ☆	WILL I RETURN? YES / NO

The Museum of Contemporary Art (MOCA) is a museum dedicated to collecting contemporary art located in North Miami. The museum is housed in a 23,000-square-foot building designed by the architectural firm Gwathmey Siegel & Associates Architects, based in New York City.

MOCA North Miami serves as a platform for presenting contemporary art and exploring its historical influences through a variety of exhibitions, educational initiatives, and collections. It draws inspiration from the surrounding communities and strives to connect diverse audiences and cultures by providing an inclusive space for encountering new ideas and voices, all while fostering a lifelong appreciation for the arts.

MOCA aims to establish itself as a welcoming hub at the heart of North Miami, where art and artistic experiences extend beyond the museum's walls, activating parks, schools, residences, and civic spaces. It seeks to facilitate the connection of local and global dialogues about art.

The museum leverages the cultural vitality of the region to introduce fresh art perspectives and experiences to the public, building upon North Miami's reputation as a cultural destination. Visitors and the community can anticipate exhibitions that challenge conventional notions, featuring lesser-explored art forms and artists, as well as amplifying diverse voices and narratives.

MOCA has gained recognition and respect both locally and nationally for its innovative curatorial approach and research-based exhibitions, which are complemented by educational programs catering to individuals of all ages. Positioned as a meeting point for cultural expressions and exchanges, MOCA aspires to become a center for promoting cross-cultural understanding and inclusivity, forging connections among diverse communities through the medium of art.

Originally starting as a modest single gallery known as the Center for Contemporary Art in 1981, the Museum of Contemporary Art North Miami underwent a significant transformation, expanding into a spacious 23,000-square-foot facility by 1996. This expansion was made possible through a substantial $2.5 million grant from the Department of Housing and Urban Development (HUD) and was executed by architects Charles Gwathmey of GSNY in collaboration with the Miami-based firm Gelabert-Navia.

In 1997, it was officially rebranded as MOCA, marking a pivotal moment when the museum began actively collecting contemporary art—a distinctive endeavor that set it apart from other cultural institutions in Miami-Dade. Today, MOCA has evolved into a prominent institution known for its role in discovering emerging artists and preserving living cultural heritage. It achieves this by curating groundbreaking exhibitions and implementing innovative educational programs, thus nurturing the growth and recognition of South Florida artists on an international scale.

MUSEUM OF SCIENCE AND INDUSTRY

REGION: CENTRAL WEST DISTRICT	COUNTY: HILLSBOROUGH	CITY: TAMPA

DATE VISITED: **WHO I WENT WITH:**

          RATING: ☆ ☆ ☆ ☆ ☆   **WILL I RETURN?** YES / NO

The Tampa Museum of Science & Industry, known as MOSI for short, offers visitors more than 100 hands-on activities in a scientific playground. MOSI features The Saunders Planetarium for stargazing, a NASA-funded Mission: Moonbase lunar colony for exploring other worlds, and Connectus for interactive experiences.

MOSI's exhibits encourage visitors to ask questions and expand their understanding of the world. The museum emphasizes the joy of curiosity, with no tests or quizzes involved. It serves as a place for sparking conversations about the world and the future, bridging generations and connecting people of all backgrounds. MOSI is a not-for-profit organization dedicated to innovation in STEAM (Science, Technology, Engineering, Arts, and Math) education, aiming to make science accessible and engaging for everyone.

Through education and outreach programs, MOSI takes its unique blend of fun and learning to the community. Summer Science Camps inspire students from kindergarten through middle school, while initiatives like mobile labs and telescopes bring science education to schools and neighborhoods. The Museums of All program, the first of its kind in Florida, offers discounted admission to low-income families.

MOSI's maker space allows families to build and launch rockets, command electricity, and create incredible chemical reactions together. The museum fosters hands-on problem-solving skills that are essential for the 21st century, not just by teaching but by celebrating and energizing them, ensuring that the learning continues beyond the museum's walls.

MOSI's history dates back to 1962 when Hillsborough County approved funding for a youth museum in Sulphur Springs. Originally named the Museum of Science and Natural History, it offered natural science exhibits and educational programs for both children and adults. The museum's name was later changed to the Hillsborough County Museum in 1967. In 1976, the museum's advisory committee and staff initiated the construction of a new facility in North Tampa, which would eventually become the Museum of Science & Industry. This new museum was completed in 1980 and officially opened its doors to the public on January 23, 1982.

In 1995, significant expansion took place with the construction of a 190,000-square-foot science center featuring extensive permanent and temporary exhibition galleries, a planetarium, and a public library. Subsequent renovations were carried out in 1996, 2001, and 2005, solidifying MOSI's position as the largest science center in the southeastern United States and the fifth largest in the entire country.

However, on August 13, 2017, MOSI faced financial challenges and made the decision to close 85% of its building to reduce costs. Numerous exhibits were removed, and the remaining ones were relocated to the previous "Kids in Charge" section of the museum.

In 2022, plans to construct a new facility in downtown Tampa were abandoned due to financial constraints. Instead, MOSI announced its intention to focus on expanding its existing North Tampa location by introducing new exhibits and programs.

NAPLES PIER

REGION: SOUTHWEST DISTRICT   **COUNTY:** COLLIER   **CITY:** NAPLES

DATE VISITED: **WHO I WENT WITH:**

RATING: ☆ ☆ ☆ ☆ ☆   **WILL I RETURN?** YES / NO

The Naples Pier is an expansive boardwalk that offers an ideal setting to enjoy the breathtaking views of the coastline and witness the stunning Florida sunset over the Gulf of Mexico. The Naples Pier is situated precisely at the west end of 12th Avenue South. Couples often visit this spot for romantic evening strolls while observing the graceful flight of pelicans and seagulls in the sky. The wooden dock is a popular location for anglers eager to cast their fishing lines, and there is a significant chance of spotting dolphins and stingrays, especially during the months of April and June.

Visitors are encouraged to capture the picturesque scenery with their cameras, and metered parking is conveniently available along the street.

The pier holds immense significance for Naples and is considered the symbol of the city. Its presence is so deeply ingrained that it is hard to imagine Naples without it. When walking along the pier, particularly during the peak season, it feels like a gathering of various cultures, resembling a "United Nations" of languages. People from all around the world leisurely stroll to the end of the pier to catch a glimpse of dolphins, observe fishing activities, and relish the beauty of the Gulf and the beach. The panoramic sunsets from the pier's furthest point are simply spectacular, making it a treasure that is truly invaluable to the city's identity.

Construction of the first pier began in 1888, commissioned by Walter Halderman of The Naples Company. The pier extended 600 feet into the Gulf and was a double-deck structure, facilitating the unloading of goods and the disembarking of passengers. It played a crucial role in connecting people and goods to the area before its existence, either through boat arrivals in the Gulf or Naples Bay or through ox carts traveling from Fort Myers.

Over the years, the pier faced several challenges, enduring storms, hurricanes, and even a fire. Despite these trials, it remained standing through the 1950s and served as a popular fishing spot and a vital food source for the community. Unfortunately, Hurricane Donna struck in 1960 and completely destroyed the pier, leaving the city with difficult decisions regarding rebuilding.

The pier's revival was made possible by the generous support of Mr. and Mrs. Lester Norris, who agreed to cover the rebuilding costs. The pier reopened at its original site, becoming a symbol of hope and unity for the community. The Norris's stipulation was that there would be no charge for accessing or fishing on the pier, ensuring that everyone could enjoy this cherished gathering place.

Although the pier has needed repairs over time, it has not suffered major storm damage. In 2015, floorboard replacement using Brazilian hardwood called IPE was undertaken to maintain its integrity. Today, fishing from the pier remains license-free, and there are no charges to walk along its length. The midway concession stand is a favorite spot for families to indulge in hot dogs and ice cream while savoring the remarkable vistas.

The pier's beauty and charm extend to people worldwide, as a webcam located on the pier allows anyone to enjoy the stunning views from afar at www.naplespanorama.org.

REGION: SOUTHWEST DISTRICT   COUNTY: COLLIER   CITY: NAPLES

DATE VISITED: WHO I WENT WITH:

RATING: ☆ ☆ ☆ ☆ ☆   WILL I RETURN?   YES / NO

Naples Zoo is not just your average zoo; it is a nationally accredited institution with 501(c)(3) nonprofit status that offers much more than just a walk-through experience. The zoo provides visitors with a full day of enjoyable activities. As you explore the zoo, you'll follow a paved path that winds for nearly a mile through a historic tropical garden filled with exotic plants that were initially planted in 1919, boasting a rich and fascinating history.

Within this lush tropical environment, you can marvel at a wide variety of beloved animals, including lions, giraffes, monkeys, pythons, and bears. Furthermore, the zoo features special exhibits and the opportunity to encounter more unusual creatures, such as a giant anteater.

Naples Zoo is dedicated to combining both conservation and entertainment, ensuring that visitors of all ages have a great time. Beyond the entertainment, you'll also find various ways to actively participate in animal conservation efforts. The zoo holds accreditation from the prestigious Association of Zoos and Aquariums and is an institutional member of the American Association of Zoo Keepers.

It annually welcomes over 350,000 guests, all of whom contribute to the zoo's conservation and educational mission. The zoo plays a crucial role in preserving rare plant and animal species both locally and globally, including the planting of more than 25,000 trees annually in regions such as Africa, Asia, and the Americas.

The origins of the Naples Zoo can be traced back to botanist Dr. Henry Nehrling, who acquired the land in 1919 to safeguard his plant collection, which had suffered severe damage during a freeze in 1917 at his initial garden in central Florida. Following Dr. Nehrling's passing in 1929, the gardens fell into neglect for more than two decades. In 1954, they were reopened to the public under the name "Caribbean Gardens" by Julius Fleischmann, Jr. At that time, they were described as located "just north of Naples."

The transition to becoming a zoo began in 1967 when Col. Lawrence and Nancy Jane Tetzlaff, renowned as Jungle Larry and Safari Jane, visited the Gardens while searching for a winter residence for their rare animal collection. Although the property was not available at that time, the Tetzlaffs were subsequently approached to house their animals within the garden following Fleischmann's passing. The zoo officially opened with the animals in place on September 1, 1969.

Despite the passing of Larry Tetzlaff in 1984, Nancy Jane Tetzlaff and her family continued to operate, improve, and expand the Zoo and gardens. In 2002, the Fleischmann family, who owned the land at the time, expressed their intention to sell it. The Tetzlaffs initiated efforts to encourage the county to acquire the land, and the Fleischmann family waited to provide the community an opportunity to take action. In 2004, a referendum to purchase the land received approval from 73% of voters. To facilitate the purchase, the Tetzlaffs transformed the Zoo into a 501(c)(3) charitable organization and transferred control to the newly established Naples Zoo Board of Directors in 2005.

Today, led by President and CEO Jack Mulvena, the zoo is home to an expanding number of critically endangered species, actively supports conservation initiatives in the wild.

REGION: NORTHEAST DISTRICT   COUNTY: ST. JOHNS   CITY: ST. AUGUSTINE

DATE VISITED: WHO I WENT WITH:

RATING: ☆ ☆ ☆ ☆ ☆   WILL I RETURN? YES / NO

The Oldest Wooden School House represents the transformation of St. Augustine from a small town into a city, thanks to the resilience and determination of early settlers who sought to establish a community rooted in their traditions, customs, culture, and faith. The Minorcans, who were impoverished people from the Mediterranean, arrived in Florida in 1768 as indentured servants, initially working on a plantation in New Smyrna. After enduring nine strenuous and deadly years in servitude, the survivors sought sanctuary 70 miles to the north in the British-controlled St. Augustine. They were permitted to settle in the northern part of St. George Street, just inside the city's gates. They continued to reside there even as the Spanish regained control of the city and remained when Florida became part of the United States in 1821.

Property records provide evidence of ownership dating back to 1740. Jesse Fish, a real estate agent acting on behalf of Spanish officers and residents who were leaving Florida when the British assumed control, completed the sale of the property to Juan Genopoly on October 1, 1780. The Genopoly family established and maintained their homestead on this land for more than a century. Juan Genopoly, a Greek carpenter hailing from Mani, constructed a new residence at the site around 1800-1810, and this building still stands today.

The primary room on the ground floor served as a classroom and had a direct entrance from the street. An additional, smaller room was later added to the floorplan, intended as the family's sitting room and featuring a backdoor for easy access to the kitchen, which was a separate structure made of wooden siding and had a coquina chimney. The garden area behind the house was utilized for cultivating vegetables, fruits, herbs, and spices. Water for cooking and drinking was drawn from the old well located next to the house.

Juan Genopoly, who had become a free citizen in the British settlement, recognized the significance of acquiring English language skills. He generously welcomed children from the Minorcan Quarter into his own home to provide them with education in reading, writing, and arithmetic. Remarkably, two of the four children born to Juan Genopoly and his wife in St. Augustine went on to become teachers at the Old School.

In the 1850s and 1860s, students attending the school left behind certified notes and letters that vividly captured their memories of their time there. Both boys and girls were enrolled in this small school, where tuition fees were 12 1/2 cents per week for younger students and 25 cents per week for older ones. These fees covered the cost of parchment, quill pens, and ink for the students to practice their writing. It's worth picturing these students learning while seated on log benches, old chairs, and sometimes even on the floor. They also spoke of the discipline enforced at the school and the consequences of misbehavior.

The school's final class was held in 1864. However, in November 1931, a heartwarming reunion took place, bringing together nine former students who hadn't gathered in over fifty years. During this reunion, these former students meticulously recreated the classroom environment as they remembered it, leading to the opening of the Genopoly House to the public as The Oldest School House.

The school welcomes tourists every day of the year except for Christmas, and during the summer, it has extended opening hours. Visitors can explore the facility through a self-guided tour that includes an animatronic teacher and student (created by Sally Corp.), who provide a brief history of the house. Additionally, there are numerous items and informative signs placed throughout the building to enhance the visitor's experience.

The gardens located behind the house offer exhibits related to the kitchen, a reconstructed outhouse, an old well, and a sculpture garden featuring busts of renowned educators. These statues are part of a larger initiative called The Grove of Educators, which aimed to collect sculptures of educators from all countries in the Americas, although only a few countries participated in the project.

ORLANDO MUSEUM OF ART

REGION: CENTRAL EAST DISTRICT   **COUNTY:** ORANGE   **CITY:** ORLANDO

DATE VISITED: **WHO I WENT WITH:**

RATING: ☆ ☆ ☆ ☆ ☆   **WILL I RETURN?**   YES / NO

Established in 1924 and officially recognized as a 501(c)(3) institution, the Orlando Museum of Art (OMA) holds the distinction of being Orlando's foremost museum, playing a prominent role in providing visual art education and experiences across a four-county region. Accredited by the American Alliance of Museums (AAM) since 1971, OMA serves as a valuable regional resource and a driving force behind ongoing learning initiatives, catering to both the central Florida community and a global audience of visitors.

The core mission of the Orlando Museum of Art (OMA) revolves around the interpretation and presentation of art to a diverse and inclusive public. OMA is dedicated to making a positive impact on people's lives through innovative and inspiring educational programs, fostering a cultural legacy in Central Florida. Additionally, OMA strives to ignite creativity, passion, and intellectual curiosity by connecting individuals from various backgrounds and experiences with compelling art and fresh ideas. The goal is to teach, influence, and expand the collective worldview and shared experiences of the community through art exhibitions and educational programming.

Annually, OMA hosts approximately a dozen exhibitions, which encompass special and visiting exhibitions as well as those curated from the museum's own collections. These exhibitions are complemented by a wide range of programs, including gallery tours, lectures on art appreciation, studio classes catering to both youth and adults, tailored community access initiatives designed for special populations, and community events such as family days and cultural celebrations. OMA welcomes over 130,000 visitors each year, and its education programs reach out to approximately 16,000 individuals annually.

OMA's collection encompasses an impressive array of more than 2,400 artworks, including holdings in various categories such as Contemporary Art, American Art spanning the 18th century to 1945, Art of the Ancient Americas, and African Art. Notably, the Art of the Ancient Americas collection is recognized as one of the finest of its kind in the Southeastern United States.

In 2014, the museum introduced an exhibition initiative known as The Florida Prize in Contemporary Art. This initiative highlights the work of emerging and mid-career artists who are pushing boundaries and sparking meaningful discussions within the artistic landscape of Florida today.

It's important to note that OMA holds accreditation from the American Alliance of Museums (AAM) and is a member of the North American Reciprocal Museums program.

This recognition underscores the museum's commitment to maintaining high standards of operation and its participation in a network of cultural institutions.

REGION: SOUTHEAST DISTRICT   **COUNTY:** MIAMI-DADE   **CITY:** MIAMI

DATE VISITED: **WHO I WENT WITH:**

RATING: ☆ ☆ ☆ ☆ ☆   **WILL I RETURN?**   YES / NO

Situated on a sprawling four-acre site within the waterfront Maurice A. Ferré Park in Downtown Miami, the Phillip and Patricia Frost Museum of Science boasts an impressive 250,000-square-foot facility, which is divided into four distinct buildings: the Aquarium, the Frost Planetarium, and the North and West Wings. This distinctive campus-like setup offers visitors a comprehensive journey, spanning from the depths of the ocean to the vastness of the Everglades, and from the intricate workings of the human cell to the mysteries of outer space. The museum delves into the exploration of life as we understand it, all while highlighting the scientific processes and innovations that drive our understanding.

Frost Science has received the prestigious LEED (Leadership in Energy and Environmental Design) Gold Certification, recognizing its exceptional commitment to sustainable and energy-efficient practices in the design, construction, and operation of the facility. Located within Miami's Arts and Entertainment District, the museum serves as a vital component of a constellation of downtown cultural organizations, alongside institutions such as the Pérez Art Museum Miami, the Adrienne Arsht Center for the Performing Arts, YoungArts, and others.

Before the current Frost Science Museum was established, the museum team at its previous location took the initiative to create an interactive exhibition aimed at understanding the community's desires for a science museum. Through this effort, they gathered valuable insights from the public, which included a strong preference for an outdoor, sunlit space dedicated to exploring South Florida's unique ecosystems, a planetarium, and exhibitions focusing on outer space and human health. All of these community preferences were incorporated into the criteria provided to architectural firms.

Additionally, there was a desire to expand the museum's already robust marine science programs by incorporating an aquarium, and to ensure that both the building and its surrounding grounds would serve as integral components of the scientific exploration experience. In 2007, following a global search, the selection committee responsible for choosing an architectural firm, which included representatives from Miami-Dade County and the City of Miami, ultimately selected Grimshaw Architects. Grimshaw was renowned for its sensitivity to local conditions and its strong commitment to sustainability. The firm had earned more than 170 international design awards, including the Lubetkin Prize for their work on the Southern Cross Station in Melbourne, Australia.

Modern technology empowers science museums to craft captivating educational encounters. Frost Science seizes this opportunity by integrating cutting-edge innovations across the entire museum, from the captivating aquarium experience to the immersive multimedia offerings within the Frost Planetarium, and even the interactive virtual representation of the Everglades in the River of Grass exhibit. Notably, the museum's structure itself serves as an exhibition, and many of its technological features are readily accessible to the visiting public.

Frost Science comprises a collection of highly distinctive buildings that demanded pioneering engineering accomplishments. These achievements are evident in various aspects of the site, including the monumental Gulf Stream Aquarium, the dome of the Frost Planetarium, and the museum's overall resilience to storms, serving as an exemplar of innovation and engineering triumph.

At the heart of the museum lies the Gulf Stream Aquarium, a remarkable 100-foot wide, cone-shaped structure containing 500,000 gallons of water. Its design eliminates corners, enabling open-water marine species like tuna and sharks to swim continuously, mimicking their natural habitat in the Gulf Stream. Constructed entirely from concrete and devoid of construction joints, this aquarium boasts 9,000 square feet of tank surface area and bears the weight of 4.5 million pounds of water.

Building this vessel presented significant challenges. A continuous 25-hour concrete pour was required, involving the distribution of 1,200 cubic yards of concrete through 131 cement trucks and the labor of two teams, each comprising 150 people. The steep angles of the vessel's sides, reaching up to 44 degrees, posed a challenge as regular concrete would simply slide down. Engineers had to develop a concrete mixture with the right consistency to stay in place yet be fluid enough to surround a checkerboard of rebar reinforcement. Prior to the actual pour, numerous trial runs were conducted to refine the methods and concrete recipes, ensuring the perfect viscosity and adherence. Vibrating the concrete properly during the pour, even on steep angles, was crucial to ensure complete settling and bonding. Workers even customized their equipment to vibrate at the correct angle without damaging the surface, marking a first in the industry.

During the pour, the concrete was brought in with less water initially and water was incrementally added as needed, depending on the pouring location within the vessel. Ultimately, the pour utilized 5 million pounds of concrete, resulting in walls with varying thicknesses ranging from 28 to 56 inches.

To prevent cracking and counteract outward and downward forces on the cone, engineers internally wrapped the structure with 9.5 miles of post-tension cable, which they stretched and secured, generating nearly 20 million pounds of compression force.

The entire structure, weighing 9.5 million pounds (5 million in concrete and 4.5 million in water), is supported above the Baptist Health South Florida Gallery by six concrete columns with an extraordinary compression capacity of 10,000 pounds per square inch (whereas standard bridge abutments typically have a compression capacity of 5,000 pounds per square inch).

The base of the Gulf Stream Aquarium features a massive viewing portal created by a 31-foot wide, 13.5-inch thick, 60,000-pound oculus lens manufactured outside of Rome, Italy. Designers used a liquid acrylic pour instead of the conventional bead fabrication process to achieve maximum clarity, bonding two layers and multiple pieces together to form the entire lens. This oculus lens was transported from Italy to Miami via barge and lowered into the Gulf Stream Aquarium using a crane. Once the vessel was filled with water, the weight of the water helped secure the epoxy seal between the concrete vessel and the acrylic lens. The lens is angled at 21 degrees to provide guests with astonishing unobstructed views into the aquatic world above.

The Frost Planetarium, boasting a diameter of 67 feet, is a unique architectural marvel. It combines cast concrete for the lower half with 32 pre-cast sections resembling "orange peel" patterns, manufactured offsite and then placed on top of the precast base to form a perfect dome. Each of these precast panels weighs a substantial 50,000 pounds and necessitated the use of a 550-ton crane for installation. During assembly, engineers erected a 50-foot-tall central shoring tower and meticulously attached the precast dome panels one by one, in opposing pairs to prevent lateral loading on the dome cap. This installation process operated around the clock, with a 24-hour-a-day, seven-day-a-week schedule, spanning two and a half weeks.

Frost Science was purposefully designed to withstand the challenges posed by a hurricane-prone area and a city grappling with the consequences of rising sea levels. The foundation of the site and its open parking area are elevated to 9 feet and 6 inches above sea level. This design choice places the first floor of the building at a considerable height of 21 feet and 8 inches above sea level, surpassing the necessary requirements by more than 50%. Anything situated below this first level, including storage areas behind the scenes, is protected by a foundation constructed from waterproof concrete, with enclosed spaces further safeguarded by water-tight storm surge doors.

The Aquarium at Frost Science consists of six substantial aquatic systems and various smaller environments, all of which support a diverse range of aquatic life, spanning from sharks to shrimp to alligators. The museum employs closed aquarium systems, which means that although they draw water from nearby Biscayne Bay to supply natural seawater to their exhibits, they do not release used water back into the bay. Instead, this used water is routed to a sewage treatment facility to prevent the introduction of diseases or parasites into the wild ecosystem, where it could harm native fish.

To ensure pristine water quality, the museum times the water intake with incoming tides. They pump in 35,000 gallons of seawater at a time through a large pipe located a few hundred yards away at the sea wall of Biscayne Bay. This water is then stored in a raw water basin and undergoes sand filtration to enhance clarity, followed by ozone filtration to eliminate parasites and bacteria. The result is exceptionally clear and high-quality saltwater, which is used in various aquatic habitats.

REGION: CENTRAL EAST DISTRICT   **COUNTY:** VOLUSIA   **CITY:** DAYTONA BEACH

DATE VISITED: **WHO I WENT WITH:**

RATING: ☆ ☆ ☆ ☆ ☆   **WILL I RETURN?**   YES / NO

The Ponce de Leon Inlet Light Station proudly boasts Florida's tallest lighthouse and is widely recognized as one of the best-preserved historic light stations in the nation. For over 130 years, its powerful beacon has provided essential guidance to mariners.

In the 1920s, the area was renamed Ponce de Leon Inlet. Initially, the Ponce de Leon Inlet Light Station was operated by the United States Light House Establishment (USLHE). From 1887 to 1939, dedicated lighthouse keepers diligently ensured that the tower's light was illuminated every evening and remained so throughout the night, regardless of the challenging weather conditions. Much like the legendary Greek couriers described by the ancient historian Herodotus, these keepers were unwavering in their commitment: "Neither snow, nor rain, nor heat, nor gloom of night" could deter them from their duty.

For over half a century, the USLHE (later known as the US Lighthouse Service/USLHS) maintained the light station. However, in 1939, with the dissolution of the Lighthouse Service, responsibility for the light station was transferred to the United States Coast Guard. Even though civilian keepers were no longer responsible for daily maintenance, the Ponce Inlet Lighthouse remained a manned facility until its automation in 1953.

With the beacon no longer requiring daily attention from resident keepers, the Coast Guard reclassified the Ponce Inlet Light Station as an unmanned facility. Personnel stationed there were reassigned to other duties, and the operation of the beacon was handed over to the Aids to Navigation (ATON) team at the Coast Guard station in New Smyrna Beach. Unfortunately, the lack of proper maintenance and the harsh coastal environment took a toll on the historic lighthouse. By the late 1960s, this once-immaculate facility, which had been a source of pride for so many years, had fallen into a state of advanced deterioration.

The Ponce Inlet Lighthouse continued to serve as an active aid for navigation until 1970 when a newly installed pole-mounted light on the south side of the inlet made it possible to decommission the old lighthouse. After being decommissioned, the light station was left abandoned, exposed to various destructive forces. These included the ravages of wind and weather, acts of vandalism, theft, and more.

During this period of neglect, the light station endured significant damage, including fires set in the tower's counter-weight well, break-ins by vagrants into the keeper's dwellings, theft of valuable artifacts, the burning down of the oil storage building, and even pieces of the rusted iron from the tower being thrown onto the roofs of nearby buildings. In 1972, the site was classified as surplus property by the Department of the Interior, and there were discussions about potentially demolishing the historic light station.

Concerned by the rapid deterioration of the Light Station and the rumors of its possible demolition, a group of residents from Ponce Inlet took action. They urged the newly incorporated Town of Ponce Inlet to acquire the property to save it from destruction. The town agreed to their request, but with one important condition: a non-profit organization had to be established to assume full responsibility for the restoration, preservation, and management of the site, with little or no financial burden on the municipality.

On June 2, 1972, the Department of the Interior officially transferred ownership of the Lighthouse Reservation to the Town of Ponce Inlet. Shortly thereafter, the non-profit 501(c)(3) organization known as the Ponce de Leon Inlet Lighthouse Preservation Association was officially incorporated. This all-volunteer group immediately embarked on the daunting task of restoring the light station's buildings, grounds, and tower to their former glory. Funding sources for the Association's early restoration efforts were limited, relying on donations, small admission fees of 25 cents, and the sale of homemade souvenirs. With little financial support from the local, state, or federal levels, the Association collected materials for restoration from various sources, including local businesses, members' garages, and even discarded items. The dedication of these individuals in achieving what they did with such limited resources was truly remarkable.

The Ponce de Leon Inlet Lighthouse Preservation Association has evolved significantly from its modest beginnings to its current status as a professional non-profit organization supported by volunteers. It has gained recognition for its groundbreaking achievements in historic preservation, restoration of Fresnel lenses, public education, and museum development, making it one of the most esteemed lighthouse preservation groups in the nation.

While the museum's day-to-day operations are overseen by professional staff, the governance of the organization remains the exclusive responsibility of the Association's all-volunteer Board of Trustees. This board consists of eleven dedicated Ponce Inlet residents who are committed to preserving and sharing the history of the Ponce Inlet Lighthouse. They receive support in their efforts from an Advisory Committee made up of like-minded town residents. Collaborating with museum staff and program volunteers, the Board of Trustees and Advisory Committee work tirelessly to fulfill the Association's enduring mission, originally established by its founding members nearly half a century ago, which is to safeguard and promote the maritime and social history of the Ponce Inlet Lighthouse.

Since its inception, the Preservation Association has maintained a steadfast commitment to the ongoing restoration and upkeep of this historic property. It is renowned not only for its expertise in restoration but also for its dedication to advancing the cause of historic preservation. All restoration work at the Light Station is carried out by qualified staff who have undergone extensive training in historic masonry restoration and 19th-century construction techniques. Moreover, all restoration efforts at the Light Station strictly adhere to the Federal Standards for Rehabilitation of Historic Properties.

Over the past five decades, the Association has successfully carried out preservation and restoration projects at the historic light station, amounting to millions of dollars in value. Additionally, they have enhanced the site by constructing several modern structures, including the Ayres Davies Lens Exhibit Building, the Gift Shop and Conference Building, the Rest Room/Group Entrance Facility, and the Administration Building. Trained Association employees and licensed contractors have painstakingly restored the once deteriorated keepers' dwellings and outbuildings, transforming them into one of the nation's most comprehensive lighthouse museums. Remarkably, all these improvements have been executed by the Preservation Association with minimal or no cost incurred by the residents of the Town of Ponce Inlet, who are granted free admission.

While the organization has sought government grants in the past to support major projects, the light station has operated independently without any tax-funded assistance from the local, state, or federal levels for more than a decade. The organization's remarkable achievements have been primarily funded through its own resources. The museum's annual operating budget, covering 100% of its expenses, is generated internally through the sale of merchandise in the gift shop, daily admission fees, annual membership fees, and contributions from private individuals and corporations.

With an annual visitor count of nearly 150,000 people, the Ponce de Leon Inlet Light Station continues to be a central pillar of the Halifax area's tourism-driven economy. Recognized as Daytona's Best Learning Experience by the Daytona Beach Area Convention and Visitors Bureau, the Preservation Association is held in high regard not only for its exhibits and historic structures but also for its outstanding educational programs. These educational programs, provided free of charge to all Volusia County school groups, have garnered praise from educators in the local community and have set a standard for lighthouse organizations across the country.

The Ponce de Leon Inlet Light Station received the official designation of a National Historic Landmark in 1998. This recognition is quite prestigious, as only 11 other lighthouses out of approximately 760 surviving ones in the United States have received this honor.

National Historic Landmarks (NHLs) are important historic properties that hold significant cultural value and contribute to the understanding of the nation's heritage. There are currently 2,618 NHLs across the United States, encompassing a wide range of historic sites, buildings, structures, objects, and districts. The Secretary of the Interior designates these places as exceptional because they play a vital role in illustrating the history of the United States.

Earning the status of a National Historic Landmark is a rigorous process. First, a property must meet strict qualification criteria set by the Department of the Interior to even be considered for nomination. Those that qualify must then undergo a comprehensive National Historic Landmark Study, conducted by the organization that nominates them. These studies are typically part of a larger thematic assessment that evaluates the comparative significance of numerous resources. The National Park Service, for instance, includes lighthouses and other navigation aids in its thematic study called "The Maritime Heritage of the United States."

SALVADOR DALI MUSEUM

REGION: CENTRAL WEST DISTRICT   **COUNTY:** PINELLAS   **CITY:** ST. PETERSBURG

DATE VISITED: **WHO I WENT WITH:**

RATING: ☆ ☆ ☆ ☆ ☆   **WILL I RETURN?**   YES / NO

Since its inauguration in 1982, The Dalí Museum in St. Petersburg, has held a special place in the Tampa Bay area's fine arts scene, unofficially serving as its heart. The introduction of a new building in January 2011 played a significant role in the area's cultural revival, marked by a surge in artistic institutions and venues that both residents and visitors can enjoy.

The mission of The Dalí Museum is to curate and preserve a meticulously chosen collection of Salvador Dalí's artwork, ensuring that his legacy endures for future generations. Furthermore, through events, exhibitions, and experiences inspired by Dalí, the museum actively contributes to the cultural vitality of our community and the wider world.

Museum collections often have various themes, such as styles, media, historical periods, or the life and work of a particular individual. The Dalí Museum, however, stands as an exemplar of an "Artist's Museum." It is dedicated to celebrating the vision, talent, and life of one extraordinary person.

The Dalí Museum is dedicated to commemorating the life and artistic contributions of Salvador Dalí (1904-1989). It showcases works from every phase of the artist's career, encompassing more than 2,400 pieces spanning various mediums and moments of his creative activity. The collection features a wide range of art, including oil paintings, original drawings, book illustrations, artists' books, prints, sculptures, photographs, manuscripts, and an extensive archive of documents. Founded with the initial collection gathered by A. Reynolds and Eleanor Morse, the museum has continually expanded its holdings, celebrating the life and artistry of one of the most influential and innovative artists in history.

The Morses, A. Reynolds and Eleanor, developed a fascination with Salvador Dalí's work after visiting a traveling Dalí retrospective at the Cleveland Museum of Art in 1942, organized by the Museum of Modern Art in New York. Their first acquisition of a Dalí painting, "Daddy Longlegs of the Evening, Hope!" (1940), occurred on March 21, 1943. This marked the beginning of a series of acquisitions that would culminate in the formation of the most prominent collection of Dalí's work in America, 40 years later. On April 13, 1943, the Morses met Salvador Dalí and his wife Gala in New York, initiating a long and fruitful friendship.

Initially, the Morses displayed their Dalí paintings in their own home, but by the mid-1970s, they decided to donate their entire collection. The attention-grabbing Wall Street

Journal article titled "U.S. Art World Dillydallies Over Dalí" drew the St. Petersburg, Florida community's interest, prompting them to rally and bring the collection to the area. Consequently, the Dalí Museum in St. Petersburg, Florida, was inaugurated in 1982. The museum's impressive new building, which officially opened on January 11, 2011, significantly enhances its ability to safeguard and exhibit the collection, welcome the public, and provide education and enjoyment. On a broader scale, it serves as a place of beauty that, much like Dalí's art, is devoted to fostering understanding and transformation.

A remarkable new Dalí Museum building was unveiled on January 11, 2011. Designed by architect Yann Weymouth of HOK, this structure seamlessly blends rationality with fantasy: it features a straightforward rectangular shape with hurricane-resistant walls that are 18 inches thick, from which emerges a large, free-form geodesic glass structure known as the "enigma." The Enigma, composed of 1,062 triangular pieces of glass, reaches a height of 75 feet at its tallest point, serving as a twenty-first-century homage to the dome that graces Dalí's museum in Spain. Inside, the museum boasts another unique architectural element—a spiral staircase, reminiscent of Dalí's fascination with spirals and the double helical form of the DNA molecule.

Situated on the Tampa Bay waterfront, The Dalí's garden offers a distinctive environment that promotes both learning and serenity. The Mathematical Garden provides a hands-on experience for students to understand the connection between mathematics and nature while encouraging exploration and well-being.

Visitors enter the museum through The Dalí Museum Store, which features the world's most extensive collection of Dalí-inspired merchandise. Café Gala offers Spanish-themed light cuisine and provides both indoor and outdoor seating. The museum's theater regularly screens a short film about Dalí, occasionally showcasing other films, and serves as the venue for special concerts and lectures. Families can engage in self-guided activities in the Stavros Education Classroom, while the Raymond James Community Room serves as a space for community-oriented exhibitions, including the renowned Student Surrealist Exhibitions, as well as various museum programs and private events.

The Dalí Museum's center for avant-garde art serves as a unique resource for scholars, art professionals, collectors, and students interested in the study of Salvador Dalí, Surrealism, and the avant-garde.

All of the galleries are located on the third floor. An overlook area is positioned between the two primary wings of the museum, offering a breathtaking view of the gardens and waterfront through the Enigma structure. The James Family Wing houses the permanent collection of Dalí's works, while the Hough Family Wing hosts special exhibitions.

SANIBEL ISLAND

REGION: SOUTHWEST DISTRICT   **COUNTY:** LEE   **CITY:** SANIBEL

DATE VISITED: **WHO I WENT WITH:**

RATING: ☆ ☆ ☆ ☆ ☆   **WILL I RETURN?**   YES / NO

Sanibel is both an island and a city located in Lee County, Florida, within the United States. As of the 2020 census, the population of Sanibel was recorded at 6,382 residents. The island is part of the Cape Coral-Fort Myers, Florida Metropolitan Statistical Area. Sanibel Island, often referred to simply as Sanibel, makes up the entirety of the city. It is categorized as a barrier island, consisting mainly of sand on the sheltered side of the more solid coral-rock formation of Pine Island.

The majority of the city is situated at the eastern end of Sanibel Island. Following the construction of the Sanibel causeway in May 1963, replacing the need for a ferry, the city was formally incorporated in 1974. At that time, residents took charge of development control by establishing the Sanibel Comprehensive Land Use Plan, aimed at maintaining a delicate balance between development and the preservation of the island's natural ecology. In September 2022, the causeway suffered significant damage from Hurricane Ian.

Sanibel is a well-known tourist destination, largely due to its convenient access via the causeway. It is celebrated for its picturesque shell beaches and abundant wildlife refuges. More than half of the island is designated as wildlife refuges, with the largest being the J. N. "Ding" Darling National Wildlife Refuge. Additionally, Sanibel is home to the Sanibel Historical Village and several museums, including the Bailey-Matthews National Shell Museum.

Sanibel and Captiva originally formed as a single island approximately 6,000 years ago. The first known inhabitants of the area were the Calusa people, who arrived around 2,500 years ago. The Calusa established themselves as a powerful indigenous nation in Southwest Florida, mainly through their advanced system of canals and waterways, facilitating trade and transportation. Sanibel was an important Calusa settlement until the decline of their empire, which occurred shortly after the arrival of European settlers.

During the 1700s, Cuban fishermen would periodically journey from their homes to set up fishing camps along the Gulf Coast, known as "ranchos." Some of these camps were established on Sanibel Island.

In 1765, the first documented reference to a harbor on Sanibel appeared on a map as "Puerto de S. Nibel" (the interchangeability of "v" and "b" is noted). Therefore, the island's name may have evolved from "San Nibel." Alternatively, it is believed by many that the name may have originated from "(Santa) Ybel," which is preserved in the old place name "Point Ybel," where the Sanibel Island Light is situated. However, the exact origins of this name remain a matter of speculation. One theory suggests that it might have been named by Juan Ponce de León in honor of Queen Isabella I of Castile. The island may indeed have been named after this queen or the saint she was named after, either by Ponce de León or by someone else at a later time. Another legend attributes the name to Roderigo Lopez, the first mate of José Gaspar (known as Gasparilla), who supposedly named it after his beautiful lover named Sanibel, whom he had left behind in Spain. However, it's important to note that much of the lore surrounding Gasparilla is considered apocryphal, as the aforementioned references to variations of the name predate the supposed reign of the buccaneer.

Sanibel is not the sole island in the vicinity that features prominently in the legends associated with Gaspar; Captiva, Useppa, and Gasparilla are also intertwined with these tales. Another story involving Sanibel revolves around Gaspar's ally-turned-rival, Black Caesar, who was believed to be a former Haitian slave that escaped during the Haitian Revolution and turned to a life of piracy. According to folklore, Black Caesar arrived in the Gulf of Mexico during the War of 1812 to avoid British interference. In the Gulf, he formed a friendship with Gasparilla, who permitted him to establish himself on Sanibel Island. Eventually, Gasparilla discovered that Black Caesar had been pilfering from him and chased him away, albeit after his ill-gotten treasure had been buried.

In 1832, the Florida Peninsular Land Company established a settlement on Sanibel, spelled "Sanybel" at the time. However, the colony failed to thrive and was deserted by 1849. This group initially sought the construction of a lighthouse on the island. After the enactment of the Homestead Act in 1862, the island was resettled, and once again, there was a request for a lighthouse. The Sanibel Island Lighthouse was completed in 1884, but the community remained relatively small.

In May 1963, a causeway connecting Sanibel and Captiva to the mainland was opened, resulting in a rapid population increase. The City of Sanibel implemented new development restrictions after its incorporation, and these regulations were challenged by developers but without success. Currently, the only structures on the island taller than two stories date from before 1974. In 2007, a new causeway was completed to replace the aging 1963 spans, which were not designed to handle heavy loads or a large number of vehicles. The new bridge includes a "flyover" span high enough to allow sailboats to pass underneath, replacing the old bridge's bascule drawbridge section. The original bridge was dismantled, and its remnants were submerged in the water to create artificial reefs in the Gulf of Mexico.

Sanibel's beaches are a major draw for visitors from across the globe, largely due to the frequent appearance of large quantities of seashells. Many sand dollars can also be found along these shores. The reason for the abundance of shells on Sanibel is attributed to the island's unique geological features. Sanibel is considered a barrier island, part of a vast plateau that extends far into the Gulf of Mexico. This plateau acts like a shelf, allowing seashells to accumulate.

Additionally, Sanibel possesses an unusual east-west orientation, unlike most islands that run north-south. This orientation contributes to the island's sandy beaches and shell-rich shores.

The discovery of an elegant brown-spotted shell of a Junonia on a Sanibel beach is a remarkable and celebrated event, often resulting in individuals being featured in local newspapers. While Junonia volutes are relatively common in deep waters, they rarely wash up on the beach. Finding a whole Junonia shell on the shore is considered a prized treasure. Junonia shells can be purchased at local shell shops and can also be seen on display at the Bailey-Matthews National Shell Museum, in some glass display tables at the Sanibel Cafe, or at the Sanibel Shell Fair held in early March.

Throughout the year, many people flock to Sanibel's beaches to collect seashells, a popular activity known locally as the "Sanibel Stoop." Beaches are plentiful all around the island, including those along the Sanibel causeway, which are excellent for fishing and windsurfing. However, parking on Sanibel itself can be quite limited, particularly during the peak season, making it a challenge to find a convenient parking spot.

Lighthouse Beach derives its name from the famous Sanibel Lighthouse and features a popular fishing pier and nature trails. Bowman's Beach, on the other hand, is the most secluded beach on the island, devoid of visible hotels, and offers a pristine and tranquil atmosphere.

Sanibel and Captiva Islands have been recognized by Barron's as one of the "10 Best Places for Second Homes."

SIESTA BEACH

REGION: SOUTHWEST DISTRICT **COUNTY:** SARASOTA **CITY:** SARASOTA

DATE VISITED: **WHO I WENT WITH:**

RATING: ☆ ☆ ☆ ☆ ☆ **WILL I RETURN?** YES / NO

Siesta Beach, also known as Siesta Key Beach, is situated on Siesta Key, a barrier island. What sets Siesta Beach apart from many other beaches is the composition of its sand. While other beaches often consist mainly of crushed coral, Siesta Beach's sand is composed of 99% quartz, with a significant portion originating from the Appalachian Mountains. Over time, natural processes removed feldspar and mica from the rock, leaving behind nearly pure quartz sand. This unique sand is so reflective that it remains pleasantly cool even on scorching days. Geologists from Harvard University estimate that the sand found on Siesta Beach and Crescent Beach, both located on Siesta Key, is millions of years old, originating in the Appalachian Mountains and being transported by rivers before settling along the shores of Siesta Key.

The southern section of Siesta Beach is sometimes referred to as Crescent Beach. This portion extends to the seawall and includes an area known as Point of Rocks, which features coral formations and a thriving marine ecosystem.

Siesta Beach is not only renowned for its length but also for its remarkable width, particularly around the Siesta Key Beach Pavilion area. The beach is so broad that the city has installed walking mats to assist beachgoers in reaching the shoreline. Once there, visitors can walk on firmer wet sand, enhancing their overall beach experience.

Siesta Beach is an ideal destination for those seeking a relaxing and enjoyable beach experience. Whether individuals are looking to rent a beachfront house, discover excellent dining options, or simply bask in the sun and sand, Siesta Beach offers a comprehensive range of amenities. Siesta Beach, situated in Sarasota, Florida, is a stunning and award-winning beach.

Siesta Beach caters to a diverse audience, offering something for everyone. Whether individuals want to unwind on the shore or engage in various beach activities, Siesta Beach provides all the necessary resources to help plan a perfect day. Visitors can choose to rent a beach umbrella or chair, enjoy a meal at one of the many restaurants, or participate in a game of beach volleyball. Regardless of the choice made, Siesta Beach offers an ideal setting for spending quality time with family and friends.

For those dreaming of the perfect vacation destination, Siesta Key beckons with paradise-like offerings. Siesta Key boasts breathtaking beaches, vibrant sunsets, and warm hospitality, making it the ultimate destination for relaxation and rejuvenation. In terms of accommodations, visitors will find themselves spoiled for choice, with a wide array of beautiful vacation rentals available. From cozy beachfront cottages to luxurious waterfront villas, Siesta Key offers options to suit every taste and budget.

Before the 20th century, Siesta Key was a sparsely populated area known by various names such as Clam Island, Little Sarasota Island, or Sarasota Key. The island was not connected to the city of Sarasota in any way, and the sole means of access was by boat. It was characterized by dense vegetation, a variety of snakes (including venomous species like rattlesnakes, copperheads, water moccasins, and coral snakes), sand fleas, wildcats, and wild boars.

This isolation continued until 1906 when Mr. and Mrs. Roberts established the Roberts' Inn, later known as the Siesta Inn. This hotel gained popularity among people seeking refuge from the cold northern winters. The reputation of Mrs. Roberts' cooking, particularly her seafood dishes, attracted many guests. Mr. Roberts collaborated with Mayor Harry Higel to create the Siesta Land Company, which developed Siesta Village and officially renamed the island Siesta Key approximately a year after opening the hotel. In 1914, Higel opened his own hotel called Higelhurst and used his boat to transport guests to and from the city. Higel also played a pivotal role in persuading the Army Corps of Engineers to construct a bridge connecting the key to the city of Sarasota. This bridge was completed in 1917, linking the northern part of the key to the city. In 1927, a second bridge was constructed at the southern end of the key on Stickney Point.

In 1954, Sarasota County acquired its first parcel of land on the key to establish a public beach. Gradually, Siesta Key's population began to grow, and it now attracts approximately 350,000 tourists annually.

In 2018, the beaches of Siesta Key were affected by Karenia brevis, a harmful algal bloom commonly known as red tide. This event resulted in the accumulation of several tons of dead fish on the beach at different times, most of which were removed during the early morning hours. The toxins produced by red tide not only pose respiratory discomfort to humans but also have detrimental effects on marine life, including fish, turtles, and manatees. In the past, red tide events have lasted up to eighteen months.

SILVER SPRINGS STATE PARK

REGION: CENTRAL WEST DISTRICT   **COUNTY:** MARION   **CITY:** SILVER SPRINGS

DATE VISITED: **WHO I WENT WITH:**

RATING: ☆ ☆ ☆ ☆ ☆   **WILL I RETURN?** YES / NO

The main spring is surrounded by serene gardens and historic structures reminiscent of the days when Silver Springs was a major destination for Northerners arriving by steamship. At the park, you can see one of the largest and best-loved springs in America by taking the famous glass-bottomed boats. The park continues to be a favorite site and location for the annual Springsfest celebrating the protection and restoration of all of Florida's springs and waterways. Silver Springs is part of the Great Florida Birding & Wildlife Trail's east section. In the upland habitats of the park, you may see wild turkey, quail, hairy woodpecker, and American kestrel. Armadillos, deer, turkey, fox, Sherman fox squirrel, and gopher tortoises are common in the park. Less frequently seen are coyotes, bobcats, and the Florida black bear. The river is home to alligators, turtles, and many species of fish.

The park has limited opportunities for bicycling on paved trails. There are many trails for mountain biking. Silver Springs State Park has 4.5-miles of dedicated off-road bicycling trails suitable for fat tire bicycles. Additionally, mountain bicycles may use another 10-miles of hiking trails. At the campground and museum entrance, the paved road between the ranger station and the picnic area is 1.1 miles and offers opportunities for wildlife viewing beneath the shade of pines and scenic oak trees. Bicycling is permitted at the main entrance, on the sidewalks around the springs and gardens. However, due to potential congestion, bicycling is not permitted in the immediate vicinity of the entrance promenade, downtown, or the glass-bottom boat area. Additional opportunities for bicycling on paved trails are available on the nearby Marjorie Harris Carr Cross Florida Greenway. All cyclists are advised to wear helmets, and Florida law requires helmets to be worn by cyclists 16 years of age and younger. The entrance to the equestrian trails can be found on State Road 40 near the intersection with State Road 326, 1.3 miles east of the main entrance.

The Fort King Paddling Trail allows visitors to take their canoe or kayak on a leisurely 1.1-mile round-trip loop around Ross Allen Island. There are no motorboat launches available inside the park. However, a launch is available downstream at Ray Wayside County Park. Admission fees may apply.

The park has 59 spacious sites on two camping loops that easily accommodate large camping units with a maximum recreational vehicle length of 50 feet. Each site offers access to water and electricity with a recently upgraded 50-amp connection. All sites include a fire pit, grill and picnic table. The park has a separate dump station for water tanks. Well-behaved pets are allowed in the campground, but not in the cabins or cabin areas. Set close to the Silver River, the primitive group camping area is for organized groups only, with preference given to youth groups. Many picnic tables are available at picnic pavilions and throughout the grounds of the park at the main entrance and the camping entrance.

SOUTH BEACH

REGION: SOUTHEAST DISTRICT   **COUNTY:** MIAMI-DADE   **CITY:** MIAMI

DATE VISITED: **WHO I WENT WITH:**

RATING: ☆ ☆ ☆ ☆ ☆   **WILL I RETURN?** YES / NO

If you want to experience the true essence of Miami, visit South Beach. This Miami Beach neighborhood, often referred to as SoBe, is inhabited by over 40,000 residents and attracts visitors from around the globe. Located just a short 10 to 15-minute drive from downtown Miami, South Beach offers something for everyone. Whether you're into an active lifestyle with activities like yoga, biking, and vegan dining or fascinated by the glitzy and glamorous shopping, architecture, and nightlife, South Beach has it all.

South Beach, commonly known as SoBe, is a neighborhood situated in Miami Beach, Florida. It is located east of Miami, between Biscayne Bay and the Atlantic Ocean, encompassing the southern part of Miami Beach below Dade Boulevard.

South Beach was the first section of Miami Beach to be developed, with construction beginning in the 1910s. The development efforts of individuals such as Carl G. Fisher, the Lummus Brothers, and John S. Collins, who built the Collins Bridge, played a significant role in establishing this area as a vital land link between mainland Miami and the beaches.

Over the years, South Beach has undergone various changes, both natural and artificial, including a thriving regional economy, increased tourism, and the destruction caused by the 1926 hurricane.

Originally, South Beach was farmland, with the Lum brothers purchasing 165 acres for coconut farming in 1870. In 1886, Charles Lum built the first house on the beach. John Collins took control of the plantation in 1894 and used it for farming, discovering fresh water on the land. In 1912, the Lummus Brothers acquired 400 acres of Collins' land with the aim of building an oceanfront city of modest single-family residences. Collins began constructing a bridge from Miami to Miami Beach in 1913, but due to financial constraints, he couldn't complete it. In the same year, Carl G. Fisher, a successful entrepreneur, arrived at South Beach with a vision of establishing it as an independent and successful city separate from Miami. It was also the year when the famous restaurant, Joe's Stone Crab, opened. Fisher loaned money to Collins to finish the bridge, which was completed in 1913 and later replaced by the Venetian Causeway.

On March 26, 1915, Collins, Lummus, and Fisher incorporated the Town of Miami Beach. In 1920, the County Causeway (now known as the MacArthur Causeway) was completed. The Lummus brothers sold their oceanfront property to the city, which is now known as Lummus Park.

In the 1920s, the Miami Beach land boom brought significant growth to South Beach. The main streets, such as 5th Street, Alton Road, Collins Avenue, Washington Avenue, and Ocean Drive, became accessible for automobile traffic. The population continued to grow, and notable individuals built homes in the area.

Until the mid-1920s, South Beach had anti-Semitic covenants that excluded Jews from living or staying in certain neighborhoods. These policies targeted Jewish property owners, tourists, and tenants through racial covenants in property deeds and hotel policies.

In the 1930s, an architectural revolution brought Art Deco, Streamline Moderne, and Nautical Moderne styles to South Beach, making it a hub of Streamline Moderne Art Deco architecture.

The 1940s saw the beach's population reach 28,000, and tourism increased after the attack on Pearl Harbor. In the 1960s and 1980s, South Beach became known as a retirement community, and drug-related activities also surfaced during this period.

Barbara Baer Capitman and activists played a crucial role in preserving South Beach's unique Art Deco buildings, leading to the designation of the Miami Beach Architectural District in 1979.

In the late 1980s, a renaissance began in South Beach, attracting fashion industry professionals. Thomas Kramer's construction boom contributed to the gentrification of the area, turning it into a popular destination for the wealthy. The high-rise buildings and development faced criticism, but they also transformed the area into a pedestrian-friendly and low-crime neighborhood.

During both day and night, South Beach in Miami Beach is a vibrant entertainment destination, offering a wide array of nightclubs, restaurants, boutiques, and hotels. Tourists from various parts of the world, including Canada, Europe, Israel, and the entire Western Hemisphere, visit the area, with some even having permanent or second homes there. The diverse backgrounds of South Beach residents are evident in the many languages spoken.

One of the unique features of South Beach is the colorful and distinct lifeguard stands along the beach. After Hurricane Andrew, Architect William Lane contributed his design services, creating lifeguard towers that became symbols of the revitalized Miami Beach.

South Beach, along with a few other neighborhoods like Downtown and Brickell, is known for embracing a car-free lifestyle. Many residents prefer walking, cycling, using motorcycles, trolleys, buses, or taxis to navigate the urban and pedestrian-friendly neighborhood. Pedestrian streets like Lincoln Road, Ocean Drive, Washington Avenue, and Collins Avenue are popular for shopping, dining, and entertainment. Lincoln Road is exclusively for pedestrians, and Collins Avenue around 5th Street offers upscale retail options.

Automobile congestion is common in the area, making it often easier to get around on foot or by bicycle. Miami Beach has implemented bicycle initiatives with citywide bike parking and lanes, making cycling a popular choice for both residents and tourists. The Venetian Causeway serves as a well-used bicycle commuter route connecting South Beach to Downtown.

Public transportation plays a vital role in South Beach life. Although there are no direct Metrorail stations, numerous Metrobus lines connect South Beach to Downtown Miami and Metrorail. The Airport-Beach Express (Metrobus line 150) offers quick access to Miami International Airport from several South Beach bus stops, operating every 30 minutes from 6:00 a.m. to 11:00 p.m. daily.

The City of Miami Beach-operated trolley routes offer free rides throughout South Beach, connecting it to other major areas of Miami Beach. The South Beach Loop, Middle Beach Loop, and Collins Express serve various parts of the city, providing convenient transportation options for residents and visitors alike. All trolley lines operate from 8 a.m. to midnight on Sundays and from 6 a.m. to midnight on other days of the week.

Lincoln Road is a vibrant open-air pedestrian mall, known as South Beach's premier shopping destination. In the 1980s, it underwent a renaissance and transformed into an arts and cultural center, attracting visitors with its trendy and chic atmosphere. Running between 16th Street and 17th Street, Lincoln Road stretches from east to west, and in the past, it allowed automobile traffic. However, access for cars was restricted in the 1950s, with the western part reserved for pedestrians only. The renovation of the SunTrust building and the development of the 1111 Lincoln Road parking garage further enhanced the area.

Ocean Drive, located on the easternmost side of South Beach, runs from South Pointe Drive to 15th Street in a north-south direction. It embodies the iconic South Beach aesthetic that visitors often expect. This tourist hotspot is home to various restaurants, including popular spots like "A Fish Called Avalon," "Mango's," and the famous "Clevelander." Moreover, it is the site of the former oceanfront mansion of Gianni Versace.

Collins Avenue, located one block west of Ocean Drive, runs parallel to it and is also known as State Road A1A. This avenue is dotted with historic Art Deco hotels and is known for its vibrant nightlife, boasting nightclubs like Mynt and Rokbar.

Española Way, stretching from Collins Avenue to Pennsylvania Avenue, was conceived as "The Historic Spanish Village" in 1925, inspired by Mediterranean villages in France and Spain. Today, it features an array of restaurants, bars, art galleries, and shops.

Alton Road, situated 1-3 blocks from Biscayne Bay on the westside, serves as the primary north-south street. It hosts various local businesses, including dry cleaners, small furniture stores, grocery markets, and a mix of non-chain and fast-food restaurants. Once it crosses Michigan Avenue north of South Beach, Alton Road mainly becomes residential.

Washington Avenue is a famous street in South Beach, running parallel to Ocean and Collins. It is renowned for housing some of the world's largest and most popular nightclubs, like Cameo and Mansion. The street is bustling with traffic until the early morning during the "season," with club-goers enjoying the nightlife. In the 1990s, South Beach's nightclub scene experienced a boom, attracting nightclub moguls like Ingrid Casares, who had the singer Madonna among her investors. Besides its vibrant nightlife, Washington Avenue is home to various shops, hotels, and architectural landmarks like Temple Emanu-El.

The West Avenue Corridor extends from 5th Street to 17th Street, bordered by Alton Road and Biscayne Bay on the east side. Originally home to grand hotels like The Flamingo, The Fleetwood, and the Floridian in the 1920s, this area became popular among celebrities like Al Capone and wealthy vacationers. Over time, the hotels fell into disrepair, and the area was somewhat neglected. However, it has since transformed into a mixed-use residential neighborhood, featuring a variety of architectural styles, from art deco buildings to contemporary high-rises. Today, it is a desirable place to live, attracting residents, vacationers, and renters with its diverse housing options and close proximity to amenities, parks, shopping, and entertainment areas like Lincoln Road and Ocean Drive. The Shoppes at West Avenue, located at 10th Street and West Avenue, complements the residential community with various shops and a disguised parking garage. The neighborhood's appeal is further enhanced by its vicinity to other popular areas like South of Fifth, Sunset Harbor, Belle Isle, Venetian Islands, and North Bay Road.

Whether you opt to explore The Bass, a contemporary art museum in Miami established in 1964, located in a historic art deco building with a beautiful garden, or The Wolfsonian - FIU, a museum, library, and research center boasting an extensive art collection, South Beach has a museum that will pique your curiosity. If you're looking for something a bit more unconventional in the art world, The World Erotic Art Museum is a unique destination. It serves as a museum, library, and education center, focusing on the history of erotic art and showcasing a collection owned by Naomi Wilzig. You'll find a diverse range of artworks here, including paintings, drawings, photos, and sculptures, featuring renowned artists such as Salvador Dali, Picasso, Fernando Botero, and Rembrandt.

South Beach is a very dog-friendly destination, so if you're traveling with your furry companions, they can join in on the fun. Dogs are allowed on the boardwalk and Ocean Drive, as well as in most restaurants with outdoor seating. Many hotels, such as the W and 1 Hotel South Beach, also welcome dogs. If you want to take your dog to the beach, Haulover Beach Park is a short car ride away, and they are allowed to play and swim there until 3 p.m. daily.

When it comes to dining options, Planta South Beach offers vegan cuisine in a stunning setting, while Yardbird serves up delicious Southern-style dishes like mint juleps and fried chicken. For a taste of South Florida, Joe's Stone Crabs offers seasonal specialties like stone crabs, lobster, and key lime pie. If you're craving sushi, Katsuya is a reliable choice with fresh and impeccably presented dishes. And if you're in the mood for steak frites and people-watching, Prime 112 is the go-to spot. The Prime family of restaurants also includes Prime Italian, Prime Fish, and Big Pink, offering a variety of dining experiences to suit your preferences.

If you're up for some water adventures, you can rent stand-up paddleboards or kayaks and explore the Miami waters on your own. The calm waters, weather permitting, make it an enjoyable experience. Alternatively, you can opt for a guided tour, especially if it's your first time out on the water. Sunset excursions are popular and worth the extra cost. You can also take a two-hour guided tour to Monument Island Beach, a secluded spot accessible only by water.

For a relaxing time outdoors, take a leisurely stroll through the expansive 17-acre South Pointe Park. The park offers playgrounds, a dog park, a fishing pier, and more. Take a break for meditation or simply sit on one of the benches, listen to the ocean waves, and enjoy a good book. If you're in the mood for some physical activity, you can rollerblade or jog on the sidewalk. And when hunger strikes, you can walk to Smith and Wollensky, which offers great steaks, wine, and excellent views.

ST. ANDREWS STATE PARK

REGION: NORTHWEST DISTRICT   **COUNTY:** BAY   **CITY:** PANAMA CITY BEACH

DATE VISITED: **WHO I WENT WITH:**

RATING: ☆ ☆ ☆ ☆ ☆   **WILL I RETURN?**   YES / NO

Besides boasting a mile-and-a-half of pristine beaches for fishing and swimming, St. Andrews also offers the chance for visitors to stroll through pines and along dunes and coastal plant communities or stay overnight in the campground. There are two half-mile trails in the park to choose from: Heron Pond (takes you on a hike through the flatwood pine forest and out toward Sandy Point) and Gator Lake trails (provides a scenic lakeside view). A popular activity in the park is a leisurely ride along the park's two-mile paved road. To preserve the natural areas of the park, bicycles are limited to roadways and are not permitted on footpaths, boardwalks, or the trail that leads to the beach. All bicyclists are advised to wear helmets, and Florida law requires helmets to be worn by bicyclists 16 years of age and younger.

In the spring and summer, shuttles are offered from the park's mainland to Shell Island. Boaters enjoy access to St. Andrews Bay, Shell Island, and the inlet to the Gulf of Mexico. Fishing opportunities include deep-sea jetty and surf fishing. The fishing piers and jetty rocks provide excellent vantage points year-round. Catches include Spanish mackerel, redfish, flounder, sea trout, bonito, cobia, dolphin, and bluefish. All fishing within the park must comply with regulations regarding size, number, method of fishing, and season. A Florida saltwater fishing license is required. Other popular activities include kayaking, hiking, canoeing, picnic areas, scuba diving, snorkeling, swimming, wildlife viewing, and full camping facilities. The gulf side of the park is very popular for surfing. Kayaks are available during the summer season via the park's boat rental shack located just beside the boat ramp. Opportunities are unlimited from just paddling around Grand Lagoon or across the boat channel to Shell Island.

The West Loop of the campground is open for reservations (sites 93 through 158). This was formerly called the Pine Grove Campground. Most sites have a view of Lower Grand Lagoon. Each campsite is equipped with water, 30- and 50-amp electric, and sewer. Each campsite has a picnic table and grills. Trails, beaches, a boat launch, and concessions are located a short distance from the campground. Pets are welcome in the campground but are not permitted in swimming areas or buildings. A dump station is located on the entrance road to the campground. Laundry facilities are available. Youth camping is available for Scouts, faith groups, and other small nonprofit groups. The campground can accommodate up to 25 people. The campground has picnic tables, a fire pit, portable restroom and outdoor shower.

There are three picnic areas in the park: the jetties use area, gulf pier use area, and at the boat basin. The Gator Lake Trail and Overlook provide visitors with a beautiful vantage point for spotting alligators and a variety of waterfowl, wading birds, and other small animals. Throughout the interior of the park, you will see raccoons and white-tailed deer. The park is a popular migration stop for many species of birds and butterflies.

REGION: NORTHEAST DISTRICT	COUNTY: ST. JOHNS	CITY: ST. AUGUSTINE

DATE VISITED:	WHO I WENT WITH:

RATING: ☆ ☆ ☆ ☆ ☆   WILL I RETURN?   YES / NO

The St. Augustine Town Plan Historic District holds the prestigious status of being a U.S. National Historic Landmark District and encompasses the heart of the city with its colonial heritage. The district largely includes the original street plan of the city, which was enclosed within walls built between the 16th and early 19th centuries (although these walls no longer stand). Its boundaries are Cordova, Orange, and St. Francis Streets, as well as Matanzas Bay. The designation as a National Historic Landmark was granted in 1970, but the exact boundaries were officially defined in 1986.

Its historical significance dates back to Ponce de León's claim to La Florida in 1513. St. Augustine, established in 1565 by Don Pedro Menéndez de Avilés as a Spanish military base, soon flourished as a town around the fort and became the center of Spanish power in Florida. During the 16th, 17th, and 18th centuries, free blacks and slaves sought refuge in Florida, as the Spanish Crown offered safety to blacks who converted to Catholicism. Today, the district preserves the characteristic layout of a 16th-century Spanish Colonial walled town. The colonial buildings within the district primarily date from the period between 1703 and 1821. Its colonial history stretches back to 1822, when Spanish East Florida became part of the United States as a portion of the Florida Territory. The street plan of the city's core, featuring narrow streets, originated during the initial period of Spanish control, which ended in 1763 when Florida was ceded to Great Britain. Florida was later returned to Spain in 1784. Approximately half of the buildings in this district were constructed before 1925, with a considerable number designed in either Spanish Colonial or Moorish Revival architectural styles.

The district is adorned with several notable landmarks that trace their origins back to the Spanish settlement. One such landmark is the Castillo de San Marcos, located at the northeastern end of the district. It was built during the city's founding and remains a significant historical site. Another defining feature is the central plaza, which was established early on. Today, the plaza is graced by the Cathedral Basilica of St. Augustine, constructed during the second Spanish period in 1793–94, as well as a 1930s post office designed to resemble the original Spanish governor's palace it replaced. Further south in the district, visitors will find a cluster of some of the city's oldest surviving residences, including the González–Alvarez House (also known as the Oldest House, which is the oldest surviving house in the city) dating back to around 1723, and the Llambias House.

Notable buildings within the district include the Plaza de la Constitución, serving as the focal point of the colonial community on King Street. The Basilica Cathedral of St. Augustine, found at 36 Cathedral Place, incorporates the 1797 parish church and remains one of the oldest Catholic religious buildings in the United States.

Other significant landmarks include the Villa Zorayda, an exotic Moorish Revival residence featuring courtyards and towers, situated on King Street and dating back to 1883. Lastly, the Gothic Revival style Stanbury Cottage on St. George Street also adds to the district's architectural richness and historical value.

ST. GEORGE ISLAND

REGION: NORTHWEST DISTRICT   **COUNTY:** FRANKLIN   **CITY:** EASTPOINT

DATE VISITED: **WHO I WENT WITH:**

RATING: ☆ ☆ ☆ ☆ ☆   **WILL I RETURN?**   YES / NO

St. George Island, located in the Gulf of Mexico, is a picturesque barrier island stretching over 22 miles. Known for having some of the most pristine and tranquil beaches in Florida, St. George Island offers a wide range of activities for all its visitors. Notably, you won't find any tall buildings or high rises on this untouched island; instead, it boasts a relaxed atmosphere, stunning shorelines, and untouched natural beauty. The uncrowded beaches are ideal for family-friendly pursuits, including swimming, fishing, and paddling in the crystal-clear Gulf waters, as well as seashell collecting, building sandcastles, and simply relaxing on the sugar-white sands. If you're eager to immerse yourself in nature, explore St. George Island's unspoiled bay marshes, where you can encounter extraordinary wildlife and witness breathtaking sunset vistas. For those seeking adventure, there's the option to rent kayaks, boats, bicycles, or scooters to explore the island's diverse landscapes. St. George Island offers a variety of lodging options, from charming beach cottages to luxurious Gulf-front homes, as well as local hotels and inns.

Whether you're in search of a romantic weekend escape, a family-friendly vacation, or a tranquil haven for the winter season, St. George Island has something to offer everyone.

St. George Island boasts an assortment of art galleries, boutiques, and delightful shops stocked with beachwear, handcrafted treasures, jewelry, and unique gifts.

Bring your furry friend along and enjoy a fantastic time on St. George Island. Without a doubt, St. George Island is a perfect destination for pet owners, being one of the few pet-friendly beaches in Florida. Many vacation homes, stores, and restaurants extend a warm welcome to four-legged guests. There are numerous pet-friendly accommodations available, whether you prefer camping at the State Park, reserving a hotel room, or renting a villa or spacious home by the bay, beach, or somewhere in between.

Whether one is a novice angler or a seasoned fishing enthusiast, St. George Island is a paradise for both fishermen and fisherwomen. Casting a line into the bay promises catches such as sheepshead, speckled trout, flounder, whiting, redfish, and tripletail. On the Gulf side, anglers can anticipate hooking snapper, grouper, amberjack, sea bass, mackerel, mahi-mahi, cobia, and even sharks. St. George Island offers abundant opportunities for both inshore and offshore fishing. Whether you choose to fish from the shore, skim the shallows, or venture into deeper waters with a charter boat captain, the island has you covered. There are several bait and tackle shops on the island, as well as two public boat ramps. For those seeking adventure, numerous businesses on St. George Island rent kayaks, paddleboards, and boats. If you prefer guided experiences, consider chartering a fishing excursion with one of the island's experienced fishing and tour guides

For biking enthusiasts, St. George Island offers miles of scenic bike paths. The island features a six-mile paved trail that runs parallel to Gulf Beach Drive, the island's main road. Cyclists can explore the island and even ride all the way to St. George Island State Park. The park itself offers hiking trails and the opportunity to explore serene dunes, forests, and marshes, all teeming with local wildlife.

When it's time to dine, St. George Island boasts a variety of restaurants that serve fresh, locally sourced seafood. Enjoy beachfront dining with stunning Gulf views or opt for a casual bayside eatery where you can savor cocktails and delectable pub fare. If you're exhausted after a day of adventures, you can order dinner or lunch from one of the island's pizzerias. And if you prefer to cook your own meals at your vacation rental, St. George Island's two grocery stores stock everything you need, including specialty and gourmet items.

St. George Island is a nature lover's dream destination. At St. George Island State Park, situated on the eastern end of the island, visitors can explore nine miles of unspoiled shoreline, majestic dunes, bay forests, and salt marshes. The State Park offers a network of serene hiking trails, boardwalks, and observation platforms.

During early summer mornings, a walk along the beach might offer glimpses of nesting sea turtles. Be sure to visit the visitor center for a close look at the historic lighthouse, the Cape St. George Light.

St. George Island emerges as an idyllic haven for nature enthusiasts. Situated at the eastern tip of the island, St. George Island State Park beckons visitors with the allure of nine miles of untouched coastline, grand dunes, a bay forest, and serene salt marshes. Within the State Park, a network of tranquil hiking trails, boardwalks, and observation platforms awaits exploration.

Don't forget to pack your binoculars. Birdwatching is a popular pastime on St. George Island, where you may have the opportunity to spot various migratory birds using the island as a stopover during their journeys. There have even been rare sightings of a flamingo and a snowy owl.

Starting in early summer, loggerhead sea turtles arrive on the shore to create their nests and lay eggs along the beach. The hatchlings emerge at night and make their way to the Gulf, guided by the moonlight. During the nesting season in summer, visitors are encouraged to assist these baby turtles in safely reaching the sea by clearing the beach of all items, filling in any man-made holes in the sand, and turning off outdoor lights.

Throughout the year, St. George Island hosts a diverse range of live music events at various venues. Additionally, the island hosts several special events, including the annual Chili Charity Cook-Off every March, which draws over 5,000 chili enthusiasts to the island for a delectable culinary experience. During the summer and fall, the Rock By the Sea

Festival gathers the region's finest musicians to raise funds for charitable causes.

ST. PETERSBURG PIER

REGION: CENTRAL WEST DISTRICT   **COUNTY:** PINELLAS   **CITY:** ST. PETERSBURG

DATE VISITED: **WHO I WENT WITH:**

RATING: ☆ ☆ ☆ ☆ ☆   **WILL I RETURN?**   YES / NO

St. Petersburg boasts a rich history of piers, with several of these structures extending into Tampa Bay during the city's early years. Here's an overview of the city's storied pier heritage:

The city's very first pier was established in 1889, thanks to the efforts of railroad entrepreneur Peter Demens. The Railroad Pier, constructed by the Orange Belt Railway, stretched half a mile into Tampa Bay from the terminus of the railroad at the foot of 1st Ave S. This 3,000-foot-long pier was initially lined with warehouses and loading docks, but it quickly gained popularity among anglers and swimmers. As a result, a bathing pavilion and toboggan slide were added to the pier.

To compete with the Railroad Pier, boat builder D.F.S. Brantley constructed the 1,500-foot Brantley Pier, although it never achieved the same commercial success. A horse-drawn flat car was used to transport goods and passengers between the water's edge and moored ships at the head of the pier. The pier's 34-room bathing pavilion became a significant attraction. The Brantley Pier laid the groundwork for the tradition of piers along 2nd Ave NE. However, it was eventually replaced in 1906 by the Electric Pier.

Edwin H. Tomlinson built a 2,000-foot pier and an artesian well near the east end of 3rd Ave S. In 1908, Dr. Jessie F. Conrad visited and sampled the well water, which he found exceptional. Dr. Conrad liked it so much that he purchased the pier. He promoted the well as "The Fountain of Youth," and the water, containing substantial amounts of lithium, became highly sought after by visitors. Unfortunately, the pier was dismantled in 1927, and the Fountain of Youth is now located at 4th Ave and 1st St SE, providing regular tap water.

In the years leading up to World War I, the Electric Pier became a prominent tourist attraction and symbolized the new St. Petersburg. Renowned for its hundreds of electric lights and streetcar lines, the Electric Pier extended 3,000 feet into Tampa Bay. Publisher Frank Davis, who also owned the St. Petersburg Electric Light & Power Company and the St. Petersburg & Gulf Electric Railway, played a pivotal role in developing this pier, which became a major tourist draw. However, it was eventually demolished in 1914.

The Recreational Pier in St. Petersburg, which opened in December 1913, holds the distinction of being the first pier designed to accommodate automobiles. On January 1, 1914, a historic moment occurred when Tony Jannus conducted the world's inaugural flight for the first-ever airline, taking off from the Central Yacht Basin adjacent to the pier and crossing Tampa Bay to Tampa. The pier approach featured several early amenities, including a hangar for the first airline and future aviation activities, an indoor swimming pool known as the Spa, an aquarium (which later transformed into a history museum in 1922), and a dance hall and banquet facility. Over time, additional public facilities were introduced, such as Spa Beach, a sandwich shop, tennis courts, the Solarium for nude sunbathing, and a senior citizen's center. Unfortunately, the wooden pier sustained damage during the October 1921 hurricane and was subsequently replaced by the Million Dollar Pier in 1926.

The Million Dollar Pier, inaugurated in 1926, became a prominent attraction and social gathering spot for the city. Along with features like Spa Beach, a solarium, and bait houses, the pier incorporated a two-lane roadway, a streetcar line, an observation deck, and even housed the WSUN radio station. Architecturally, the Million Dollar Pier followed the popular styles of the 1920s in St. Petersburg, combining Spanish, Italian, and Moorish elements, thus contributing to the city's Mediterranean Revival architectural heritage. Regrettably, the Million Dollar Pier faced deterioration issues and was ultimately demolished in 1967.

The Inverted Pyramid, featuring its innovative and unconventional design, was constructed atop the Pier head dating back to 1926. This unique structure was envisioned and created by the renowned architect William Harvard, Sr. It was completed and made accessible to the public in 1973, carrying forward the tradition of an overwater public gathering place and a tourist attraction in downtown St. Petersburg for a span of four decades. Throughout its existence, it hosted three restaurants, snack bars, a miniature golf course, novelty shops, an aquarium, and offered breathtaking views of Tampa Bay. However, the Inverted Pyramid was closed to the public in 2013 to make room for the new St. Petersburg Pier.

The design of the new Pier was the result of extensive collaboration between the design team and the community to ensure that it would cater to the evolving needs of St. Petersburg's growing population. The St. Pete Pier District was planned to remain as vibrant and relevant in the next twenty, fifty, and even more years as it is today.

As a testament to its exceptional design, the Pier has garnered numerous prestigious awards from various regional, national, and international organizations. Notably, the Urban Land Institute honored the Pier with the 2022 ULI Global Awards for Excellence, a prestigious recognition highlighting outstanding new urban designs. The St. Pete Pier was one of just two designs in the United States to receive this accolade and one of only six globally. Additionally, in 2022, the Pier Approach received the International Architecture Award for Excellence, presented by the world's oldest and first global design awards program.

SUNKEN GARDENS

REGION: CENTRAL WEST DISTRICT   **COUNTY:** PINELLAS   **CITY:** ST. PETERSBURG

DATE VISITED: **WHO I WENT WITH:**

RATING: ☆ ☆ ☆ ☆ ☆   **WILL I RETURN?** YES / NO

The Sunken Gardens cover an area of 4 acres (1.6 hectares) and are well-established botanical gardens situated in the Historic Old Northeast neighborhood of St. Petersburg, Florida. You can find them at 1825 4th Street North. These gardens have been around for over a hundred years and hold the distinction of being one of the oldest tourist attractions alongside the road in the United States. Nowadays, they are managed by the City of St. Petersburg and are kept up with the help of volunteers.

The oldest existing museum in St. Petersburg is a botanical haven nestled within the bustling city. Sunken Gardens, which has been flourishing for a century, houses some of the most ancient tropical plants in the area. Winding pathways lead guests through a living assortment of over a thousand plant species, featuring tropical plants and vibrant flowers, along with well-maintained showcase gardens, enchanting waterfalls, a group of graceful flamingos, and a diverse array of previously rehomed tropical birds such as macaws and cockatoos. The Sunken Gardens are accessible to the public every day, but there's an entrance fee for visitors, and you can also opt for an annual membership.

The historical significance of Sunken Gardens lies in their representation of a typical commercial attraction from the 1930s in Florida, particularly on the west coast of the state. These gardens welcome the public for various educational programs, guided tours, and special events. Notably, they have been a popular venue for weddings for many decades, with ceremonies taking place on the Wedding Lawn and in the banquet facilities located in the Garden Room, providing a unique and picturesque garden backdrop.

In 1911, a plumber named George Turner Sr. made a significant purchase of 4.1 acres of land, which would later become a world-renowned botanical attraction. To transform this land, he employed an intricate network of clay tiles to drain what was originally known as Curlew Pond. This drainage process left behind nutrient-rich muck soil, which proved to be perfect for George's beloved hobby - gardening. The beauty of Mr. Turner's garden captivated his neighbors so much that by the early 1930s, he began charging fifteen cents for guided tours.

Mrs. Eula Turner, George's wife, shared her husband's passion for plants and played a pivotal role in establishing the gardens as a prominent landmark. Their dedication to horticulture was passed down through generations, with their children and grandchildren continuing the family legacy by creating this exceptional tropical garden, complete with its meandering ponds.

In 1999, the City of St. Petersburg acquired Sunken Gardens through funds obtained from a tax that had been approved by the voters. Staying true to the original vision, the City's aim is to safeguard this historically significant botanical garden and utilize it as a source of cultural and educational enrichment for the community.

Today, Sunken Gardens attracts thousands of visitors each year, offering them a peaceful and serene garden experience. The gardens cater to both local residents and tourists by providing guided garden tours, horticultural programs, and hosting special events. More than a century after George Turner Sr. first began nurturing his gardening passion, Sunken Gardens endures as a tranquil haven nestled right in the heart of St. Petersburg, serving as a timeless oasis for all to enjoy.

Being one of the few remaining roadside attractions in Florida, this historical treasure warrants some special attention when you visit. Visitors to Sunken Gardens are encouraged to stay on designated paths, avoid touching or climbing on plants and structures, and maintain a respectful distance from the animals while observing them. Please note that the gardens may close temporarily during unfavorable weather conditions.

TALLAHASSEE

REGION: NORTHWEST DISTRICT	COUNTY: LEON	CITY: TALLAHASSEE

DATE VISITED:	WHO I WENT WITH:

RATING: ☆ ☆ ☆ ☆ ☆   WILL I RETURN?   YES / NO

Tallahassee, pronounced as TAL-ə-HASS-ee, serves as the capital city of the state of Florida in the United States. It holds the distinction of being the county seat and the only officially incorporated municipality in Leon County. Tallahassee is situated in the central part of the northern panhandle region of Florida, approximately halfway between Pensacola to the west and Jacksonville to the east. Tallahassee assumed the role of Florida's capital, initially as part of the Florida Territory, back in 1824. As of 2022, the city's population stood at 201,731, making it the eighth-most populous city within the state of Florida. In 2018, the population of the broader Tallahassee metropolitan area reached 385,145. Tallahassee takes the lead as the largest city within the Florida Big Bend and Florida Panhandle region, serving as a primary hub for trade and agriculture in these areas, as well as in Southwest Georgia.

Tallahassee boasts a substantial student population, exceeding 70,000, making it a vibrant college town. It's home to prestigious institutions such as Florida State University, recognized as the nation's 19th-best public university according to U.S. News & World Report. Additionally, Florida A&M University, which holds the distinction of being the nation's top public historically black university according to the same report, contributes to the city's educational landscape. Tallahassee Community College, a sizable state college, primarily acts as a feeder school for Florida State University and Florida A&M.

As the state capital, Tallahassee hosts a variety of important government institutions, including the Florida State Capitol, the Supreme Court of Florida, the Florida Governor's Mansion, and nearly 30 state agency headquarters. The city is also notable for its abundance of law firms, lobbying organizations, trade associations, and professional groups, including the Florida Bar and the Florida Chamber of Commerce. Tallahassee is recognized as a regional hub for scientific research and is home to the National High Magnetic Field Laboratory. In 2015, it received the All-American City Award from the National Civic League for the second time, highlighting its community and civic achievements.

The area has a historical significance dating back to the exploration of Spanish adventurer Hernando de Soto, who camped in this region during the winter of 1539-1540. Initially, it was inhabited by the Apalachee people and later by the Creek peoples. Seven Franciscan missions were established in the area, with Fort San Luis serving as their headquarters in 1633. Unfortunately, during Queen Anne's War (1702-1713), Fort San Luis was destroyed in 1704 by forces led by Governor James Moore of Carolina.

When Florida became a U.S. territory in 1821, it had two capitals: St. Augustine and

Pensacola. Tallahassee, deriving its name from a Creek word meaning "old town," was chosen as the capital in 1824 due to its central location between the two existing capitals. The iconic capitol building, with its porticoed design, began construction in 1839 and later received its dome in 1902. It was eventually restored after a new skyscraper-style capitol was completed in 1977.

Notable early residents of Tallahassee included Prince Achille Murat, a nephew of Napoleon I, and his wife Catherine Willis, who was a great-grandniece of George Washington. During the American Civil War, Tallahassee was relatively distant from major battle zones and remained the only capital of a Confederate state east of the Mississippi River that was not captured by Union forces. There was an engagement on March 6, 1865, at Natural Bridge, located about 10 miles southeast of the city (now a state historic site), where local militia successfully repelled a Union advance toward Tallahassee.

Tallahassee serves as a significant trade and distribution hub for the surrounding regions engaged in lumbering, agriculture, and livestock. Additionally, the city plays a role in the industries of printing, publishing, electronic equipment manufacturing, and metal product production. Services, particularly those associated with government and the area's higher education institutions, constitute a substantial portion of the local economy.

Among the local attractions, you'll find the Tallahassee Museum of History and Natural Science, the Museum of Florida History, and the Columns, which is the city's oldest building dating back to 1830. The annual Springtime Tallahassee festival, held over a month from March to April, commemorates the city's founding.

Tallahassee is surrounded by natural treasures, including the Apalachicola National Forest to the southwest, Alfred B. Maclay State Gardens, and the Lake Jackson Mounds State Archaeological Site on the northern edge of the city. Further south, you'll discover Edward Ball Wakulla Springs State Park, and along Apalachee Bay lies the St. Marks National Wildlife Refuge.

THE BASS MUSEUM OF ART

REGION: SOUTHEAST DISTRICT   **COUNTY:** MIAMI-DADE   **CITY:** MIAMI

DATE VISITED: **WHO I WENT WITH:**

RATING: ☆ ☆ ☆ ☆ ☆   **WILL I RETURN?**   YES / NO

The Bass Museum of Art is a contemporary art institution. Its inception dates back to 1963 when it was founded and subsequently opened to the public in 1964. The museum's origins are closely tied to John Bass (1891-1978) and Johanna Redlich, who were immigrants from Vienna, Austria, residing in Miami Beach. John Bass, in addition to his role as President of the Fajardo Sugar Company of Puerto Rico, was an amateur journalist, artist (particularly known for his painting and etching), and a composer with published musical works. The couple had an extensive collection of both fine art and cultural artifacts, which included a substantial manuscript collection now housed in the Carnegie Hall Archives. In 1963, the Basses made a significant bequest to the City of Miami Beach, consisting of over 500 works that encompassed Old Master paintings, textiles, and sculptures. This generous donation came with the stipulation that a public Bass Museum of Art be established and maintained indefinitely.

The museum officially opened its doors on April 7, 1964, becoming the sole municipally operated art gallery in South Florida at the time. The city allocated $160,000 for the renovation of the museum building, which had previously housed the Miami Beach Public Library. John Bass played a pivotal role in leading the museum from its inception until his passing in 1978.

However, in 1969, concerns regarding the authenticity of many artworks within the Bass collection were raised, leading to a request for an independent appraisal by a group of concerned citizens, as reported by several publications. The Art Dealers Association conducted an assessment in September 1969 and concluded that the Bass collection featured "the most flagrant and pervasive mislabeling by any museum known to this association." Subsequently, in 1973, the Miami Beach City Council decided to close the John Bass Art Museum.

In 1980, the museum brought in art historian Diane Camber as the Executive Director. Over the following three decades, Camber worked diligently to professionalize the museum's operations, attain accreditation from the American Alliance of Museums (AAM), curate scholarly exhibitions, and successfully manage a capital campaign for expanding the museum, thereby transforming it into a significant cultural institution. Renovations took place in 2001, and in 2002, a 1,500 square meter (16,000 square feet) expansion designed by Arata Isozaki was unveiled, coinciding with the exhibition "Globe Miami Island."

In 2013, the Bass Museum announced a substantial $7.5 million grant from the City of Miami Beach to initiate a second phase of transformation and expansion. Consequently, the museum temporarily closed for construction in May 2015 and reopened on October 29, 2017. The $12 million expansion, designed by David Gauld, augmented the programmable space by nearly 50 percent. This expansion included the addition of four new galleries, each spanning 380 square meters (4,100 square feet), with Isozaki serving as a design consultant. As part of a rebranding effort, the museum dropped "Museum of Art" from its name.

In 2022, the Bass received $20.1 million in city-issued funds, as part of a municipal general obligation bond that was authorized by voters during the US midterm elections.

The Bass Museum integrates its original collection into a program of international contemporary exhibitions. The museum's permanent collection encompasses a diverse range of artistic categories, including European painting and sculpture spanning from the 15th century to the present day, textiles, tapestries, and ecclesiastical vestments and artifacts from the 7th to the 20th century, 20th and 21st-century art from North America, Latin America, Asia, and the Caribbean, as well as photographs, prints, drawings, and modern and contemporary architecture and design. It places a particular emphasis on the design history of Miami Beach, both pre- and postwar.

One of the unique features of the museum is the "Open Storage" gallery, which is dedicated to showcasing the museum's permanent collection. It hosts a series of rotating artist projects that engage with and respond to the collection. The first artist to intervene in this space was Pascale Marthine Tayou with his exhibition titled "Beautiful."

In the period from August 21, 2015, to July 17, 2016, a selection of artworks from the permanent collection was presented in an exhibition at the Lowe Art Museum at the University of Miami, titled "Dürer to Rubens: Northern European Art from the Bass Museum." This exhibition featured works in various media, including oil on canvas, tempera on panel, enamel on porcelain, and textiles.

In September 2016, The Bass initiated a ten-year program aimed at expanding the museum's holdings of international contemporary art within its permanent collection. This initiative commenced with two significant public art acquisitions: "Miami Mountain" (2016) by Ugo Rondinone and "Eternity Now" (2015) by Sylvie Fleury. In August 2017, the museum announced its third major acquisition for this initiative, "Petrified Petrol Pump (Pemex II)" (2011) by Allora & Calzadilla.

In 2017, the museum inaugurated its Creativity Center, which stands as the largest art museum education facility in Miami-Dade. This center is equipped with three classrooms and various adaptable spaces that are dedicated to facilitating a comprehensive curriculum of programs designed to engage individuals of all generations in the realm of art and creativity.

93

THE FLORIDA AQUARIUM

REGION: CENTRAL WEST DISTRICT   **COUNTY:** HILLSBOROUGH   **CITY:** TAMPA

DATE VISITED: **WHO I WENT WITH:**

        RATING: ☆ ☆ ☆ ☆ ☆   **WILL I RETURN?** YES / NO

The roots of The Florida Aquarium trace back to the Clearwater Marine Science Center (CMSC), a private non-profit educational organization located in Clearwater Beach, Florida, established in 1977. In 1985, the CMSC Board approved an expansion plan aimed at creating a world-class facility that could effectively compete in the Florida market. This move was driven by the aspiration to transform into a nationally recognized educational institution. Consequently, on December 12, 1986, The Florida Aquarium, Inc. was officially incorporated as a distinct not-for-profit entity.

After years of negotiations, meticulous planning, and design efforts, The Florida Aquarium finally opened its doors in Tampa on March 31, 1995. In its inaugural year of operation, it served one million residents and visitors to the Tampa Bay area, delivering a significant positive economic impact of $60 million to the local community.

Over the years, The Florida Aquarium has continually evolved, consistently improving the guest experience through the introduction of new and captivating animal ambassadors, innovative exhibits, entertainment options, and educational programming aligned with its mission. Throughout this journey, The Florida Aquarium has embraced its dual role as not just an educational institution but also a prominent leader in conservation efforts. Today, visitors can enjoy an immersive experience that both entertains and inspires, underscoring the institution's commitment to its mission and the community it serves.

The Florida Aquarium, operating as a 501(c)(3) non-profit organization, actively fulfills its role as a conservation-driven attraction with a multifaceted mission program encompassing conservation, research, education, and outreach. It operates with a primary focus on providing exemplary care to a diverse array of aquatic and terrestrial animals, extending a warm welcome to visitors to engage with and learn about these animals. The overarching objective is to raise awareness and inspire action for the conservation of species and their natural habitats.

In pursuit of the goal of "edutainment," guests are offered the opportunity to explore intricate ecosystems, interact with informative and interactive exhibits, and even embark on dolphin-watching excursions in Tampa Bay. Beyond being a mere tourist attraction, The Florida Aquarium is dedicated to safeguarding and rejuvenating our planet's aquatic environments. This commitment is translated into tangible conservation efforts, including groundbreaking research initiatives and rescue operations aimed at revitalizing Florida's coral reefs and sea turtle populations.

The layout of The Florida Aquarium's exhibits is thoughtfully designed to illustrate the journey of a single drop of water, starting from one of Florida's numerous freshwater springs and culminating in the vast expanse of the Gulf of Mexico. These exhibits encompass various elements, such as a substantial simulated wetlands exhibit situated beneath a towering glass atrium, a lifelike beach simulation, and a thriving coral reef community contained within an impressive 500,000-US-gallon (1,900,000-liter) tank.

94

THE RINGLING

REGION: SOUTHWEST DISTRICT   **COUNTY:** SARASOTA   **CITY:** SARASOTA

DATE VISITED: **WHO I WENT WITH:**

RATING: ☆ ☆ ☆ ☆ ☆   **WILL I RETURN?** YES / NO

The John and Mable Ringling Museum of Art is the official state art museum of Florida. The Ringling stands as one of the foremost arts institutions within the United States. What sets it apart is the extraordinary breadth of its collections, which encompass a wide range of fields, including art, circus memorabilia, history, architecture, performance arts, and meticulously maintained gardens. These diverse collections serve as a testament to the institution's distinct origin.

Central to the narrative of The Ringling is the prominent figure of circus impresario John Ringling and his wife, Mable. Together, they shared a common vision to elevate Sarasota into a globally renowned destination. This ambition laid the foundation for the remarkable institution that exists today.

John Ringling was one of the five Ringling brothers who embarked on their first circus tour in 1884. Initially starting on a modest scale, their circus enterprise expanded rapidly in both size and prosperity, with each brother taking on distinct managerial roles.

In 1907, the brothers achieved a significant milestone by purchasing the renowned Barnum & Bailey show, a testament to their astute business acumen. Among the brothers, John emerged as the most financially successful, diversifying his investments into various ventures, including railroads, ranching, and real estate.

John and Mable tied the knot in 1905, and much like John, Mable hailed from humble origins in the Midwest. The couple did not have children, opting instead to fill their home with social gatherings, visits from loved ones, numerous pets, and an ever-expanding collection of exquisite furniture and artwork.

In 1911, the Ringlings acquired a winter residence situated on a 20-acre waterfront parcel in Sarasota. At the time, Sarasota was a small fishing village, but John and Mable envisioned its potential for development. As the 1920s rolled around, John's wealth had grown substantially, prompting the couple to construct a new, grandiose home on their property that would befit their elevated status.

John and Mable Ringling enlisted the services of architect Dwight James Baum, based in New York, to design their opulent mansion, which came to be known as Ca' d'Zan, translating to "House of John" in the Venetian dialect. Baum's design for the mansion was a fusion of various architectural influences, ranging from the Venetian Gothic to the Mediterranean Revival style. He incorporated a diverse array of materials, including glazed terracotta, colored marble, and stained glass, resulting in a visually stunning and impressive structure. Ca' d'Zan spanned a sprawling 36,000 square feet and featured an impressive 56 rooms. Remarkably, the mansion was completed in a mere two years, with construction concluding in 1926.

During the period when Ca' d'Zan was under construction, John and Mable Ringling made two pivotal decisions that would leave a lasting impact on the Sarasota community:

Firstly, they chose to establish an art museum that would serve as their enduring legacy to the people of Florida. John embarked on a passionate pursuit of art collection, amassing over 400 paintings by both renowned and lesser-known artists in just under six years. This expanded his collection to include over 600 works.

Secondly, in 1927, John relocated the winter headquarters of his circus from Bridgeport, Connecticut, to Sarasota. During the winter months, visitors had the opportunity to pay a nominal admission fee and visit the circus grounds, where they could witness acts rehearsing for the upcoming season. This decision left an indelible mark on the identity of Sarasota, establishing it not only as a circus town but also as a prominent national tourist destination.

The year 1929 marked a challenging period for the Ringlings. Tragically, Mable Ringling passed away at the age of 54, having enjoyed only three winter seasons at Ca' d'Zan. Additionally, the stock market crash of that year inflicted significant financial hardships upon John Ringling. Nevertheless, in 1930, The John and Mable Ringling Museum of Art was opened to the public, finally realizing the couple's long-planned legacy. Five years later, upon John's own passing in 1936, he bequeathed the museum and his entire estate to the people of Florida.

However, the Great Depression and John's unsuccessful business ventures had left him in considerable debt. Legal disputes and eager creditors prolonged the settlement of his estate until 1946. Throughout this decade, the Museum of Art was sporadically open and inadequately maintained, while Ca' d'Zan remained closed to the public.

When the state ultimately gained control in 1946, the estate required substantial attention, including weatherproofing, mechanical upgrades, and the preservation of Mable's gardens. Some private donors stepped forward to assist in keeping the museum operational, although the institution's dedicated staff, though committed, struggled with limited funding to fulfill the museum's potential. Gradually, under the leadership of The Ringling's inaugural Director, A. Everett 'Chick' Austin, Jr., the museum began to regain its footing and momentum.

In 1948, A. Everett 'Chick' Austin took a pioneering step by creating the first museum in the United States dedicated exclusively to the circus. This museum was filled with an array of artifacts, photographs, costumes, and props, many of which were obtained from local circus performers who had established Sarasota as their home. This unwavering dedication to preserving the history of the circus has since become a fundamental pillar of The Ringling's mission.

Austin was also a strong advocate for the performing arts, and he played a pivotal role in shaping The Ringling's commitment to live performances. In 1952, he oversaw the reassembly of the Historic Asolo Theater, originally constructed in 1798 in Asolo, Italy, on the grounds of The Ringling in Sarasota. This venue provided The Ringling with a dedicated space for a wide range of performing arts events. The U-shaped theater features three tiers of boxes adorned with ornate decorative panels and serves as a platform for plays, concerts, operas, lectures, films, and various other cultural programming.

In the year 2000, following an extended period of negotiations, the governance of the museum was officially transferred to Florida State University (FSU). This significant development ushered in a new era for The Ringling, characterized by fresh sources of funding and dynamic leadership. During this transformative period, The Ringling experienced a remarkable resurgence. Ca' d'Zan, the mansion, underwent an extensive $15 million restoration, revitalizing this iconic structure. Furthermore, the Historic Asolo Theater was meticulously restored and relocated inside the newly constructed John M. McKay Visitors Pavilion, one of several new buildings added to the complex during this phase of rejuvenation.

In January 2006, the Circus Museum saw the addition of the Tibbals Learning Center, which quickly captivated visitors with its remarkable centerpiece: the 3,800-square-foot Howard Bros. Circus Model, an intricate and historically accurate model circus comprising an astounding 42,000 individual pieces. Subsequently, in 2012, interactive galleries were integrated into the Tibbals Learning Center, offering visitors an immersive experience in the world of the circus arts. Here, visitors could try their hand at various circus activities, such as walking the high wire, fitting into a clown car, or mastering the art of balancing on the back of a horse. The Tibbals Learning Center also houses The Ringling Archives, which boast one of the nation's most significant collections of rare handbills and art prints, circus-related documents, business records, heralds, and photographs.

Continuing to evolve, The Ringling has consistently made additions to its estate, ensuring that it remains a welcoming space for individuals of all ages and interests. The state-of-the-art Johnson-Blalock Education Center, equipped with storage facilities, offices, and an art library, has proven to be an invaluable resource for scholars, educators, and students alike. In 2013, the David F. Bolger Playspace was introduced, encouraging families and school groups to engage in spontaneous play during their visits.

The Ulla R. and Arthur F. Searing Wing, an extension of the museum's north wing added in 2007, contributed more than 20,000 square feet of exhibition space. In 2011, a significant addition to The Ringling's modern and contemporary art program came in the form of Joseph's Coat: A Skyspace by James Turrell, which was integrated into the Searing Wing.

In 2016, the Ting Tsung and Wei Fong Chao Center for Asian Art was unveiled with the aim of fostering appreciation for Asian history and culture through a variety of exhibitions, programs, and publications. The same year saw the establishment of the Keith D. Monda Gallery for Contemporary Art, a 2,400-square-foot gallery space dedicated permanently to modern and contemporary art, marking a first for the museum.

The Kotler-Coville Glass Pavilion, completed in 2018, serves as a showcase for The Ringling's expanding collection of vibrant studio glass. This 5,500-square-foot facility is open to the public free of charge and also functions as the entry point for visitors to the Historic Asolo Theatre. Distinguished by its sculptural glass façade and innovative design, the Kotler-Coville Glass Pavilion stands as the latest landmark architectural addition to The Ringling campus.

VENETIAN POOL

REGION: SOUTHEAST DISTRICT   **COUNTY:** MIAMI-DADE   **CITY:** CORAL GABLES

DATE VISITED: **WHO I WENT WITH:**

RATING: ☆ ☆ ☆ ☆ ☆   **WILL I RETURN?**   YES / NO

Swimming in the crystal-clear, blue-green waters of the Venetian Pool, you might momentarily forget that you're in Florida. This unique oasis, located just 20 minutes outside of Miami, transports visitors to a distant Mediterranean locale with its wrought iron balconies, stucco buildings, and terra cotta roofs that surround the pool. The Venetian Pool, situated in Coral Gables, has become a popular destination for both locals and tourists, cherished not only for its relaxing waters but also for its rich history.

Notably, the Venetian Pool holds the distinction of being the only swimming pool listed on the National Register of Historic Places. Since its inception in 1924, it has been a cherished asset to the City of Coral Gables and a beloved attraction for countless visitors.

The pool, originally known as the "Venetian Casino," was born out of an abandoned rock quarry that had once been a source of limestone for the construction of the burgeoning city of Coral Gables. Real estate developer George Merrick, who funded the entire project, envisioned a community pool that would embrace the Mediterranean Revival architectural style, a popular aesthetic choice at the time, especially in Coral Gables. In its early years, the Venetian Pool drew Hollywood celebrities and the affluent elite, solidifying its status as a luxurious retreat.

During its early history, the pool was often emptied for special events, particularly concerts. The orchestra would take their place within the empty pool, capitalizing on its remarkable acoustics for unforgettable performances. Today, the pool is still periodically drained, but the primary purpose is for maintenance and cleaning, ensuring its continued pristine condition.

Upon entering the Venetian Pool, visitors will encounter a captivating display of photos and images chronicling the pool's extensive and storied history. It's worth taking a moment to peruse these visual narratives as you make your way to the pool area.

Once inside the Venetian Pool, you'll quickly realize that it consists of one large, expansive pool. What sets this pool apart is the refreshing quality of its water, which is continually pumped in and out of the pool through artesian wells and an aquifer. This unique circulation system contributes to the pool's exceptional clarity and purity, requiring minimal chlorine usage. As a result, the water is gentle on the eyes and maintains a pleasantly cool temperature, enhancing the overall swimming experience.

Within the pool itself, swimmers have various options for enjoyment. Two grottos offer secluded spots for relaxation, while the presence of a cascading waterfall adds an exciting element to the swimming experience. Additionally, a short pedestrian bridge connects to a small island, providing an ideal place for visitors to bask in the sun or take exhilarating leaps into the water. In close proximity to the pool, there are separate facilities including a kiddie pool for younger visitors and a sandy beach area for sunbathing enthusiasts.

The Venetian Pool provides essential facilities commonly found at public swimming pools; however, it's advisable to bring your own towels, as the availability may be limited. While there are chairs available, they tend to be occupied quickly. The restroom facilities are generally well-maintained, but it's recommended to wear footwear when using them.

For those who require lockers, they can be rented on-site. Additionally, there is a café stand within the pool area offering a selection of light snacks and lunch options, including hot dogs, hamburgers, and pizza. Visitors are allowed to bring their own food, but it's important to note that alcoholic beverages and coolers are not permitted within the pool premises. There is a small picnic area where you can enjoy your own snacks or meals.

The operating hours and days of the week during which the pool is open may vary depending on the season. It's advisable to check the official website for the most up-to-date information regarding hours of operation. Due to its popularity, the pool tends to reach its capacity quickly, so arriving early is recommended. Once the pool reaches its capacity, admission may be restricted.

The Venetian Pool is conveniently located at 2701 De Soto Boulevard, Coral Gables, Florida 33134. If you're traveling from Miami, you can follow these directions: Take US-1 South until you reach SW 40th Street/Bird Road. Drive approximately 1.5 miles, and when you reach Granada Boulevard, make a right turn. You'll come across a traffic circle, where you should take the second exit onto De Soto Boulevard. The pool will be located on your right just up the street.

While the Venetian Pool Café offers food options, if you're seeking a delicious lunch, you may want to explore the surrounding city. Downtown Coral Gables, also known as the Miracle Mile, is an excellent choice. It's a vibrant outdoor shopping area filled with restaurants, boutiques, galleries, and numerous shops.

For an enjoyable afternoon, consider visiting the Coral Gables Museum, which celebrates the rich history of the city of Coral Gables. This community was one of the earliest planned developments in the United States, established during the Florida land boom of the 1920s.

If you're looking for evening entertainment, the Coral Gables Art and Cinema house is a great destination. It offers a rotating selection of independent films, documentaries, and international cinema. The theater has been in operation since 2010 and proudly holds the distinction of being the highest-grossing art house cinema in South Florida.

VERO BEACH

REGION: CENTRAL EAST DISTRICT   **COUNTY:** INDIAN RIVER   **CITY:** VERO BEACH

DATE VISITED: **WHO I WENT WITH:**

RATING: ☆ ☆ ☆ ☆ ☆   **WILL I RETURN?**   YES / NO

Vero Beach, an elegant city situated along the Atlantic Coast of Florida, is renowned for its attractions related to golf, water sports, and fishing.

Vero Beach is situated along Florida's Treasure Coast, known for its beautiful beaches. The city offers three primary public beaches: South Beach, which is accessible at the eastern end of Florida State Road 656 and the eastern end of 17th Street; Humiston Park, located in Vero's Central Beach Business District on Ocean Drive; and Jaycee Park, adjacent to Conn Beach. In Indian River County, there are a total of 26 miles (42 km) of oceanfront shoreline. Additionally, Vero Beach provides other free public access points to the beach through trails and walkways, including Riomar Beach, Sea Cove, Sea Grape Trail, Sexton Plaza, and Turtle Trail.

This tranquil destination boasts serene beaches, museums, nature tours, and a diverse range of hotels, making it an ideal vacation spot and a significant part of the region known as the Treasure Coast.

Visitors to Vero Beach can also enjoy a wide variety of shopping options, from those located along the oceanfront and in the historic downtown area to large shopping malls. The city offers delectable dining choices catering to various budgets.

Additionally, Vero Beach boasts museums, art galleries, and numerous parks, some of which provide access to a captivating network of rivers and inlets inhabited by manatees.

Positioned on Florida's eastern coast, Vero Beach is conveniently located between West Palm Beach and Cape Canaveral, making it a central hub for relaxation seekers. With access to both the Atlantic Ocean and the Indian River Lagoon, the city provides ample opportunities for aquatic adventures.

Vero Beach seamlessly blends the historic with the modern, as it was once home to the first integrated Major League Baseball spring training site in the southern United States. Consequently, there is an abundance of activities to suit every visitor's interests in this city on Florida's Treasure Coast.

In 1915, parts of a human skeleton were discovered north of Vero Beach in conjunction with the remains of Pleistocene animals. This discovery was met with controversy, and for many years, it was believed that the human remains were from a much later period than the Pleistocene. However, in 2006, an image of a mastodon or mammoth carved on a bone was found in the vicinity of the Vero man discovery. A scientific forensic examination of the bone suggested that the carving had likely been done during the Pleistocene era. Subsequently, archaeologists from Mercyhurst University, in collaboration with the Old Vero Ice Age Sites Committee (OVIASC), conducted excavations at the Old Vero Man site in Vero Beach between 2014 and 2015. Starting in 2016, archaeologists from Florida Atlantic University joined the excavations at the Old Vero Man site.

In 1715, a Spanish treasure fleet encountered disaster off the coast of Vero when eleven out of twelve Spanish ships carrying significant quantities of silver sank during a hurricane. The presence of the sunken silver attracted the attention of pirates. A group of 300 unemployed English privateers, led by Henry Jennings, seized approximately £87,500 worth of gold and silver in their initial acts of piracy. To this day, coins from this treasure fleet continue to wash up on the shore.

In 1872, Captain Allen W. Estes, who had settled in the area in 1870, officially established the first land patent between the Atlantic Ocean and the Indian River Lagoon. In 1893, Henry Flagler's Florida East Coast Railway commenced operations in the region.

The town of Vero was granted a charter on June 13, 1919. It was later officially renamed "Vero Beach" and transitioned from being part of St. Lucie County to becoming the county seat of Indian River County, which was formed in June 1925. The origin of the city's name remains a subject of debate, with no consensus.

The Indian River Lagoon, which runs through Vero Beach, constitutes a substantial segment of the Intracoastal Waterway. This lagoon serves as a central location for various water-related activities such as boating, fishing, water skiing, diving, kayaking, and other recreational activities involving small watercraft.

Vero Beach is renowned for its picturesque beaches, and among them, Round Island Oceanside Park stands out as a top attraction. Situated approximately 8 miles southeast of Vero's downtown area, this beach park offers a comprehensive array of amenities to ensure a pleasant visit. Visitors will discover shaded pavilions equipped with grilling facilities, a playground for children, as well as restroom facilities, among other conveniences. Moreover, even when specific areas are cordoned off to safeguard sea turtle nests, the expansive shoreline provides ample room for sunbathing and relaxation.

What truly distinguishes Round Island Oceanside Park from other beaches is its close proximity to the Indian River Lagoon. For those seeking a change of scenery, a short walk across State Road A1A will take you to Round Island Riverside Park, its sister park. This adjacent park boasts a unique set of attractions, including a 400-foot-long boardwalk, winding nature trails, a fishing pier, and an observation tower. Ascend the observation tower for an opportunity to spot manatees, or opt for paddleboarding or kayaking to observe these gentle creatures up close. It's important to note that water sports equipment rentals are not available on-site, so be sure to bring your own gear or arrange for equipment delivery if you plan to explore the water.

Located less than 2 miles north of the Pelican Island National Wildlife Refuge, nestled between the Indian River Lagoon and the Atlantic Ocean, Sebastian Inlet State Park is a veritable haven for surf enthusiasts. This protected area boasts world-renowned surf spots such as First Peak and Monster Hole, which are renowned for offering some of the most exceptional and consistent surf breaks in the state. In fact, the surfing conditions at this inlet are so exceptional that professional surfers like Kelly Slater, C.J., and Damien Hobgood frequented this location during their youth to refine their skills. However, the incredible waves are just one of the park's many attractions.

Sebastian Inlet State Park also features pristine, untouched beaches that are perfect for shell hunting and observing sea turtle nesting sites. The park's jetties provide outstanding fishing opportunities, while the Bayside Marina serves as an excellent vantage point for wildlife enthusiasts hoping to catch glimpses of dolphins and manatees. Additionally, the lagoon offers calm waters, making it an ideal spot for kayaking. Visitors can also explore the Hammock Trail, a one-mile-long path that winds through diverse subtropical vegetation, including mangrove, palm, and oak trees.

For history enthusiasts, a visit to the Sebastian Fishing Museum is a must. This free museum showcases various exhibits dedicated to the fish houses that operated in the area during the 19th and 20th centuries. Exhibits include a replica of an original fish house, a handcrafted fishing boat, and various fishing equipment. Another noteworthy historical attraction is the McLarty Treasure Museum, located just outside the park's southern entrance.

Established in 1986 and situated along the Indian River, the Vero Beach Museum of Art (VBMA) serves as a vibrant platform for an extensive array of artistic expressions, spanning from drawings and glassworks to sculptures and photography. The museum frequently hosts temporary exhibitions, which have showcased American folk art and highlighted the works of Picasso. In addition to these changing exhibitions, VBMA boasts a remarkable collection of permanent pieces, including several artworks created by the renowned artist Dale Chihuly.

Recognized as the foremost artistic institution on the Treasure Coast, VBMA goes beyond visual art exhibitions and diversifies its offerings by presenting musical events, organizing a children's arts festival, and conducting art classes that are accessible to the general public.

When you step foot into Pelican Island National Wildlife Refuge, you'll instantly feel like you've escaped the hustle and bustle of civilization. Established in 1903 as the very first national wildlife refuge in the United States, this expansive sanctuary covers over 5,400 acres and serves as a sanctuary for a diverse range of wildlife. This includes migratory birds, various fish species, sea turtles, alligators, and an array of mammals such as manatees, dolphins, and bobcats. Additionally, over ten different pelican species choose this refuge as their nesting grounds.

With such abundant wildlife, it's no surprise that the refuge's primary activities revolve around bird-watching and fishing. For those who prefer a more active experience, there are three trails spanning approximately 7 miles in total for leisurely hikes. If you're seeking the most breathtaking view of Pelican Island, the refuge's most iconic feature, previous visitors highly recommend embarking on the Centennial Trail. This trail, measuring almost 1 mile in length, boasts an impressive 18-foot-tall observation tower equipped with two mounted spotting scopes. Moreover, it features a boardwalk adorned with informative signs featuring QR codes that can be scanned with a smartphone for additional insights.

While exploring these trails, it's essential to bring an ample supply of drinking water, as no water sources are available on-site. Additionally, considering the warm climate and the presence of mosquitoes, it's wise to apply sunscreen and insect repellent generously to ensure protection from the sun's rays and pesky insects.

The Indian River Lagoon Greenway is a publicly accessible trail system maintained by the Indian River Land Trust, providing a captivating window into the distinctive ecosystem of the region. This trail network is open to bicyclists, pedestrians, walkers, and joggers, allowing them to explore the area's natural beauty. Notable trails within this system include the 1-mile boardwalk, which serves as an out-and-back path, culminating in a scenic overlook offering picturesque views of the Indian River Lagoon. Another trail option is the approximately 2.5-mile Loop Trail.

Regardless of which trail you choose, you can anticipate encountering an abundance of wildlife, particularly various bird species, as well as the striking presence of mangrove forests. It's important to note that motorized vehicles are strictly prohibited from using these trails. Additionally, visitors with dogs must ensure that their pets are kept on leashes while on the trail and must diligently clean up after them. These trails are open throughout the year, providing visitors with the opportunity to explore the natural beauty of the area regardless of the weather conditions.

Established on land that was initially acquired for the purpose of establishing a citrus grove, McKee Botanical Garden serves as both a historical homage to classic roadside attractions and a serene haven for the appreciation of plants and the natural world. This garden, which was previously known as McKee Jungle Gardens, is not only steeped in history but also a place of tranquility.

Recognized for its historical significance, McKee Botanical Garden has earned a spot on the National Register of Historic Places. During the 1940s, it was among the most popular tourist destinations in Florida. However, with the advent of other attractions in the state, it experienced a decline in visitor numbers and revenue, eventually leading to its closure for a span of two decades.

Fortunately, in the early 1990s, concerted efforts by local preservationists led to the rescue of 18 out of the original 80 acres. These individuals worked to clear the overgrown trails, preserving the essence of the garden. In its present form, the garden was reintroduced in 2021, featuring an impressive collection of over 10,000 plants, a dedicated children's garden, and an onsite cafe that offers a diverse menu encompassing salads, sandwiches, and desserts.

97

VIZCAYA MUSEUM AND GARDENS

REGION: SOUTHEAST DISTRICT   **COUNTY:** MIAMI-DADE   **CITY:** MIAMI

DATE VISITED: **WHO I WENT WITH:**

RATING: ☆ ☆ ☆ ☆ ☆   **WILL I RETURN?** YES / NO

The Vizcaya Museum and Gardens, originally referred to as Villa Vizcaya, stands as the former residence and estate of James Deering, a prominent figure associated with the Deering McCormick-International Harvester fortune. This exquisite property is situated on the shores of Biscayne Bay, in the modern-day Coconut Grove neighborhood of Miami, Florida. Dating back to the early 20th century, the Vizcaya estate encompasses not only an opulent villa but also extensive gardens in the Italian Renaissance style, a natural wooded landscape, and a collection of historic village outbuildings.

The story of Vizcaya began in 1910, a period less than 15 years after the incorporation of Miami as a new city. Since then, the histories of Vizcaya Estate and the city of Miami have remained closely intertwined.

James Deering, an industrialist born in 1859 who passed away in 1925, oversaw the construction of Vizcaya between 1914 and 1922. His first winter residence in the Main House at Vizcaya commenced on December 25, 1916.

Vizcaya is situated in the Coconut Grove neighborhood of Miami, and the estate was entirely enveloped by subtropical forest along the shores of Biscayne Bay.

The concept behind Vizcaya was to create a modern and subtropical interpretation of an eighteenth-century Italian villa, specifically drawing inspiration from the country estates located in the Veneto region of northern Italy. The designers of Vizcaya skillfully adapted traditional Mediterranean architectural elements to suit the subtropical climate, demonstrating a remarkable understanding of environmental considerations.

Despite its Baroque aesthetics, Vizcaya was, in fact, an exceptionally modern residence. It may come as a surprise to many that the construction primarily employed reinforced concrete, incorporating cutting-edge technology of that era, such as generators and a water filtration system. The house featured various amenities for the utmost comfort and convenience, including heating and ventilation systems, two elevators, a dumbwaiter, refrigerators, an automated telephone switchboard, a central vacuum-cleaning system, and a partially automated laundry room.

Featuring enduring Mediterranean-style architecture and housing collections spanning from the early 20th century to ancient Pompeii, Vizcaya's Main House emerged as a prominent symbol of burgeoning Miami during its construction from 1914 to 1922.

A hundred years later, Vizcaya continues to hold significance. It serves as a cultural attraction drawing tens of thousands of visitors from around the globe annually. Furthermore, it remains a focal point for locals seeking opportunities for learning, personal growth, and community engagement, all within the distinctive ambiance of "Miami's home."

The architectural and landscape design of Vizcaya was heavily influenced by the Italian Renaissance, drawing inspiration from the regions of Veneto and Tuscany. The Mediterranean Revival architectural style, infused with Baroque elements, characterizes the estate. The team behind this grand project included F. Burrall Hoffman as the architect, Iwahiko Tsumanuma (also known as Thomas Rockrise) as the associate architect, Paul Chalfin as the design director, and Diego Suarez as the landscape architect.

The Vizcaya property is now under the ownership of Miami-Dade County, operating as the Vizcaya Museum and Gardens, open for public visitation. Access to this location is facilitated by the Vizcaya Station on the Miami Metrorail system.

Today, Vizcaya remains an undisturbed haven of tranquility and lush greenery, miraculously preserved just south of Miami's contemporary skyline. The focal point and primary living area of the house is the Courtyard, which originally lacked a roof. The design of the house was carefully orchestrated to make the most of its location along the shores of Biscayne Bay. James Deering intended for Vizcaya to be approached and admired from the sea, with the eastern façade facing the bay being the most grandiose and the sole symmetrical one. This part of the house opens onto a broad terrace that gradually descends toward the water.

The other sides of the house establish distinct relationships with the surrounding landscape. The west façade, which has served as the main entrance since Deering's era, exudes simplicity and stands in contrast to Vizcaya's ornate interiors. The north façade features one of Vizcaya's most charming features—the swimming pool that emerges from vaulted arches at the lower level of the house. The south façade connects to the formal gardens and features enclosed loggias on both the first and second floors.

The first floor encompasses various reception rooms, including the Library, the Music Room, and the Dining Room, all surrounding the Courtyard. The second floor housed Deering's private suite of rooms, guest bedrooms, as well as a Breakfast Room and the Kitchen.

The interiors of the Main House were meticulously arranged around various pieces of furniture, paneling, and architectural elements, such as gates and fireplaces. Each object served to enhance the decorative ambiance of the specific room it occupied, effectively shaping the architectural design of the house.

Paul Chalfin possessed a profound expertise in Italian furniture and interiors, which is readily apparent in the diverse styles of rooms found in the Main House. The primary source of inspiration for Vizcaya was the eighteenth century, encompassing the asymmetrical and creatively innovative Rococo style, as well as the more linear and austere Neoclassical aesthetic.

Chalfin aimed to capture the essence of various Italian cities, resulting in rooms inspired by Milan (Music Room), Palermo (Reception Room), and Venice (the Cathay and Espagnolette bedrooms). Within Deering's personal suite, Chalfin curated masculine yet ornate furniture from the Napoleonic era. In the Living Room and Dining Room, he followed the trend of "modern" Renaissance interiors favored by art collectors in Europe and the United States.

Chalfin did not adhere strictly to historical accuracy; instead, he masterfully integrated new design elements into old artifacts, creating eclectic arrangements. Vizcaya was, after all, intended as a vacation residence, and its décor consistently exudes a sense of playfulness and whimsy.

Nevertheless, Vizcaya boasts one of the most significant collections of Italian furniture in the United States today.

Vizcaya's gardens, inspired by European aesthetics, stand as some of the most intricate in the United States. These gardens evoke the styles of seventeenth- and eighteenth-century Italy and France, with an overarching design that resembles a series of distinct rooms.

The central area is dominated by meticulously arranged geometric hedges, known as parterres. Beyond this central space, you'll discover a range of enchanting gardens, including the secretive Secret Garden, the cozy Theater Garden, the whimsical Maze Garden, and the former aquatic realm of the Fountain Garden. Flanking this meticulously planned landscape are the untouched native forests, preserved by James Deering.

Vizcaya's lush gardens are adorned with an abundance of architectural features, intricate fountains, and both antique and specially commissioned sculptures. The use of sculptures crafted from aged, porous coral stone was a deliberate choice, lending the gardens a weathered appearance shortly after their completion. To enhance the perception of age, Deering and Paul Chalfin strategically planted mature trees, along with vines and foliage that would gracefully drape over the garden structures.

Many individuals are familiar with Vizcaya's magnificent bayfront residence and gardens, which have played a significant role in Miami's cultural scene for more than a century. However, just across South Miami Avenue lies a lesser-known but equally noteworthy part of our community's history—the Vizcaya Village. Today, a mission is underway to restore the Village and create dynamic new programs accessible to all residents of Miami-Dade County.

The Vizcaya Village, once the bustling core of the estate, is currently undergoing revitalization to tell fresh stories about our community's heritage and introduce innovative programs. Nestled beneath the shade of majestic banyan trees, the Vizcaya Village comprises 11 architecturally significant buildings spread across 12 acres. Originally constructed in 1916 with the goal of making Vizcaya self-sufficient, the Village included housing for staff, a garage, workshops, barns, greenhouses, and cultivated fields that supplied fresh flowers, fruits, and vegetables. The restoration of the Village aims to unlock Vizcaya's full potential as a cultural hub, offering year-round innovative programming and green spaces for both residents and visitors.

98

WEEKI WACHEE SPRINGS STATE PARK

REGION: CENTRAL WEST DISTRICT   **COUNTY:** HERNANDO   **CITY:** WEEKI WACHEE

DATE VISITED: **WHO I WENT WITH:**

RATING: ☆ ☆ ☆ ☆ ☆   **WILL I RETURN?**   YES / NO

Weeki Wachee Springs State Park, one of Florida's oldest roadside attractions, has been captivating audiences since 1947. Its name, "Weeki Wachee," was bestowed by the Seminole Indians and translates to "little spring" or "winding river." This remarkable spring is renowned as one of the deepest naturally formed underwater caverns in the United States.

Since 1947, Weeki Wachee Springs State Park has captivated visitors with its captivating mermaids, who gracefully swim in the refreshing, crystal-clear waters of this legendary enchanted spring. This unique attraction, the only one of its kind globally, stands as one of Florida's most distinctive roadside destinations.

In addition to its mesmerizing mermaids, the park offers various activities such as kayak rentals, paddling adventures, and relaxing river boat cruises.

Weeki Wachee Springs State Park serves as a magical portal to an enchanting underwater realm, teeming with mermaids, manatees, turtles, and enchanting bubbles. As you sit in the submerged Mermaid Theater, which accommodates 400 people, you'll feel as though you've been transported into the flowing spring itself, evoking a sense of simpler times before the advent of super theme parks and massive highways.

This breathtaking 538-acre park offers an abundance of attractions beyond its mermaids. Buccaneer Bay, Florida's sole spring-fed waterpark, boasts a sandy white beach, a swimming area, and four exhilarating waterslides designed to cater to thrill-seekers of all ages. Embark on a tranquil River Boat Cruise to immerse yourself in the natural beauty of Florida, where you can observe the state's native wildlife, flora, and fauna. Alternatively, rent a kayak or canoe to embark on your self-guided aquatic adventure. Don't miss the entertaining and educational Animal Show, which provides an opportunity to get up close with indigenous wildlife such as alligators, snakes, and turtles.

In 1946, Newton Perry, a former U.S. Navy serviceman responsible for training Navy Frogmen in underwater swimming during World War II, identified Weeki Wachee as a promising location for a new venture. During this period, U.S. Route 19 was a modest two-lane road, and most other roads in the area remained unpaved. Essential amenities such as gas stations, grocery stores, and movie theaters were conspicuously absent, and the region was more populated by alligators and black bears than by humans.

Regrettably, the spring itself was marred by discarded, rusted refrigerators and abandoned cars. Perry undertook the task of clearing this debris and embarked on experiments with underwater breathing techniques. He devised a method for individuals to breathe underwater using a continuous air hose connected to an air compressor, rather than relying on conventional tanks strapped to their backs. This innovation enabled people to appear as though they were thriving twenty feet beneath the water's surface without visible breathing apparatus.

Utilizing the natural limestone, Perry constructed an 18-seat theater submerged six feet below the water's surface, providing spectators with a direct view of the spring's natural beauty.

Perry recruited and trained young women to swim with air hoses while maintaining cheerful smiles. He taught them to consume Grapette, a non-carbonated beverage, and eat bananas underwater while performing aquatic ballets. Subsequently, he erected a sign along U.S. Route 19 that read: "WEEKI WACHEE." On October 13, 1947, the inaugural show at the underwater theater in Weeki Wachee Springs made its debut. This event coincided with the first broadcast of "Kukla, Fran and Ollie" on the new medium of television and preceded Chuck Yeager's historic breaking of the sound barrier. During this debut, the mermaids executed synchronized ballet routines underwater while relying on concealed air hoses within the scenery for breathing.

However, during those early days, traffic along U.S. Route 19 was sparse. When the mermaids detected an approaching vehicle, they would hastily run to the roadside in their bathing suits to entice drivers into the parking lot, akin to the sirens of ancient mythology who lured sailors to their peril. Subsequently, they would dive into the spring to commence their performance.

By the 1950s, Weeki Wachee had become one of the nation's most popular tourist destinations, achieving international recognition. Movies, including "Mr. Peabody and the Mermaid," were filmed at the spring. The park offered an array of attractions, including mermaid shows, orchid gardens, jungle cruises, an Indian encampment, and a newly established beach. The mermaids even received instruction in etiquette and ballet.

The peak era of Weeki Wachee commenced in 1959, following the acquisition of the spring by the American Broadcasting Co. (ABC), which initiated an extensive promotional campaign. ABC was responsible for constructing the current theater, boasting a seating capacity of 400, ingeniously embedded into the spring's side at a depth of 16 feet below the surface. ABC also introduced thematic elements to the underwater shows, featuring intricate props, elevators, musical accompaniments, and storylines.

During the 1960s, aspiring mermaids traveled from as far as Tokyo to audition for the privilege of joining this glamorous troupe. The mermaids, bedecked in one-piece swimsuits, delivered an astounding eight shows daily to consistently packed audiences. The attraction drew up to half a million visitors annually. Weeki Wachee Springs boasted a roster of 35 mermaids who took turns performing in the shows. They captivated audiences with underwater football matches and picnic scenes. Some of the mermaids resided in cottages specially designated for them on the attraction's premises. These mermaids were treated with great reverence wherever they went in Florida.

Weeki Wachee's allure extended to a wide range of personalities, including notable figures such as Elvis Presley, Don Knotts, Esther Williams, and Arthur Godfrey, who made the journey to witness the enchanting performances of the Weeki Wachee mermaids.

The City of Weeki Wachee was officially incorporated in 1966, a milestone that placed the small city of Weeki Wachee on regional maps and state road signs. In 1982, Buccaneer Bay made its debut, featuring exhilarating waterslides and a pristine white sand beach for visitors to enjoy. In 1997, the immensely popular "Former Mermaid" shows were introduced, reuniting former mermaids and bringing them back to Weeki Wachee Springs to participate in the "Mermaids of Yesteryear" performances. These shows consistently played to capacity crowds, and the allure of Weeki Wachee Springs continued to beckon these former mermaids, drawing them back time and again, much like an unforgettable dream that refuses to fade. For these former mermaids, the motto rings true: "Once a mermaid, always a mermaid."

99

YBOR CITY

REGION: CENTRAL WEST DISTRICT   **COUNTY:** HILLSBOROUGH   **CITY:** TAMPA

DATE VISITED: **WHO I WENT WITH:**

RATING: ☆ ☆ ☆ ☆ ☆   **WILL I RETURN?** YES / NO

Ybor City is a historic neighborhood situated just northeast of downtown Tampa, Florida, in the United States. Its establishment dates back to the 1880s when Vicente Martinez-Ybor, along with other cigar manufacturers, founded the neighborhood. Ybor City saw an influx of thousands of immigrants, primarily from Cuba, Spain, and Italy, who settled in the area. Over the next five decades, the cigar factories in Ybor City produced hundreds of millions of cigars annually.

What made Ybor City unique in the American South was its status as a prosperous town predominantly inhabited and owned by immigrants. This neighborhood boasted distinctive characteristics not commonly found in other contemporary Southern communities, particularly its diverse multiethnic and multiracial population and the presence of numerous mutual aid societies. The cigar industry, which employed a substantial workforce with good wages, played a pivotal role in transforming Tampa from an economically struggling village into a thriving city in just about two decades, earning it the nickname "Cigar City."

The growth and prosperity of Ybor City persisted from the 1890s until the onset of the Great Depression in the 1930s. During this economic downturn, reduced demand for premium cigars led to a decline in the number of cigar factories. Furthermore, the introduction of mechanization in the cigar industry substantially reduced job opportunities in the neighborhood. This trend escalated after World War II, leading to a continuous outmigration of both residents and businesses. By the late 1970s, large sections of what was once a vibrant neighborhood had become nearly deserted.

Efforts at revitalization remained unsuccessful until the 1980s when an influx of artists initiated a gradual process of gentrification. In the 1990s and early 2000s, a portion of the original neighborhood, particularly around 7th Avenue, transformed into a nightlife and entertainment district, with many historic buildings undergoing renovation for new purposes. Since then, the local economy has diversified to include more offices and residences, marking the first significant population growth in over half a century.

Ybor City has earned recognition as a National Historic Landmark District, with several structures within the area listed in the National Register of Historic Places. In 2008, 7th Avenue, the primary commercial street in Ybor City, was honored as one of the "10 Great Streets in America" by the American Planning Association. Additionally, in 2010, the Columbia Restaurant, Florida's oldest restaurant located in Ybor City, was named one of the "Top 50 All-American icons" by Nation's Restaurant News magazine.

Indulge your palate with a myriad of flavors as you venture through Ybor City, either on your own or with Ybor City Food Tours. A visit to the Columbia Restaurant, Florida's oldest restaurant, is a must, not only for its cultural significance but also for its exceptional cuisine. You can experience the tastes of Sicily at Casa Santo Stefano or savor a Cuban-inspired coffee at Café Quiquiriqui. For nearly a century, La Segunda Central Bakery has faithfully followed the same hand-baked process and traditional recipes, ensuring a unique taste and texture that cannot be replicated.

You can conveniently hop on the TECO Line Streetcar for a free ride to historic Ybor City, located just over a mile from Downtown. Take your time exploring the local cigar shops, including Tabanero Cigars, Sweetheart Cigars, and J.C. Newman Cigar Co., which also features a new on-site museum. Here, you can find the perfect complement to your leisurely evening stroll through these cherished streets.

Delve into the rich local sports history by visiting the Tampa Baseball Museum, which is located in the childhood home of Tampa's first MLB player, Al López. Right next door, you'll find the Ybor City Museum, situated within an urban park at the heart of Tampa's National Historic Landmark District. This park encompasses a primary exhibit area housed within a bakery building dating back to 1923, a lush Mediterranean-style garden, and a faithfully recreated cigar worker's home known as a casita. If you're interested in live music, head down the block to The Ritz Ybor, where you can catch performances by local musicians. Photography enthusiasts should make a point to visit the expansive Florida Museum of Photographic Arts.

ZOO MIAMI

REGION: SOUTHEAST DISTRICT   **COUNTY:** MIAMI-DADE   **CITY:** MIAMI

DATE VISITED: **WHO I WENT WITH:**

RATING: ☆ ☆ ☆ ☆ ☆   **WILL I RETURN?** YES / NO

Zoo Miami, also known as The Miami-Dade Zoological Park and Gardens, holds the distinction of being Florida's largest zoo and the fifth largest in the United States. Situated in South Florida, it enjoys a unique subtropical climate that enables the care of a diverse range of animals hailing from Asia, Australia, Africa, and the Americas. This collection represents an unparalleled mix of species, setting it apart from other zoos in the country.

The zoo's approach to organizing animals involves grouping them based on their natural geographic territories, mirroring the peaceful coexistence observed in the wild. Exhibits are meticulously designed to replicate the native habitats of the animals, with trees, foliage, and soil closely matching those found in their homelands.

The origins of Zoo Miami date back to 1948 when it was initially established as the Crandon Park Zoo on Key Biscayne, an island located near downtown Miami. At its inception, the zoo covered 48 acres within the park and housed its first animals, including lions, an elephant, and a rhinoceros that had been left stranded when a circus ceased operations in Miami.

Today, Zoo Miami has expanded to occupy nearly 750 acres, featuring 4 miles of walkways and providing a home for over 2,500 animals representing more than 400 diverse species. Among these inhabitants, over 130 species face threats in their natural habitats, with many classified as endangered or critically endangered. Additionally, the zoo boasts a vibrant botanical collection, encompassing more than 1,000 species of trees, palms, and other plants, along with over 100 specialized exhibits covering a wide array of species and scientific themes.

Zoo Miami proudly holds accreditation from the Association of Zoos and Aquariums (AZA), underscoring its commitment to the highest standards of animal health and welfare, fundraising, staffing, and participation in global conservation initiatives. As a leader in wildlife and environmental conservation, the zoo actively engages in around 30 programs annually across five continents, contributing to the preservation of endangered species and the protection of our planet's natural treasures.

PHOTOS   PARK NAME...

PHOTOS   PARK NAME...

PHOTOS   PARK NAME...

PHOTOS   PARK NAME...

PHOTOS   PARK NAME...

PHOTOS   PARK NAME..

PHOTOS   PARK NAME...

PHOTOS   PARK NAME...

PHOTOS   PARK NAME..

PHOTOS   PARK NAME...

Thank you for taking the time to read my book. I hope you found it enjoyable.

Your feedback is important to me, and I would greatly appreciate it if you could take a moment to share your thoughts by leaving an online review.

Your review will not only help me improve as an author but also assist other potential readers in making informed decisions.

Once again, thank you for your support and for considering leaving a review.

Warm regards,

Max Kukis Galgan

Write to me if you think I should improve anything in my book:

maxkukisgalgan@gmail.com

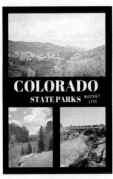

COLORADO
STATE PARKS ^{BUCKET LIST}

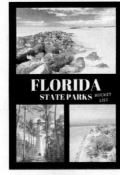

FLORIDA
STATE PARKS ^{BUCKET LIST}

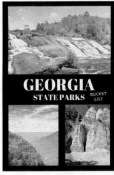

GEORGIA
STATE PARKS ^{BUCKET LIST}

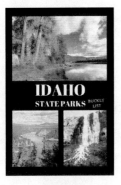

IDAHO
STATE PARKS ^{BUCKET LIST}

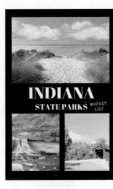

INDIANA
STATE PARKS ^{BUCKET LIST}

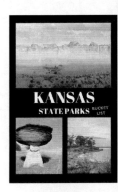

KANSAS
STATE PARKS ^{BUCKET LIST}

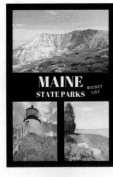

MAINE
STATE PARKS ^{BUCKET LIST}

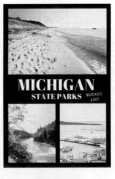

MICHIGAN
STATE PARKS ^{BUCKET LIST}

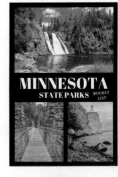

MINNESOTA
STATE PARKS ^{BUCKET LIST}

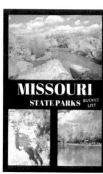

MISSOURI
STATE PARKS BUCKET LIST

NEW YORK
STATE PARKS BUCKET LIST

OHIO
STATE PARKS BUCKET LIST

OREGON
STATE PARKS BUCKET LIST

PENNSYLVANIA
STATE PARKS BUCKET JOURNAL

TENNESSEE
STATE PARKS BUCKET LIST

TEXAS
STATE PARKS BUCKET LIST

UTAH
STATE PARKS BUCKET LIST

VIRGINIA
STATE PARKS BUCKET LIST

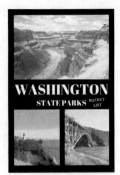

WASHINGTON
STATE PARKS BUCKET LIST

WISCONSIN
STATE PARKS BUCKET LIST

Made in United States
North Haven, CT
28 February 2024